# Self-Literacy

*Self-Literacy: Writing Out Personhood* offers fifty perspectives on gaining an understanding of what 'personhood' may mean through various disciplines. Literature is a key medium through which selves are mapped as humans are written into being. Such literature is intimately tied to health such as within self-help literature, written accounts of illness, or of characters who are defined by their afflictions – physical, psychological, and moral. This book adopts an essay approach to aspects of selfhood, including disciplines of psychology (personality), sociology (social selves), anthropology (cultural selfhood), literary (the self as portrayed in literature), and history (notions of self through time). Each chapter can be read in isolation, and a comprehensive list of works on self is provided as a bibliography. This book will appeal to researchers and postgraduates engaged in the fields of Literature and Health Humanities, as well as psychology, sociology, and anthropology academics and students.

**Alan Bleakley** is Emeritus Professor of Medical Education and Medical Humanities at Plymouth Peninsula School of Medicine, Faculty of Health, University of Plymouth, UK. He is a leading international figure in medical education and medical humanities and is widely published as both an academic and poet.

# Routledge Studies in Literature and Health Humanities

**Canadian Literature and Medicine**
Carelanding
*Shane Neilson*

**Narrative Fiction and Death**
Dying Imagined
*Sabine Köllmann*

**Sensation Novels and Domestic Minds**
Mental Health in Victorian Literature
*Mathilde Vialard*

**Gut, Brain, and Environment in Nineteenth Century French Literature and Medicine**
*Manon Mathias*

**Experiencing Epiphanies in Literature and Cinema**
Arts and Humanities for Sustainable Well-being
*Bradley Lewis*

**Narratives of Injury**
Nineteenth-Century Coalfields Fiction
*Rosalyn Buckland*

**Self-Literacy**
Writing Out Personhood
*Alan Bleakley*

To learn more about this series, please visit: https://www.routledge.com/
Routledge-Studies-in-Literature-and-Health-Humanities/book-series/RSHH

# Self-Literacy
Writing Out Personhood

**Alan Bleakley**

NEW YORK AND LONDON

First published 2026
by Routledge
605 Third Avenue, New York, NY 10158

and by Routledge
4 Park Square, Milton Park, Abingdon, Oxon, OX14 4RN

*Routledge is an imprint of the Taylor & Francis Group, an informa business*

© 2026 Alan Bleakley

The right of Alan Bleakley to be identified as author of this work has been asserted in accordance with sections 77 and 78 of the Copyright, Designs and Patents Act 1988.

All rights reserved. No part of this book may be reprinted or reproduced or utilised in any form or by any electronic, mechanical, or other means, now known or hereafter invented, including photocopying and recording, or in any information storage or retrieval system, without permission in writing from the publishers.

*Trademark notice:* Product or corporate names may be trademarks or registered trademarks, and are used only for identification and explanation without intent to infringe.

*Library of Congress Cataloging-in-Publication Data*
Names: Bleakley, Alan (Alan Douglas), author.
Title: Self-literacy: writing out personhood / Alan Bleakley.
Description: New York, NY: Routledge, 2025. |
Series: Routledge studies in literature and health humanities |
Includes bibliographical references and index.
Identifiers: LCCN 2025000958 (print) | LCCN 2025000959 (ebook) |
ISBN 9781041025429 (hardback) | ISBN 9781041025726 (paperback) |
ISBN 9781003619901 (ebook)
Subjects: LCSH: Self. | Self-perception. | Self in literature. |
Self-perception in literature.
Classification: LCC BF697 .B573 2025 (print) |
LCC BF697 (ebook) | DDC 808.8/0384—dc23/eng/20250520
LC record available at https://lccn.loc.gov/2025000958
LC ebook record available at https://lccn.loc.gov/2025000959

ISBN: 9781041025429 (hbk)
ISBN: 9781041025726 (pbk)
ISBN: 9781003619901 (ebk)

DOI: 10.4324/9781003619901

Typeset in Sabon
by codeMantra

# Contents

| | |
|---|---|
| *List of illustrations* | *ix* |
| *Preface* | *x* |
| *Acknowledgements* | *xiii* |
| Introduction: the self, not a given but a problem | 1 |
| 1  The camouflaged self | 5 |
| 2  Authentic and inauthentic selves: duty of candour and whistleblowers | 10 |
| 3  Ancient Greek practices of self-forming | 13 |
| 4  Self as *flâneur* | 17 |
| 5  Authenticity with muscle: the ancient Greek hero | 20 |
| 6  Familiars | 23 |
| 7  Renaissance self fashioning | 25 |
| 8  The alchemical self as outlaw: an experiment in embodied metaphor | 29 |
| 9  Animal or plant self?: geography matters | 34 |
| 10  The enlightenment self as 'subject to' King and Divinity | 37 |
| 11  The enlightened self: beyond subjection | 40 |

vi  *Contents*

12  Unique identifiers: fingerprints and ears          44

13  Talking yourself up: illeism          46

14  Possessed and absent selves          48

15  The modern ego: the all-seeing 'I'          51

16  The origins of 'self-help'          56

17  The relational self          61

18  Self stripped of rights          64

19  Self engulfed by panic          68

20  The self-righteous narcissist          71

21  Paranoia: beside oneself          75

22  The translational self: an attractor in a dynamic, complex system          77

23  The narrative construction of self          82

24  Personal confessional narratives constitute a confessional self          85

25  The self's new religion: secular and humanistic          89

26  ~~Writing out~~ the modern self: postmodern prescriptions          92

27  Cancelling the self: postmodern anti-narrativists          95

28  As mad as a hatter: neurodivergent selves          99

29  Self-consciousness without consciousness: tacit knowing          106

Contents vii

| | |
|---|---|
| 30 Bodies at their limits: intentional self-fashioning | 111 |
| 31 Wired for subjectivity | 113 |
| 32 Loneliness | 118 |
| 33 The fashioning of family | 123 |
| 34 Feminist selves | 126 |
| 35 Self as laboratory rat | 131 |
| 36 The self in pieces: the yips | 136 |
| 37 Mods | 139 |
| 38 Politicised junior doctors | 144 |
| 39 The progressively absent self | 147 |
| 40 A roof over yourself | 149 |
| 41 From carbon to silicon | 152 |
| 42 Différance | 155 |
| 43 Lacanian subjectivities | 158 |
| 44 The neurological self | 162 |
| 45 The linguistic transactional self in surgical settings | 167 |
| 46 Subject to power/power runs through the subject | 171 |
| 47 Bodies that are no-bodies: the biological self | 174 |
| 48 The universal SELF | 178 |

viii *Contents*

| | | |
|---|---|---|
| 49 | Subject to the abject | 180 |
| 50 | The final straw: the self's last sip of life's juice | 182 |

*Appendix: The disposable self as 'worm'* 186
*Further reading* 189
*Index* 207

# Illustrations

| | | |
|---|---|---|
| 0.1 | Inspired by Magritte (unattributed) | 1 |
| 6.1 | 'Eat up, my beauties!' | 24 |
| 7.1 | Albrecht Durer's grid c.1600 | 28 |
| 10.1 | Hobbes' 1651 *Leviathan*. The populace is contained in the figure of the King | 38 |
| 14.1 | Anton Mesmer's tub – collective animal magnetism at work | 48 |
| 19.1 | Pan | 69 |
| 32.1 | 'Lonely' by Moghadam Khamseh | 119 |
| 37.1 | Mods | 140 |
| 40.1 | The Elemental House, Melbourne. Photograph: Jack Lovel | 150 |
| 43.1 | The Triquetra Knot: the Real, the Symbolic, and the Imaginary | 161 |
| A.1 | Appendix | 187 |

# Preface

Nothing is more central to health humanities than self-worth, and literature is the primary medium through which we debate what 'self-worth' means. But what is the 'self'? How do we come to know ourselves? Clearly through observation of how others respond to us as we reflect on our own actions – or, talking to others and talking to oneself. Immediately, there are problems with such a view – narcissists only talk to themselves and those with paranoid dispositions think others are talking about them when they are not. A realist would accept that there are multiple approaches to selfhood – indeed, we might say that every self is unique, but that does not get us very far in understanding what selfhood means and what it is to 'write out' or author selfhood. The writer DH Lawrence, famously a sceptic, said in 1932 that questing for knowledge of self is fruitless, where: 'At last, we escape the barbed wire enclosure of know thyself, knowing we can never know'.

The psychoanalyst Jacques Lacan famously described the 'mirror stage' of development – at around age one a child recognises herself in a mirror as a first indication of an emergent selfhood. Lacan points out that this is a misrecognition: the self the child sees in the mirror is not necessarily the self that is mirrored back to that child through her immediate social group such as family and friendship circles. As we grow up, so we bear the expanding conundrum of dislocation between felt self and self as shaped by the responses of key others. This is why Lacan settled on the term 'knot' – as primary metaphor – to best describe an adult character, where the psychologist and educationalist Yrjö Engeström describes social relations as forms of 'knotworking'. Importantly, we not only talk, but write, ourselves into being in various modes and styles making literature a key medium through which selves are mapped. Such literature is intimately tied to health: its manifestations as in a vast contemporary literature on self-help, and its decline as in written accounts of illness, or of characters who are defined by their afflictions – physical, psychological, and moral.

Identities can be stolen ('identity theft'), unintentionally forgotten through illness (amnesia, Alzheimers, dementia), traded or sold (selling

Preface xi

privacy and recognition online), maligned (malice), or purloined (character assassination). Identity theft can have serious psychological consequences. For example, at the time of writing, a best-selling popular author – Coco Mellors – supposedly invented a drug-abusing character in one of her novels. This character was recognised by a poet acquaintance of hers as based on him, leading to what was described in the press as a 'mini identity crisis'. Perhaps this is an effect of the so-called 'snowflake generation', formally described in the *Collins English Dictionary* as 'the young adults of the 2010s, viewed as being less resilient and more prone to taking offence than previous generations'. Identities or selves are then historically sensitive within cultures and advertise mass effects or trends.

Considering these introductory remarks, how dear reader can you best navigate this idiosyncratic text? I would say in the same way that we navigate our various selves, as paths at once both certain and uncertain, steady and ambiguous. While a stable sense of 'who I am' may permeate your life, of course expressions differ from moment to moment because we play roles – as parent, partner, or lover; through occupation, profession, or hobby; in sports, as competitors; and feigned or forced in negotiating awkward social contexts – within wider prescriptions of ethnicity and gender, and (increasingly) as settlers or forced migrants. By 'self' I embrace role, person, personhood, identity, subject, and subjectivity. I use the word as both noun and verb, and to embrace both the literal and metaphorical.

First educated as a zoologist, I am interested in the life-form that is the human – the strange position we find ourselves in as an end point of biological evolution now morphing into cultural evolution and in the unique position of slowly destroying the very ecological niche that has supported our development. Standing upright while developing large brains within heavy, protective skulls has produced a need for deep anatomical compromise. As we age, our spines and knee joints can barely take the strain and wear readily. Our internal organs want to drop through gravity and must be suspended by a mass of connective tissue. We are all born prematurely, in vulnerable states, because our heads that accommodate such large brains would be too big for a woman to bear the passage of birth if allowed to develop any further in the womb. Mothering and fathering are not guaranteed to run smoothly – maternal and paternal instincts do not necessarily kick in and are complicated by social forces shaping childcare.

Later educated as a psychologist and psychodynamic psychotherapist, I became interested in the psychological trauma that these biological restrictions bring, but also in the sense of freedom and innovation that a life lived well promises. As Sigmund Freud first postulated, it seems natural to subscribe to a life instinct – Eros – and pursue a path that draws on life force and life-enhancing activity. But, as Freud later thought, a bigger force – at once oppressive and frightening – is Thanatos, a death instinct. We are by nature running down or subject to entropy, moving ever closer

xii  *Preface*

to death. Further, we are attracted to risk that flirts with death. Not all of us are big wave surfers, skydivers, or racing drivers, but we engage in daily unhealthy intake through diet, recreational drugs and alcohol, and emotionally sapping work and relationships that breed stress and anxiety.

And so, we form, reform, and perform selves. Multiple selves across multiple contexts. And yet, according to certain dominant cultural templates, we must entertain a continuous and stable sense of self. Already, as we have seen, this is compromised – or rather complicated – by psychological and social factors. Today's self – globally – is further extended or augmented by technologies. Personal computers, tablets, and mobile phones are both extensions of self and dictate the shapes and styles of selves. Today's self is shaped by relative wealth and poverty, and this is related to location – where we live, the nature of our houses, shelters, and households, and whether we are settled or in transit (the latter now often forced by conflict and climate change).

I have been entangled professionally with notions of selfhood for over half a century, primarily as a psychologist, psychotherapist, and educator developing psychotherapy training programmes, working as a psychotherapist, and more recently, as a medical educator. I have also been a student of cultural studies and literature and am a widely published poet. My readings of selfhood have generally been through a literary lens where I strive to bring literary flair to my more technical academic books. Over that time, I have accumulated a library of books on selfhood and often promised myself that I would give something back to academic culture by addressing the multiple notions of self within a Western cultural framework. This urge recently came to a head and this slightly quirky book of essays is the result. I decided early on that while maintaining academic rigour, each essay would not be encumbered by references. Rather, I would simply list all the books on selfhood that I have on my shelves as a final bibliography. I wanted this book to appeal to a wide academic audience but to maintain a focus of literary interest. The reader is invited to navigate the text in any way that you like – sections do contain cross-referencing but there is no overarching narrative to the text.

# Acknowledgements

My life partner Sue brings a brilliant visual imagination to bear on my meagre literary skills and for this I am eternally grateful. We both agree that conditions of creativity must be challenging and should never afford an easy ride. Thanks also to my loving family who provide a caring cradle but also a nexus of imagination and productivity.

Professor Paul Crawford has long been an ally in promoting thoughtful practice in healthcare and has given me great support for this book. Taylor & Francis/Routledge editors Iola Ashby and Bryony Reece have provided unconditional support for this project – thank you both.

# Introduction
## The self, not a given but a problem

First, a note on method. In her article 'Situated Knowledges: The Science Question in Feminism and the Privilege of Partial Perspective' the feminist scholar Donna Haraway (1988) challenges the privileged perspective of scientific 'objectivity' (as gendered male). Rather than thinking of science as impartial, Haraway argues that science – indeed all knowledge – is necessarily partial or situated. The more we argue for impartiality, the more we dig a hole for ourselves by mistaking objectivity for inclusivity. Every statement must be relative, where every maker of statements is situated. Ironically, where scientists situate themselves in geographies of 'objectivity', they merely advertise the historical, cultural, and personal 'subjective' (Figure 0.1).

*Figure 0.1* Inspired by Magritte (unattributed).

DOI: 10.4324/9781003619901-1

## 2   Self-Literacy

In the case of the 'self' – role, person, personhood, identity, subject, subjectivity – the problem of objectivity is of course highlighted. There is no one 'right' way to describe the subject that is self. Selves offer varieties of situated knowledges. As selves contemplate the self – you, the reader, ranging over the necessarily arbitrary 50 kinds of selfhood that inhabit this book – you may alight on favourite or preferred versions of self, but these are never to be considered as right, or truth. They must be taken as perspectives within a multiplicity. Perhaps the best approach to this book is to read it as a set of literary essays to be appreciated before any attempt at explanation is made. Selves present first to be explored and may then be explained. Considering the above, I will give a health warning about bias: first, the variety of selves considered here are Western examples; second, I write from the point of view of a white, heteronormative North European male.

A sense of 'self' may seem unproblematic – it is surely *experienced* daily. That we have differing experiences of ourselves from moment to moment is surely less important than the more pervasive sense of a consistent sense of self running through experiences – a stable identity? In *Habits of the Heart: Individualism and Commitment in American Life* – first published in 1985 and subsequently in two new editions (1996, 2008) – Robert Bellah and colleagues note that 'self-confidence', 'self-reliance', and 'self-respect' are at the heart of the modern American psyche and yet all remain fragile, while the cultural value of individualism itself is so ingrained that it remains unexamined. This uninterrogated view of self is of course problematic. Self already affords ambiguity as the person seen in the mirror seems oddly different from the person mirrored back by others.

The self is first and foremost a product of historical, cultural, and social forces summed up in the term 'intersectionality' (the interplay between class, gender, and ethnicity). Is the self that dreams the same as the self that functions as we consciously think? Is the automatic or habitual self that switches in when we ride a bike or drive a car the same as the self that ponders, is vague, confused, or lost? 'Who' or 'what' is the other self that looks over the shoulder of the self when we reflect on things? Who is the spontaneous self that flies into an uncontrollable rage, unthinkingly jumps into a river to save a drowning child, or goes on a drink and drugs binge? Is the self that comes to after such a bender the same one that ran headlong into self-oblivion? The public self and the private self may differ considerably, while the individualism that is so cherished in democracies is formed and manipulated by a host of cultural forces: education, advertising, marketing, therapies, social media, and so forth.

Does self (no longer a thing but a process) change over time, and can it completely change as a new character – or a series of characters – emerging from the chrysalis of the old? Is the self today the same as an ancient Greek, medieval or Renaissance self? Is the 'European' self the same as a Japanese self, or an aboriginal Australian self the same as a white settler living in the suburbs of Sydney? Is the self best located in the brain or in culture, or is it better construed as a conversation between these two locations and then not a thing at all but a process or an emergent event? Is the self consistent across genders, or after a change in gender identification? Why do philosophers and psychologists in particular fuss over what 'self' means when the layperson seems to know: 'I don't feel myself today'. Where does the self go during the 'little death' of orgasm, or when a person is in a coma, a deep meditative state, or deliriously in love? In short, as the sociologist Zygmunt Bauman suggests, the contemporary self is (and must be) 'liquid'. In this sense, the self may best be described as a metaphor – not a literal thing that we can pin down but a means by which we can deepen, complexify, and intensify living. Where the poet Wallace Stevens said that 'Reality is a cliché from which we escape by metaphor' perhaps we can say that the self is also a cliché from which we escape by metaphor. Yet self-aggrandising statements persist as concrete realities, where imperialist settlers claim territory such as Israelis claiming Palestinian land, or gentrifying incursions by people of 'new money' into traditionally impoverished city quarters.

Language already problematises selfhood, where we use a range of descriptors: identity, agency, person, personhood, individual, subject, ego, the indexical linguistic 'I', and 'me'. Qualifications of the self must embrace the divergent – is a paranoid self the same as a depressed self? Selfhood includes character, personality, persona, sub-personalities, possible selves, split identity, multiple selves, displaced selves, social selves, the narrative self, the autobiographical self, the biographical self, the personal confessional self, the looking glass self, the mirror stage self, the remembered self, authentic and inauthentic selves, the pastiche personality, the performed self, the private self, the relational self, the transpersonal self, the online self, the addicted self, and the animal self. Can we say that the embryo or the baby in the womb has a sense of self? And then there is that Lacanian moment of first looking into the mirror in an act of simultaneous self recognition and alienation.

Perhaps we can locate the self somatically – in the body and its apparent boundary. Clearly not, for while we may have a sense of self from physical actions alone, it is language that gives meaning to those actions. So, do we speak and write ourselves into being? Further, our bodies are now so inscribed through fashion and medicine and extended through technologies that the body is no longer one's own. We may find ourselves in the grip of cultural fads or inexplicable urges, so that we either starve or overfeed the body, or exercise compulsively, or spend countless hours online. And then we must account for selves perceived or labelled as challenged, differently abled, neurodivergent, or with special needs.

## 4  *Self-Literacy*

The self then is slippery, unstable, difficult to pin down, untrustworthy, liable to strong fluctuations, and complex, at the same time as it won't go away, is persistent, bothers us by its hovering presence: we wouldn't be the same without it. Is the self then a lifelong affliction? Perhaps the safest way to think about a self is not to think about it at all, but to let it happen. But 'who' is the transcendent self that makes this decision? The philosopher Immanuel Kant thought that the 'real' self occupied this transcendent place. If we must describe the self's existence, then it may be multiple, and a product of bricolage, or 'do it yourself'. The bricoleur is the person who engages in bricolage, which leaves us with the dilemma that the person constructing the self is in fact the self, so that the self precedes its construction. Again, a transcendent other in conversation with a grounded self.

As Alice says in Lewis Carroll's *Alice in Wonderland*: 'It's no use going back to yesterday, because I was a different person then'. In *Hard Times*, Charles Dickens problematised the body location of self where the intolerable Mrs Gradgrind – on her sick bed – is asked by her daughter whether she is in pain: 'I think there is a pain somewhere in the room', she replies, 'but I couldn't possibly positively say that I have got it'. If we substitute 'self' for 'pain' and ask where the self is located, then we can perhaps rephrase Mrs Gradgrind as: 'I think there's a self somewhere in the room, but I couldn't positively say that I have got it'.

# 1 The camouflaged self

In the 1970s, the politically aware and politically radical post-hippy era when feminism was front and centre, young men's casual fashions in the UK turned to greens and browns. This was often called 'spinach and shit' – the green an olive drab, the brown the colour of dribbly poo. In the face of strident women wearing primary colours, this was a way for men to meld into the background or camouflage themselves. Or to pretend that they were one with nature, when in fact they were unreconstructed patriarchs. Overt camouflage clothes such as cargo pants with multiple pockets, and flak jackets, became popular geek- or nerd-wear/ware during the 1990s and early 2000s as part of Y2K fashion. Of course, while fashion supposedly advertises individuality, selves are in fact sucked into general trends where everybody of a certain age group looks like everybody else – conformists camouflaged in full view.

In the mid-18th century, Erasmus Darwin coined the term 'concealing colouration' to refer to what we now call animal camouflage. Here, 'The colours of many animals seem adapted to their purposes of concealing themselves, either to avoid danger, or to spring upon their prey'. A century later, Erasmus' grandson Charles Darwin adopted the same idea. Animals conceal themselves, cause disruption, take on disguises, and mimic to hide from predators or to surprise attack as predators because of the process of evolution through natural selection. Such camouflage or disguise is also adopted by the human animal to avoid being seen and possibly attacked, or – in contrast – to spring a surprise attack. Such behaviour is not confined to warfare, but is characteristic, for example, of clowning, stage magic, burglary, robbery, and idiosyncratic bedroom antics.

'Camouflage' is a late 19th-century word derived from the Italian *camuffare* ('to disguise, conceal, or deceive') and the French *camoufler* ('to disguise'). The word originated as thieves' slang, associated with the French *camouflet* – 'whiff of smoke in the face'. This offers a direct line not only to clowning but also to stage magicians who disguise largely through misdirection of the audience's attention. The English equivalent is 'smokescreen'.

DOI: 10.4324/9781003619901-2

## 6   Self-Literacy

Camouflage was used widely in World War I in disguising vehicles and weapons as well as the use of camouflaged clothes – the typical battle dress of mottled sludge green and brown imitating soil and tree or plant life so that the military would blend with the natural environment. Such military kit was originally called 'fatigues' where it was worn by soldiers off duty who were too tired to engage in battle or were recovering from battlefield injuries. Ironically, then, the very battle dress that served as camouflage in the war zone also served to mark out a soldier in civilian settings – camouflage as show or badge. Self is mutable according to dress. To the human eye, as observers not predators, many camouflages of animals are seen as wonderful aesthetic self-displays, or animal shows – nature less as combat and more as theatre and performance.

Such aesthetic display is squashed by instrumental biology and natural history, where camouflage is typically reduced to function: extravagant displays purely for seeking a mate to reproduce the species; melodic birdsong primarily for marking out a territory; brilliant disguises adopted only to avoid being eaten by predators. But such displays are not just functional – they also exhibit aesthetic surplus. Birdsong goes beyond mating calls or territorial imperatives where singing is just for the sake of singing or showing off. Similarly, as noted, human combat outfits are not just for disguise in war zones. 'Fatigues' have become popular, and sometimes fashionable, casual wear. Humans wear extravagant perfumes and dress with flair and brilliance not just for function but largely for show – display as proclamation of identity or advertising of self. Again, what was designed as camouflage now becomes its opposite, as self-display. Camouflage or fatigues then paradoxically afford both refusal of identity as disguise, and display of identity as combat fashion. This advertises both a combat mentality (e.g., mass shooters often wear a uniform of body armour and other tactical gear) and a combat parody as a mark of resistance through fashion (where it is illegal in most countries to wear actual military clothing as a civilian).

The human animal, like most animals, has then retained the power of camouflage as changing identity for both hiding and exclaiming presence. While functional biologists describe this as a technique for survival in a competitive world, the most impressive thing about animal camouflage is again its aesthetic nature – form before function. Camouflage – 'animal disguise' – may help in either avoiding or becoming the predator, but it can be seen primarily as show, a way of advertising beauty. The paradox of camouflage in the animal world is that many perceivers may not actually 'see' the camouflage as expressed. In other words, the optics (or other sensory modalities) of the viewer may not be able to register the nature of the camouflage, thus defeating its functional purpose but highlighting its power as aesthetic display. Also, through extensions to human

The camouflaged self 7

senses – such as cameras – we can appreciate the camouflage displays of animals that bear no immediate meaning for us biologically but are spectacular aesthetic events.

Camouflage, says the biologist Adolf Portmann, is where an animal 'pretends to be what it is not'. Doesn't this also have an immediate ring for human self-presentation? Portmann continues that an animal 'does this in order to survive'. We can object to both these statements. First, camouflage can be read not as 'pretence' but as a valid alternative form of identity; and second, camouflage, as I suggest above, is perhaps aesthetic first (as 'display') and functional second (as 'survival'). Ironically, as a student of zoology myself, it was from the work of Portmann that I first learned to see nature as form before function and then self as aesthetic display prior to functions such as survival and finding a mate.

We might think that camouflage is unusual, context-specific, and runs against the grain of advertising an identity or personality as unique or idiosyncratic. But the opposite is true. Fashion creates us all as clones in camouflage-of-the-day. Indeed, it is those who do not follow fashion who stand out, as 'nerdy', 'goofy', 'uncool', 'stiff', and so forth. Fashion dictates that we deny our differing identities in terms of body shapes and facial features as we adopt make-up or invest in aesthetic surgeries precisely to not look like ourselves and often to imitate a common – rather than idiosyncratic – aesthetic ideal, following a trend almost certainly dictated by the fashion industry in pursuit of profit. Idiosyncratic identities are denied and in denial. Here, humans echo the animal tactic of camouflage-through-mimicry. For example, certain butterflies avoid being easy prey by exuding a scent offensive to birds who may otherwise eat them. Other butterflies (who cannot exude an offensive scent) avoid being eaten by birds through camouflaging themselves in imitation of the butterflies who can exude the offensive scent. Such are evolution's convoluted paths. Human evolution has led to the fashion catwalk, a strange pinnacle.

There are two basic kinds of camouflage-through-mimicry in the insect world. The first is through imitation of offensive properties and was first described by the English naturalist Henry Walter Bates in the late 19th century after studying butterfly behaviour in the Amazon rainforest for over a decade. Its key element is mimicry. However, there is a second kind of adaptive evolutionary impulse in which the insect does not simply mimic another insect repulsive to predators but develops the same secretions that keep other insects free from predation. This is a much safer form of evolutionary impulse in the long run (advertised, for example, by the adoption of stripes in wasps who can also sting and exude nauseous chemicals). It seems that humans who adopt – inevitably transient – fashions advertise the first, and most unstable, tactic of imitation. Here, then, imitation becomes the basis for identity: not as the sincerest form of flattery, but as

## 8    Self-Literacy

victim of fashions created and manipulated by a late capitalist neoliberal industrial complex.

The fashion industry, the primary matrix for 'fast fashion' high street clothing, is predicted to be worth $185 billion by 2027. The UK fashion industry alone is currently worth nearly £30 billion and generates nearly a million jobs, as the UK's primary creative industry. But the industry may be seen to create, feed, and destroy human selves as it cycles through trends – a kind of uroboric snake that eats itself from its own tail only to regenerate. Further, the fashion industry is responsible for 10% of global carbon emissions, and a fifth of all plastic pollution annually. Production of polyesters, the most used clothing fibre, requires 1.3 billion barrels of oil annually. The human self-display that is the ephemeral animal skin (the camouflage of fashion-led clothing) must carry shame.

For the sociologist Erving Goffman, we are constantly in a state of camouflage, engaging in 'impression management'. Goffman's model of self is perhaps the most radical in the social sciences, for it hollows out any sense of an 'authentic' self or 'personality' to focus entirely on how we manage impressions in changing social contexts. Here is an example: Sally visits Harry at home. As Sally approaches Harry's door, so she adjusts her demeanour to fit with expectations of how Harry might greet her. Meanwhile, Harry (an ex-lover) has been watching Sally approach the house from an upstairs window, even noting the impression management preparation that Sally has carried out before knocking on the door. Harry and Sally adjust themselves accordingly to manage impressions in an uncertain encounter where both are conflicted about the status of their relationship. Goffman calls his model 'dramaturgical', seeing life as a play or drama in which we are all actors across a lot of familiar social contexts or scenes, with prepared 'scripts'. These are moulded by cultural norms, habits, and innovations, including use of language, signs, and symbols. Heavily scripted encounters demand adoption of formal identities, roles, and behaviours – such as a UK commoner meeting the King. There is little room for improvisation. Even in the privacy of the bedroom, sexual encounters largely demand culturally scripted roles. We are always and everywhere in camouflage, the irony being that our camouflages can easily be seen through.

The artist Cindy Sherman has, for over four decades, based her work on shifting identity through camouflage. She says, 'I wish I could treat every day as Halloween and get dressed up and go out into the world as some eccentric character'. Her initial self-portraits draw on Hollywood B-movies and stereotypical depictions such as the unhappy housewife, the jilted lover, and the jaded seductress. Later, she depicted the grotesque and the repulsive. Her wigs slip off, her make-up is sloppy. Recently she has been experimenting with artificial intelligence (AI) to generate multiple

*The camouflaged self* 9

selves. Sherman reminds us that selves are both manipulable through fashion and can be idiosyncratic aesthetic statements serving as signatures. Here, appearance – through clothes, hairstyles, make-up, and character-istic gait and demeanour – is a way of 'writing oneself out' as a semiotics of appearance. We write ourselves out through mixtures of fashion and idiosyncratic statements as characters in a narrative and so our lives are quintessentially literary.

Returning to camouflage, the profession that is most interested in the dialogue between covering up and exposure – other than biology/natural history – must be the law. Here, duplicity and conflicting readings of the evidence are commonplace, and the courts act as theatre. The profession that is least interested in camouflage is medicine. Doctors want to be able to read symptoms with clarity and uncertainty, even as they often present as ambiguous. Medical students however crave the unusual – to see rare diseases and to make a spot-on diagnosis from a complex set of presenting symptoms, imitating Sherlock Holmes' best sleuthing (from Conan Doyle's novels), or Dr Gregory House's infamous intuitions (from the highly suc-cessful TV series 'House MD'). But there is a well-known maxim in medi-cine: 'If you hear hoofbeats, don't think zebras'. In other words, go for the most obvious diagnosis and not for the rare – the latter is unlikely. Presentations of symptoms rarely come disguised or camouflaged. Odd that zebras are icons of the camouflage industry. Zebras' main predators, lions, are colour-blind and so they see zebra skin as a wavy pattern blend-ing in with the wavy grasses in its habitat: the animal self-absorbed into an accommodating background.

# 2 Authentic and inauthentic selves
## Duty of candour and whistleblowers

There is a famous description in Jean-Paul Sartre's masterwork *Being and Nothingness* that advertises the essence of Existentialism – a philosophy that asks of us: are we living an authentic or inauthentic existence? Is the self a sham or is it living out an existence in what Sartre calls 'good faith'? To be in 'bad faith' is to accept inauthenticity as natural. Sartre describes a waiter who is 'play-acting' at being a waiter – overly subservient, angling for a tip.

> Let us consider this waiter in the café. His movement is quick and forward, a little too precise, a little too rapid. He bends forward a little too eagerly; his voice, his eyes express an interest a little too solicitous for the order of the customer. Finally there he returns, trying to imitate in his walk the inflexible stiffness of some kind of automaton while carrying his tray with the recklessness of a tight-rope-walker by putting it in a perpetually unstable, perpetually broken equilibrium which he perpetually re-establishes by a light movement of the arm and hand. All his behaviour seems to us a game. He applies himself to changing his movements as if they were mechanisms, the one regulating the other; his gestures and even his voice seems to be mechanisms; he gives himself the quickness and pitiless rapidity of things. He is playing, he is amusing himself. But what is he playing? We need not watch long before we can explain it: he is playing at *being* a waiter in a café. There is nothing there to surprise us.

Such 'bad faith' cannot be camouflaged, it has become habitual, part of a role that sociologists call 'impression management'. In Sartre's (1938) novel *Nausea*, the main protagonist Antoine Roquentin becomes increasingly nauseous as he considers the condescending behaviour of those around him. He aches for authenticity. Not for narcissism, imposition, or bullying as a response to meek acceptance of the status quo, but for behaviour with 'qualities' – morally aware, deep, thoughtful, reflective, and caring. But Roquentin himself seems to be falling into a kind of melancholia that is a nausea, 'the sickness unto death' as the 19th-century philosopher Søren

DOI: 10.4324/9781003619901-3

*Authentic and inauthentic selves* 11

Kierkegaard termed it. It appears that Roquentin is aloof and judgemental. Spurned by a former English lover, Anny, Roquentin is driven further into despair and depression. He forms a relationship with a humble 'self-taught man', the bailiff's clerk Ogier, who is a socialist and shows a genuine deep love for humanity. Ogier shows a kind of wisdom that Roquentin seems to have lost, advertising Sartre's version of Existential authenticity in the face of dread (the human condition).

The ancient Greeks had pondered on such slippage into inauthenticity. Where Roquentin has slipped into melancholy, adopting an aloof and judgemental position about his fellow humans, and Ogier adopts a low-key, non-invasive empathy for humankind, the ancient Greeks describe a more active third way of crafting an authentic self: *parrhesia*, or truth-telling. We now see formal encouragement of truth-telling in professional spheres – such as healthcare – as 'duty of candour' (the need to tell the truth or expose personal and institutional malpractice) and 'whistleblowing'. The French psychologist and philosopher Michel Foucault revived study of *parrhesia* not just as an act of 'truth-telling' (whistleblowing) but as a personality disposition, a style of life, or cultivation of an authentic self.

Discussion of bold speech, speaking out against injustice, or whistleblowing as duty of candour can be traced to Euripides (487–407 BC) who coined the term *parrhesia* or 'fearless speech' to describe talk free from rhetoric speaking truth to power. *Parrhesia* literally means 'to speak everything', or to speak openly and boldly, implying not just freedom of speech but speaking truth as a public obligation even if this means bringing risk upon oneself. An Athenian orator Lykourgos drew public attention to the wrongdoings of a high-profile crooked citizen, suggesting that the law might do nothing about this, but ordinary citizens are surely free to speak out publicly to denounce wrongdoing, if they have the courage to do so. Hellenic kings had advisers skilled in *parrhesia* who would temper the rhetoric of the monarch where this was inflated or misguided. This was later echoed in the role of the fool or court jester, who tempers overblown royal rhetoric or bad behaviour. Today, we have the satirical press serving this parrhesiastical role. *Parrhesia* is a literary style advertised particularly in investigative journalism and expositional biography.

Whistleblowing in politics now has a major role in civic affairs and an international online network. The parrhesiast recognises and articulates conflicts between corporate or professional interests and those of the public where there is a perceived social injustice or abuse of privilege. The law should save whistleblowers, not silence them, although we still live in a climate in which if you spill the beans on your company's criminal activities you will not just lose your job, you could lose your career where you will be black marked. High-profile whistleblowers within WikiLeaks have

## 12 Self-Literacy

exerted moral courage in a manner that has tested governments as they enter the realm of classified secrets linked to national security. Authenticity directed at national security brings the risk of incarceration. At the time of writing, Chelsea Manning – a former US soldier who has undergone a gender identity transition from male to female – was court-martialed and has served prison time, while Julian Assange (the founder of WikiLeaks in 2006) has served prison time in the UK and has just been released as a free man, having been cajoled to confess to crimes of high treason against the US government for publishing security-sensitive data.

Whistleblowing as an act of moral courage moulding an identity can be traced beyond Euripides' coining of the term to Homer (8c BCE). Homer refers to the story of the smuggling of troops inside the wooden horse into Troy in the *Odyssey*. Pre-Homer, all members of an audience would have been familiar with the tale, sung by oral storytellers accompanied by the lyre. The Greeks' wooden horse ruse did not fool all the Trojans. Laocoon, a Trojan, blew the whistle on the whole scheme seeing it for what it was – a trick – but was ignored by fellow Trojans. As a mis-punishment for his apparent brazen lying Laocoon, with his two sons, was killed by venomous and constricting sea snakes who both bit and suffocated two of the three to death. One son was said to have escaped, depicted in a famous life-size marble sculpture now in the Vatican. Laocoon is a giant among whistleblowers as – in questioning the apparent gullibility of his comrades – he questioned fate itself, acting against the preordained script of Troy's destiny to fall. No mortal could challenge Fate, and in response Poseidon is said to have ordered Laocoon and his sons to meet the fate described above.

Metaphorically, this perhaps is what whistleblowers – from high-profile political Wiki-leakers to local protesters – feel like when governments, corporations, or even powerful seniors or peers turn on them. 'Truth-telling' is an example of deep moral courage – facing the sovereign power ('power over') of authority even when blatantly crooked, deceitful, or committing obvious error without apology. Again, truth-telling invokes truth to power, calling out wrongdoing. We should support this 'moral courage' identity rather than turning the tables to treat parrhesiasts as scapegoats for a corrupt system.

The modernist sensibility described here – drawing on value terms such as 'authenticity' and grounded in ancient Greek notions such as 'truth-telling' – has been eclipsed by a postmodern sensibility whose wayward child is the 'post-truth' gibberish spouted by Donald Trump and his followers (as 'alternative truths'). Postmodernists (of both reconstructive and deconstructive persuasions) ask legitimate questions that situate truth claims (whose truth? and how is it legitimated?), where post-truth adherents make things up as they go along to deflect critique or valuable inquiry from those who would question their assumptions – many of which seem to be grounded in wayward conspiracy theories lacking any credible evidence.

# 3  Ancient Greek practices of self-forming

The historian Norbert Elias (1939), in *The Civilizing Process*, shows how the modern self of the secular upper classes in the West dictated 'manners' and 'taste' particularly during the 17th and 18th centuries. Activities that received no censure, or were publicly acceptable, included shitting and pissing in public view, spitting, copulation, eating with hands, swearing publicly, and arguing in public. Changes in habits were shaped by inventions such as flush toilets (not widely available until the 19th century) and efficient public sewerage. Selves were formed in terms of adopting supposed civilised habits through following constraints (such as disgust introduced as a response to spitting in public) and mini technologies (such as widespread use of cutlery) during the 17th and 18th centuries. Quoted in Elias, a 17th-century French text on manners says that 'Formerly … it was permitted to spit on the ground before people of rank, and was sufficient to put one's foot on the sputum. Now that is an indecency'; and by the 19th century, an English book on manners advises that 'Spitting is at all times a disgusting habit. … Besides being coarse and atrocious, *it is very bad for the health*'.

Elias' text is partly shadowed by Barker-Benfield's (1992) *The Culture of Sensibility: Sex and Society in Eighteenth-Century Britain*, where we learn that upper-class civility and manners drip-fed changes in habits in the emerging middle classes based on cultivation of sensibility. This was focused particularly on the sensitivity of men towards women, the latter considered to be more sensitive than men and prone to suffering from 'nerves' or having a frailer disposition. Public manners of men were adjusted to care for this perception of women's selves with an emphasis on how women might seek pleasure differently from men. For example, 'tenderness' was not given in the man but had to be cultivated. Mary Wollstonecraft's (1792) *A Vindication of the Rights of Woman: with Strictures on Political and Moral Subjects* was a landmark in feminist texts, where Wollstonecraft urged men to be more tender and women to be more 'masculine' by which she meant showing assertiveness.

DOI: 10.4324/9781003619901-4

## 14  *Self-Literacy*

Such key historical shifts in cultural habits focused on shaping selves were already a feature of ancient Greek society. The renowned French psychologist and philosopher Michel Foucault's life's work was an examination of what he called 'technologies of the self' – ways in which identity is, historically, specifically marked out and cultivated through conscious technique. He traces such 'soft' technologies back to Classical Greek practices of two kinds: for the wealthy and everyday citizens. Today, the better off take out a subscription to the gymnasium or the sauna club. The less well-off may go to the local boxing club or join a running group. We are inundated by fitness regimes online, in magazines, and in the colour supplements. At the same time as we have an obesity crisis, we crave ideal body shapes. We can see from ancient Greek sculptures that they too promoted idealised, honed bodies. The Greeks invented field and track athletics and competitive sports where the cultivation of body, mind, and feelings were inseparable.

Away from the gymnasium and the athletics field, 'street philosophers' – essentially buskers of ideas – would draw crowds listening to their notions about perfecting the self through ideas and lifestyles. Among these in Athens was Socrates, who would exhort citizens to know themselves through inquiry – not just contemplation, but active questioning – where all knowledge should be subject to examination. Socratic inquiry demanded close, critical questioning of otherwise taken-for-granted beliefs and judgements to tease out enhanced ways of living. Central to this was how to cultivate a self through improvement or technique. For the wealthy or privileged, such self-improvement would be part of a lifestyle that involved the equivalent of today's mix of Pilates classes, Yoga, book groups or literary circles, discussion groups, political debate, and – again – the gymnasium.

Nearly 500 years after Socrates, Plutarch – a priest of the temple of Apollo at Delphi and a philosopher – tells the story of a wealthy Spartan who was asked why the cultivation of land was given over to slaves and not carried out by the landowners themselves. The Spartan replied 'It was by not taking care of the fields, but of ourselves, that we acquired those fields'. We get the point. Today the middle classes have nannies and cleaners or 'home help'.

Foucault notes a transition in Western culture from the Graeco-Roman notion of 'take care of yourself' to the later 'know yourself' – basically, a switch from body to mind, soma to psyche. The former is a set of muscular character-building practices as a style of life, the latter is a more cerebral and philosophical approach. Indeed, in many strands of Christianity, Islam, Hinduism, and Buddhism, renunciation of self – asceticism – is a pathway to inner peace in this life and salvation in the next. The body must be renounced (but not necessarily neglected). The Graeco-Roman 'care of self' is a different approach to identity. Nowadays it may be solely about

*Ancient Greek practices of self-forming* 15

grooming, fitness, and aesthetic surgery as a cult of the perfect body, but the classical model is about forming an ethical self in relation to others. In other words, how will you develop your ethical commitments and sensitivity to others as deep practices? Modern-day attendances at the gymnasium, nail salon, sauna, Pilates class, or surgical theatre in Turkey do not incur such an ethical commitment to improve the lot of humanity.

Identity formation in Classical times is then the cultivation of a style of life that is permanently reflexive about one's ethical commitment towards one's identity. Am I true to myself and can I be true to others? This does not imply selfishness, for ethical commitments are only realised in a community setting. Not a community of ascetics, transcending self, but of aesthetics, forming selfhood as an art of life. Self is a matter of sculpting. While this may embrace manners, appearance, and etiquette, this is not the core of self-forming that is rather a constant asking of living itself as not only 'am I doing this right?', but also 'am I doing this well?' Self is not a quantity (just muscle) but a quality or an intensity. The self is perfected or 'written out' as a tangible script of set activities – an aesthetic code.

Care of self is then an exercise of both beauty and technique. There are ground rules. First, take care of self before you attend to others. Otherwise, you will burn out. This is, however, a soul-making that is quite different from narcissistic self-interest. Second, self-knowing is lifelong. Third, self-knowing as self-making is a critical practice that also requires unlearning of bad habits. Fourth, self-making necessitates struggle or strife – it is not a straightforward path. Fifth, self-forming is self-medication involving both body and mind. Sixth, while 'self' is primary, self-forming requires the initial help of a teacher (now, perhaps a therapist or life coach) who you will eventually outgrow. The 'teacher' may extend to a supportive group or community. Seventh, and finally, such practices of self – known to the ancient Greeks as *askesis* – have limits defined by individual capacity. One must recognise and honour these limits and work within them. In fact, the notion to be 'realistic' is carried through to everyday living where one must – at one and the same time – be optimistic and work for the best, just as you should expect to be tripped up or suffer misfortune. Be prepared. But, while strife is involved, care of self is not about beating yourself up.

As far as media for cultivating the self are concerned, Classical authors call for cultivation of memory (now a lost art in the age of computers), of keeping notes or journals, and of habitual self-reflection without self-absorption (the dangerous path to narcissism). This is a 'hermeneutic' of the subject – a lifelong process of investigation and interpretation where nothing should be taken for granted. The 'I' is the self-investigating subject – not a tautology, but a life's work, an arc of growth. Such contemplation is book-ended by the 'death exercise' and this is what

## 16  *Self-Literacy*

distinguishes self-concern from narcissism. Narcissists are duped by a sense of immortality. The 'death exercise' is the constant reminder to oneself of mortality, and then of frailty. Care of self is not to toughen up against such frailty but to integrate it as the key aesthetic component of life. In other words, we must cultivate not just body and mind but also what the ancients called 'soul' and what we might call 'imagination'. A life, and then a self, must be continually invented and reinvented. Aesthetic and ethical self-forming form a compound style of life.

# 4 Self as *flâneur*

In the American fiction writer Joy Williams' disturbing short story 'The Girls', the father of two exceptionally cruel sisters – who are the main protagonists in the story – says: 'when you look death in the eye you want to do it as calmly as a stroller looks into a shop window'. Who might this 'stroller' be?

The Roman orator, poet, and philosopher Cicero (c.84–83 BCE), writing on self-conduct, describes *humanitas* as a set of techniques for both intellectual and ethical education through the forming of aesthetic qualities or attributes – such as wit, taste, grace, elegance, and subtlety. In the same tradition, the German philosopher Friedrich Nietzsche urges us to see life as a project in aesthetic and ethical 'self-forming'. This is explicitly not instrumental (nor technical) self-improvement through mechanical techniques such as breathing exercises, yoga, athletics, or bodybuilding. Rather, self-forming is an artistic project resulting in idiosyncratic personal style. It is, above all, subtle.

Such a 'writing out' of self encompasses less the huff-and-puff of sports or the gymnasium and more the cultivated quietness of the observant walk or stroll. In Europe around the middle of the 17th century, a new figure arrives called 'the man of taste' (or discrimination) – an aesthete. A clear boundary was set between good and bad taste. Indeed, the man of taste was defined in a negative sense as the person who does not show bad taste. Bad taste is to, for example, render folk art on the same level of accomplishment as a Renaissance master. By the 19th century, a refinement of this figure came about as the person of good taste who does not crow about it, indeed, who remains perfectly quiet about his quality of aesthetic discrimination as an ethical gesture. The quiet man of good taste – the role is usually described as gendered male – prefers not to publicly judge or advertise his qualities while turning his everyday life into a walking work of art whose core activity is observation (as the quiet critic).

Isabel Vila-Cabanes' (2018) landmark book *The Flaneur in Nineteenth-Century British Literary Culture: "The Worlds of London Unknown"*

DOI: 10.4324/9781003619901-5

## 18 *Self-Literacy*

does however describe 'Aspects of Female Flanerie in Nineteenth and Early Twentieth-Century Literature' where women took on the identity of *flâneuse* without being mistaken for 'streetwalkers' (prostitutes). In a literary context, 'strolling' in the city has become a contemporary method of gaining material for novels, extended to riding on public transport. The novelist Lauren Elkin (2016) engages this theme in a study of the woman writer as *flâneuse* that suggests an origin with Virginia Woolf in London looking for content for her literary work and continues with women writers of today as close observers of city life.

The poet Baudelaire describes the 'stroller' as a connoisseur of the everyday, an exquisite negotiator of space, and a magician when dealing with identity:

> Thus the lover of universal life enters into the crowd as though it were an immense reservoir of electrical energy. Or we might liken him to a mirror as vast as the crowd itself; or to a kaleidoscope gifted with consciousness, responding to each one of its movements and reproducing the multiplicity of life and the flickering grace of all the elements of life. He is an 'I' with an insatiable appetite for the 'non-I', at every instant rendering and explaining it in pictures more living than life itself, which is always unstable and fugitive.

There is no definitive catalogue of famous *flâneurs* engaged in the occupation of *flânerie* – an art of the urban embodying purposeful looking without purpose, inhabiting without engaging, and strolling rather than hurrying or lingering. As identity politics turned to a dominant model of a permanent and settled sense of self, so the *flâneur* seeks a self in motion that celebrates its transitory nature and its keen eye. As the modern person seeks settled space and regularity of time, so the *flâneur* remakes well-known spaces such as crowded city environs on every stroll and reinvents self through time in that remaking of space. The French poet Baudelaire described this as 'an ego athirst for the non-ego'. Above all, it is a sensory ego. The *flâneur* has in a sense been recreated for contemporary times through the journal *The Idler* that promotes 'slow living' as a right to be 'lazy', in turn a form of 'self mastery'. But laziness here is a synonym for leisurely but close observation.

Artists and writers such as Baudelaire – who first coined the term 'modern' in the 19th century – and later the visual artist Marcel Duchamp took their day-to-day urban lives as the material for an artwork of self-forming. Such a vocation involves an aesthetic recreation of the self without resorting to narcissistic self-interest or therapeutic self-discovery. Such a path must avoid explicit striving to form a self (thought of as vulgar, as a return to the muscular), but should be natural, relaxed, informal, to

*Self as* flâneur    19

appear invisible to others. The 19th-century French poet Charles Baude-laire described the modern *flâneur* as cultivated observer of modern life, rather than frantic exponent, following a relaxed approach of passing by rather than acting into. The *flâneur* walks the streets, sits in cafés, idles in shops (without shopping), all the time observing but never interfering or passing judgement.

Synonyms for *flâneur* are 'stroller', 'lounger', 'saunterer'. Sceptics would call the *flâneur* a 'loafer' (an old German word for 'tramp') but look at how loafers – as slip-on shoes – became cool in the 1930s when they were reinvented, and even cooler in 1950s and early 1960s America as a sign of the relaxed and hip culminating in the 'boat shoe' (associated with the yacht crew). They oozed casual style. Ivy league students popu-larised the 'penny loafer' – made with a slit at the top of the shoe's tongue that held a penny, claimed to be used for emergency phone calls, but again a fashion statement like vents in suits, a sign of cool. Loafers were twinned with sportswear and jeans. Completely uncool in the hippy and punk eras, loafers have made a comeback as the contemporary *flâneur*'s riposte to the ubiquitous and often gaudy 'trainer'. How can you 'stroll' or 'saunter' unnoticed in the 2024 summer trend of 'ugly' or 'chunky' 'dad sneakers' – gaudy, thick-soled trainers? Indeed, the whole point of wearing these is to be noticed – to advertise the self, rather than to glide by with panache unnoticed and unhurried, or loafing.

We have all been there as curious human watchers, both entranced and perplexed by humanity. But is there a point to this activity without engage-ment? At one level non-engaged gazing (never staring) is a kind of street art. At another, the *flâneur* offers an aesthetic and ethical gesture of resist-ance to an otherwise anaesthetised or dulled bourgeois culture of decency. For it is rude to stare. The great quality of the seasoned *flâneurs* is that they remain near-invisible and logically cannot be talked about. The self is permanently erased and craves no attention. You will never see the *flâneur* on the catwalk. Self is muted yet sensitively formed. A kind of idleness replaces idolatry or identity worship.

# 5 Authenticity with muscle
## The ancient Greek hero

Live fast, die young. In Homer's *Iliad* the Greek warrior Achilles ponders on life during a break from combat in the Trojan War. He compares going home and settling down to ensure a long life with the heat of battle that carries huge risk to life. The former is appealing but does not compare to the adrenaline rush of war. For the ancient Greeks, the identity of the masculine heroic self – in battle and in the Olympic games – was primary. The four years period between games – the Olympiad – was key to how time was reckoned in ancient Greece.

The ancient Greek hero, while dreaming of immortality, is usually destined to die young and in combat. What distinguishes heroes from gods is that heroes have the 'mortality gene'. The hero of song, myth and story (such as Homer's *Iliad* and *Odyssey* epic poems that book-end Western culture along with the Bible) is then a paradox who bears a burden: his life is short, an intense flame that burns fiercely, burns out, and then lives on after death where this flame both illuminates and warms the lives of others – a burning memory rekindled in differing ways across generations.

A pathological fascination with mortality is a distinguishing mark of the martial hero, who accepts fate or destiny as if a sacrificial victim dying for a greater cause. We revere war heroes, even as we despise bloody conflict. The Homeric epics detail how extraordinary humans sacrifice longevity – in recognition of their destinies – usually in combat and to be remembered forever through epic song, and then literature. The hero then gains eternal life through repetitive appearance in cultural lore – or the hero is regularly re-embodied in the body politic of a community. This counts for much in human culture as our ancestors are usually forgotten after only three generations. What do you know of your great-grandparents? There are, in Homer, accounts of 'upper case' heroes such as Achilles and 'lower case' heroes as minor characters (usually foot soldiers) – the latter constituting about one eighth of the *Iliad*. They all die young – in the poet Christopher Logue's free translation of Homer's war book, the siege of Troy is described as 'all day permanent red', referring to the brutal

DOI: 10.4324/9781003619901-6

hand-to-hand, blood-spilling combat between Trojans and Greeks. In the poet Alice Oswald's *Memorial*, the deaths of 200 lesser figures – foot soldiers – are retold from Homer's *Iliad*.

The death of the 'upper case' hero (e.g., the Trojan warrior Hector) constitutes a sacrifice for the greater good of the future body politic. Great figures, now dead, are recycled for their key qualities as ethical models. *Parrhesia* – or 'truth-telling' – is enacted on the battlefield as patriotism, fighting for a cause. As the hero is remembered – just like a sacrificial animal was once dis-membered – or put back together in memorial, the people come together to celebrate, reconstitute, and further the body politic. Here, memories act as compost for new growth. This is why the desecration of the hero's body is such a taboo, where the body must be intact when it is buried so that it can be subsequently remembered as whole – or configured not disfigured. The unforgiveable upset of tradition – committed by both Hector in desecrating Achilles' lover Patroclus' body, and Achilles in later desecrating Hector's body in revenge for the death of Patroclus – are deep moral transgressions, errors of judgement. The pristine dead, as it were, feed the living. The courage and depth of feeling of Achilles must drip-feed the procession of culture as role model.

Homeric characterisations of the hero come from song cycles composed and transmitted orally over two and a half thousand years ago in the Iron Age, about events that occurred in the much earlier Bronze Age, from around 4,000 years ago. These song cycles, that we call epic poems, celebrate the cult of the hero of which there are two types. Quick-burn Homeric heroes – of whom Achilles is the supreme model – are characterised by choosing glory over long life. Slow-burn heroes, of whom Odysseus is the supreme model, are characterised by adventure and homecoming, nevertheless filled with danger. Their way is the cumulative overcoming of obstacles through persistence. The short-term hero dies in a blaze of glory.

Homeric heroes then suffer fleshly wounds and die gloriously in war to gain a posthumous life in cult; or undertake a series of adventures and trials to emerge wiser and to rule over a kingdom. Joseph Campbell, in *The Hero with a Thousand Faces*, notes a pattern across hero myths universally. The hero (1) responds to a call or vocation, (2) to sacrifice himself for a bigger purpose, putting his life at risk. He (3) undergoes an arduous set of initiations and a journey involving trials, (4) resists a series of temptations, and (5) achieves a goal that benefits others. The perils of the journey include encounters with death and visits to the underworld.

Campbell continues: (1) heroes satisfy needs in those who are not heroes; (2) the heroic tradition celebrates masculinity; (3) heroes are individuals; (4) heroes must embrace mortality; (5) heroes have a stand-in, or ritual substitute (Patroclus for Achilles); (6) heroes have a cult after death; (7) heroes are flawed psychologically and morally; (8) heroes are

## 22   *Self-Literacy*

transgressive; (9) heroes are charismatic as well as skilled; and (10) the behaviour of heroes is excessive. Again, heroes might be seen as two types: one of force, the other of craft and adventure. Again, the *Iliad* and the *Odyssey* offer prototypes of these two types of heroes. Achilles models courage and force, while Odysseus models craft, guile, and adventure. You may be one of these kinds. Your self may have been forged or crafted as an inviolable destiny.

# 6  Familiars

Imagine how close Palaeolithic hunter-gatherers must have been to the animals they hunted. The bond is revealed in the sensitivity with which animals are depicted in Palaeolithic cave art dating back 40,000 years to the last Ice Age. The tradition continues in small hunter-gatherer and isolated forest-dwelling communities today, where a community identifies with animals that serve as staple food. The animal must be revered in order that the herd or flock returns next season. It is the role of the shaman to make a visit to the spirit world of the hunted animal, in trance, to ask for forgiveness for taking the lives of the animals who sustain the human group. This is often accompanied by drumming on an animal skin, for this music and beat offers the bridge for the journey to the animal's heart. The shaman does not just *identify with* the animal spirit, but his or her identity transforms to become the animal itself. A tribe takes on an animal as a totemic object investing power. The members of that tribe say: 'I am that animal: that animal is a part of me, I am a part of that animal'. Identity is achieved through the totemic object as identification with it. Selves are shaped by animal forms – both natural and in the spirit world visited in trance and dream.

Shamans are of both genders. It is common for male shamans to adopt a female identity. Women shamans have often been stereotyped by men as malevolent witches with unsavoury familiars. Don't fall for that trap. Women know the moon and the cycles of nature. Women give birth – they know bodies. It is the repressed woman who returns as 'witch' – to give the patriarchy a lesson in humility – 'eat up, my beauties!' (Figure 6.1).

DOI: 10.4324/9781003619901-7

24  *Self-Literacy*

*Figure 6.1* 'Eat up, my beauties!'.

# 7 Renaissance self-fashioning

The historian Stephen Greenblatt describes identity construction in the European Renaissance of the 16th century as 'self-fashioning'. This is a paradoxical description, where we debate whether there is a prior 'self' that fashions character, or if the fashioning is the process by which the 'self' if formed. Michel Foucault's account of Graeco-Roman traditions of 'self-forming' faces the same conundrum: Who or what is the impulse that shapes a 'self'? Is this a social force imposed as character development and/or a prior psychological condition of character open to further modification, as character building or self-fashioning? Shakespeare's famous line from *As You Like It* (1599) offers a dramaturgical model of self-fashioning: 'All the world's a stage, and all the men and women merely players. They have their exits and their entrances; And one man in his time plays many parts'.

With access to detailed historical records, the historian Carlo Ginzburg (1980) was able to provide a detailed account of the day-to-day life of a 16th-century Italian miller. This gives a finely grained account of the forming of a working-class European self during the Renaissance. From this account, day-to-day living is cocooned within the dogma of the Christian Church, seemingly allowing little room for an 'individuality' to develop. Ginzburg certainly describes a character, but sense of self is larger than its colouration by idiosyncratic character, and this sense of self is deeply entwined with religion.

In contrast to Ginzburg, Greenblatt (1980) says that 'in sixteenth-century England there were both selves and a sense that they could be fashioned'. There is interplay between forces of nature and nurture. Indeed, the word 'fashion' entered the English language precisely with the meaning of forming oneself (where 'fashion' in contemporary usage conjures images of catwalks, catalogues, and the high street). Forces of Christian Church and State had already squashed a sense of autonomy – or control over who one is and how character shall be expressed. The 16th century and the Renaissance period ushered in 'an increased self-consciousness about

DOI: 10.4324/9781003619901-8

## 26  *Self-Literacy*

the fashioning of human identity as a manipulable, artful process' says Greenblatt. This echoes Foucault's claim for a golden period of character building as an aesthetic and ethical process in ancient Greece (as *askesis* or strong self-disciplining) and the early Roman world – a gendered privilege among men.

Such an interest in self-forming – again perhaps a rekindling of Classical techniques of self in the Renaissance spirit of the rediscovery (or remaking) of a humanist aesthetic of the Classical world – goes against the grain of centuries of Christian asceticism, grounded in Augustine's theology of self-negation or refusal of the ego. Augustine had warned that anybody who tried to 'build themselves' would only build a 'ruin'. Instead, there is a fashioning as imitation of Christ that is a shedding of self-interest. For Greenblatt, the key catalyst in the Renaissance view of self-forming is literature, casting back to the Classics – Greek and Roman works. The archetypal force is Shakespeare, who drew on any number of extant literary works, mythology, and folklore, to create an unparalleled linguistic universe as a mirror to self-knowing.

Such literary self-knowing is a method: 'storying' oneself into existence, or a narrative self-forming. This is both to conceive of one's life as a story (with plot, subplots, characters, denouements) and to tell life as story, both for others (biography) and self (autobiography and autoethnography). In this model of storying a life, we may find ourselves constantly reinventing the narrative out of the matter of the present; or we revise ourselves through differing interpretations of the past. In this way, identity becomes a text or a series of texts. Personhood becomes a discursive representation, a product of talk and text. Indeed, the self may become a metaphor or a series of metaphors ('he burned brightly at this period in his life', 'she was leaden and depressive for most of her life').

This Renaissance model of self assumes that we are born imperfect creatures, and it is an aesthetic and moral duty to perfect ourselves, mirroring again the Graeco-Roman traditions. Such an imperative takes on an important dimension – it is not subjugation to an authority, script, or power, but rather a critical act of interrogation through art of what it means to attain human perfection. The Renaissance again returns to an idealistic vision of the Classical era to set the standard for this imperative. While sculpture, painting, architecture, and literature may have taken the sacred – Christian themes – as topics, artists and builders explicitly adopted a deep humanism as their guiding light. Perfection was embodied in the architecture of the human body and mind. 'Self' was declared as transcendence within immanence, a celebration of human potential rather than Augustinian self-negation in imitation of Christ.

If everyday humanism, set in a wider world of monotheistic belief, is the ground for self-improvement, then during the Renaissance it is also set in a binary world of good and evil. To develop a self here is essentially a moral task of overcoming evil, or temptation to immorality – quite simply being bad to others in cheating, lying, stealing, and manipulating. But the imperfection of humans is accepted as inevitable and not set against an impossible task of meeting perfection as demanded in the now idealised figure of Christ (by the 16th century, Christ's humanity had already been lost to canonisation rather than beatification). The Renaissance human self remains perfectible in an imperfectible way.

Nearly two centuries earlier than Shakespeare at his peak, in Florence in 1425, Filippo Brunelleschi set out the principles of linear perspective. A decade later, Leon Battista Alberti expanded on this finding in *De Pictura*, a treatise on painting. The leading architect of his time, Brunelleschi designed the dome of the Duomo in Florence and was also a renowned painter. Alberti was a polymath. The core of Brunelleschi's model was to combine the notions of a vanishing point and horizon. It was common up to that point to represent the world in a multi-perspectival way in painting, as Cubism recovered for modern times. Here, it is as if we stand among objects rather than gaining distance from them as isolated viewers (such isolation acting as a gaze creating a gazer or objective self). Those who represented the world, such as painters, did not actually see the world other than as a receding horizon. It was simply that they had not mastered elegant ways to represent perspective. Palaeolithic cave artists had attempted this by drawing animal herds with overlapping figures (such as bison, for example), also using the contours of the cave walls to represent depth.

Early medieval (Byzantine) art eschews perspective. It has been argued that this is because art was religious and explicitly non-representational. For example, icons were painted as 'flat' representations. In the Renaissance, human life became subject matter for artists, introducing perspective. However, religious paintings also adopted perspective. The psychotherapist and cultural commentator Robert Romanyshyn (1989) sophisticates this argument, suggesting that the codification of perspective in the Renaissance led to a new model of person as distanced observer rather than involved participant. This can be described as an isolated self, who literally has a 'viewpoint' on worldly events. Alberti did not use the term 'vanishing point' but rather 'centre point' or 'point of flight'. It is as if the 'vanishing point' and horizon move one way as the viewer moves in the opposite direction. Hence, an ego is formed as objective eye. This 'eye' becomes the detached 'I' of science – the cold, dispassionate observer who catalogues events through careful observation. This can also be described as the self that is the spectator.

Shakespeare describes the viewpoint of the 'spectator self' in a scene from *King Lear* where Edgar is describing such a viewpoint to the blind Gloucester, from the top of a cliff looking down, where 'The fishermen

28  *Self-Literacy*

*Figure 7.1* Albrecht Durer's grid c.1600.

that walk upon the beach/ Appear like mice'. Just as Renaissance painters employed a literal mathematical grid through which they could look at the subject they painted, as if looking through a window and representing the scene on that window. Here, the isolated 'I' becomes a technologised viewer, one used to adjusting sight through eyeglasses, looking down a microscope or through a telescope, or increasingly perfecting representations of depth vision through photography and film as windows on the world. As cinema captures movement in three-dimensional space (represented on a two-dimensional screen) so a new problem arises for painting – how to represent movement. Paradoxically, Cubism returns to the involved spectator of the earliest Renaissance paintings and frescoes, prior to the discovery of the rules of perspective, advertised in Marcel Duchamp's 'Nude Descending a Staircase' and exploited in Vorticism.

The Renaissance painter's grid (Figure 7.1) also advertises the male gaze. Where the Renaissance self as spectacle is fashioned or perfected through social practices, so this perfects what the earlier Renaissance had established in the detached 'I' as spectator. Shakespeare's dramas, open to the public who might wander in and out of a performance at will, perfect the meeting of the self-fashioned self (as actors on stage) and the detached 'I' (as audience members) in rehearsals of what Erving Goffman describes as the 'dramaturgical self', again Shakespeare's 'All the world's a stage'.

# 8 The alchemical self as outlaw
## An experiment in embodied metaphor

Caught between the dogma of the Church (in the West, varieties of Christianity) and the authority structures of the State (a rigid class system based on inherited ownership of property that cemented a position for you socially) how was a self to be enacted that was independent of both these dogmatic positions? This was the conundrum of those who wished to protest, speaking truth to power. Such a self may be interested in a spiritual perspective that clashed with Christian dogma (e.g., an animism that saw all of nature as blessed with an immanent rather than transcendent spirit), and a humane vision of social equality.

You would have to form a secret society and communicate with colleagues in coded ways that would outwit or confuse the authorities. In this coded, surreptitious way the selves of alchemists were nurtured, already fed by ancient spiritual teachings (e.g., from Egyptian mythology and Jewish Qabalah). By Shakespeare's time in the late 16th and early 17th centuries – the Elizabethan and early Jacobean periods – to be an alchemist as your primary identity marker or sense of self was to identify as an outlaw. Your passion or calling would be seen as that of either heretic or swindler, so you had to find ways of disguising such a passion. Your material practice (heating, dissolving, condensing) would become a forerunner to the science of chemistry, and your spiritual practice would morph into Jungian psychotherapy and New Age musings.

Jung took the view that the material approach to alchemy – literally attempting to make gold from base metals – was never the true meaning of the transformative art. While this material approach provided a forerunner to modern chemistry, for Jung alchemy was at heart a symbol system that attempted to make sense of humanity's search for meaning and greater depth of experience, again just as all religions and philosophies attempt to do. But in doing so, Jung turned away from the hands-on sensory experience of, for example, engaging with extreme heats, poisonous substances, stuff blowing up, the textures of metals, colour changes, sulphurous stinks, and the ephemeral nature of vapours – now here, now gone. This was the

DOI: 10.4324/9781003619901-9

30  *Self-Literacy*

laboratory work on matter. Jung was focused more on the library and psychic transformations.

There is a halfway house between the material aspects of alchemy (the stinks, the colours, the vaporous clouds) and alchemy as symbolic of psychological transformations: the world of *embodied metaphor*. A metaphor is where one word or phrase is used instead of another to raise the value of the latter, such as iron pyrites (a gold-coloured mineral) being called 'fool's gold'; or synapses (connections across nerve endings) originally being called 'protoplasmic kisses'; or 'the rub of the green' (as good fortune). Such metaphors are 'embodied' because they refer to tangible matter. Metaphors matter because they turn the literal and functional into poetry – something far more intense, engaging, and inspirational. Let's imagine alchemy as material poetry and metaphor factory.

Alchemy as a system of embodied metaphors does have therapeutic implications – for example, 'lead' as leaden depression, 'fire' as various kinds of emotional warmth and extreme or heightened feelings, 'sulphur' as manic behaviour, 'mercurial' as flighty and unpredictable, and 'salt' as obsession and memory. We feel the heaviness and poisonous nature of lead in a leaden depression. We are fired up, or inflamed, or merely feel warmth towards another. Extremely heated exchanges are sulphurous (and they stink). We salt away memories and feel bitter remorse. Where such alchemical activities occur, referring obliquely to the transformation of material substances from the base to the precious, so language deepens from the surface and literal to the deeper metaphoric and poetic as the innovative metaphor count increases. Let's consider some examples.

Substances can act as metaphors for personality – the self is of the earth and will return to it. This is literally true. The human body may be in-spired by a spirit – consciousness. But so is the earth herself as poets know – 'speaking' through tremors and volcanic eruptions, for example. In the triad <alchemical sulphur/salt/lead> rests a simple psychological map with profound implications. As noted, alchemical sulphur (inner fire) can be understood psychologically through metaphors of impulse, haste, and mania, whereas alchemical lead can be read as melancholia, depression, and torpidity. The first is over-excitement and lack of focus, the second is under-excitement and over-focused. Alchemical salt balances these extremes by bringing a grounding, focus, and pragmatism. While sulphur refers to rapidity of events, and lead to events grinding to a halt, salt turns events into experiences through memory, or salt makes events memorable by turning them into experiences. A fourth substance, alchemical mercury, provides experiences with reflection, or refines experiences by assessing their qualities. Mercury brings imagination to the everyday.

Salt must be touched by the mercurial imagination otherwise memories are merely stored away and not revivified. Experiences have no special

## The alchemical self as outlaw: an experiment in embodied metaphor   31

elements. Salt fixes the running on of memories and makes substance of them. Salt without mercury is rote psychotherapy – rules, no imagination, poetry by numbers. Descartes salted the soul away as pea-size in the pineal gland. Mercury allows the soul the freedom and inventiveness of the spirit Ariel in Shakespeare's *The Tempest*. Salt, says James Hillman, 'makes events sensed and felt, giving us each a sense of the personal', but 'salt is the mineral substance or objective ground of personal experience making experience possible'. Repressed salt returns as a distortion of personalism – narcissism. Selfies, self-interest, obsessions with image. The curse of our times – 'how do I look?' Personal-confessional cultures. Impulses of others (the world's sulphurs) felt as personal insult (the sulphurs salted away). Therapies can become over-salted obsessed with rooting around in memories and bitter residues, never moving on. Pickled in principles of 'regression-is-good'. Suffering becomes a cult.

Salt has cultural meanings. In *The Golden Bough*, James Frazer gives several examples of salt used in purification ceremonies. The young Inca, the Peruvian sun-god incarnate, is prepared for kingship through fasting, during which time he must not see the sun or eat salt. He must sit, suspended between the realm of the sun god and that of the ordinary people he will rule. Frazer says that the ancient Japanese bear hunters, the Ainu, banned salt in their annual honouring of the bear soul where a captured bear is sacrificed and returns to the spirit world. In hunting cultures, upholding of chastity before the hunt often includes a taboo upon eating salt. The Huichol Indians 'hunt' the peyote where the men take a vow of chastity and eat no salt. When the Romans left town, after a conquest, they salted the land so that the conquered could not farm it. Ouch! A literal bitterness and a strange cruelty, but also a meaningful gesture – the heat of sulphurous battle would be ceremonially closed over by the salting of conquered land that was of little use to the conquerors. As the Roman soldiers left for other confrontations, they were paid in salt (a 'salary') because salt was worthy (salt of the earth) – necessary but scarce.

Alchemists in their laboratories never literally turned base metals such as lead into gold. Where they claimed to do so, they were frauds, or tricksters. But in such laboratory-based experimentation, the alchemists who became known as 'puffers' (because they spent a lot of time with bellows, keeping fires alight and regulating heat) made many fascinating discoveries about how materials reacted with one another under conditions of heat and in solution, in the process establishing modern chemistry. For example, in the 16th century, Paracelsus discovered that lead-tainting water caused goitre (a swelling of the thyroid gland). Authentic alchemists never claimed to literally make gold, rather they made golden metaphors – they improved or enhanced things through enriching language both verbally and visually. Again, they were poets. They invented a tactile, sensuous language that

## 32   *Self-Literacy*

was also contradictory or ambiguous – such as oily earths, wet fires, and stones that sweat.

We must swing back and forth between the earth-bound 'puffers' and alchemy as a metaphor system. In a contemporary alchemical process, since the 1980s we have indeed been able to literally change base metals into gold through nuclear reactions. The problem is that the process costs more than the gold yield is worth (one quadrillion dollars per ounce), while the product is also radioactive and therefore useless.

We have always been fascinated with what lies beneath our feet – the geography and geology of our surroundings, as the apparent stability of what is a highly unstable *terra firma*. Some take this literal earth to be the focus of their religious zeal. Recall that humanity is a mere microsecond in the history of planet Earth that is fundamentally a history of a large, unstable rock mantle with a molten core. A planet whose resources, in an evolutionary blink of an eye, we are intent on destroying through emissions leading to global warming (a massive and misguided alchemical experiment in itself). As humans evolved so they dug up special stones from that mother rock, such as flint – thought of as the bones of the body of Earth – and learned how to knap them to create sharp-edged tools primarily used for killing animals (arrowheads and spearheads), and flensing (scraping fat from) their hides. Metals also rest in the earth's mantle, a literal spin-off product of millions of years of churning activity at the molten core of the planet. At hot spots of volcanic and seismic activity – such as granite-rich areas where the stone had been thrust up from deep in the earth millennia ago and then cooled rapidly – some metals would get thrown up to the surface and could be gathered from soil or panned from streams. This included useful metals such as tin, and rarer metals such as silver and gold, used largely in ornamentation such as jewellery where the metals are too soft for tool use. But humans soon learned that digging deeper into the earth would reveal rich seams of metals in ores (rocks or sediment containing mixtures of metal deposits). Metals such as copper and tin, used in making bronze, were sought by cultures around the world to make tools and weapons (the ten-years-long war at Troy waged by the Greeks against the Trojans documented in Homer's *Iliad* is set in the late Bronze Age, twelve hundred years BCE).

We have seen that in contrast to the more spiritually inclined alchemists were those who pursued the impossible task of 'quickening' nature by turning base metals into gold. The hedonist alchemists aimed to get rich quickly and have fun now rather than waiting for heavenly promises. Even if they could not really produce gold from base metals, they would convince (and show by a bit of trickery) potential rich patrons that they could, disappearing when they were exposed as charlatans, but pocketing their advance payments. This group of alchemists saw that metals 'grew' in

*The alchemical self as outlaw: an experiment in embodied metaphor*   33

the earth. Some were common and relatively worthless, like lead, tin, and copper. Others were rare and precious, like silver and gold, the latter used as a mark of prestige. The idea occurred to them that all metals in rocks had the same origin, but some had been 'quickened' in their development through natural forms of heating, compression, and combinations of elements. If these forces of quickening could be studied and understood, they may, perhaps, be reproduced in small ways in the laboratory, where base metals might be transformed into gold.

A small number of alchemists claimed that they had mastered these secrets through intensive laboratory experimentation. They faced a different challenge to the spiritually inclined alchemists. While the latter were hunted down and persecuted by the Church, the material alchemists were hunted down and persecuted by the State. For example, in Britain the Monarch and his State saw that if alchemists really could produce gold from base metals, then economies controlled by the King would quickly be destabilised. The Church in turn feared that its dependable income from the State might be reduced. By the end of the 13th century, Pope John XXII issued a decree declaring alchemy to be against nature – an irony, as alchemy was grounded in a principle of 'quickening' nature first by understanding the natural world and its substances. Alchemy was outlawed, and then officially declared an illegal activity in 1403 by Henry IV of England. An act was passed in parliament in 1404 that forbade the transmutation of base metals into silver or gold (if that were indeed possible). (The law was repealed in 1689 on the condition that any false precious metals produced by alchemists would be passed on to the State to be deposited in the mint in the Tower of London. In return, the depositor would be issued with the same weight of natural gold or silver. No such transactions occurred). Thus, in the early 15th century, alchemists were officially banned in England and banished as criminals. They had offended both Church and State, but more, they had offended nature herself by attempting to 'quicken' the growth of metals in unnatural ways. Alchemists now took on the identities of outlaws. They became the subject of literary texts and Jung's work on alchemy single-handedly invented a genre of literary psychology that morphed – degraded – into a mountain of New Age self-help books.

# 9 Animal or plant self?
## Geography matters

We focus a good deal on self as personality (the psychological), or self as a social construct (the sociological), but not so much on self as a product of geography – belonging to a specific place or space. Here, geographers have challenged the traditional notion that space and matter are separate or mutually exclusive. But what if we identify them – so that the matter of the body is determined by place or geography, or what matters is the body in immediate space or habitat. There is a German word, *Umwelt*, that best captures this notion of habitat shaping a self, where no English equivalent is available. Geographers call this intimacy of person and place 'natural inclusionality' and see this as a key influence in shaping self. A third factor – scale – can be added to place and space. For it is scale that affords a sense of affect in being, for example, feeling awe under an open sky or a thunderstorm, or the feeling of returning to the womb in a cosy household.

This coupling of space/place and character is today muddied by the large number of people who are migrating and cannot identify with a specific geographical location shaping character. Over 281 million persons are migrating, many of whom are displaced – 3.6% of the global population. It is further muddied by the idea of Gilles Deleuze and Félix Guattari that there are two styles of self. Those who prefer settled life are content at 'being' in their bodies, while those who prefer movement and nomadic lives are 'becoming', always in transition and more irritable in their bodies. Our current migration dilemma is a forcing of settled people into migrant lives to which they cannot adapt. This through conflict, persecution, or starvation – increasingly because of negative outcomes of climate change such as prolonged drought or flash floods.

Anthropologists and ethnographers have posited a different cut through the cake. The German self-taught ethnographer Leo Frobenius (1873–1938) posited two types of persons – those who relate to animals (hunters) and those who relate to plants (agriculturalists), in turn there is a geographical dimension: those who live in wide open spaces such as tundra, in contrast to those who live in enclosed spaces such as dense forest

DOI: 10.4324/9781003619901-10

*Animal or plant self?: geography matters*   35

(even as these have clearings allowing vision of the sky). Groups that have been closely studied by anthropologists include Inuit tundra-dwelling and seagoing hunter-gatherers, and Amazon rainforest people – such as the Yanomami – who live in heavily canopied forest environments. They can be seen to have quite different mythological structures and senses of self. Each too is subject to uninvited incursions into their cultures.

Tundra dwellers stress the importance of a strong, individual self – the vulnerable person isolated on the land with a wide horizon and open sky pitching him- or herself against this world in a struggle for survival. Not much plant life can be gathered here, and hunting may be for large animals – such as whales – whose meat can be stored. These communities are shamanic. The shaman must, in trance, visit the underworld where he or she will meet with the spirit of the dead animal, or the Overlord Spirit of that animal realm, to ask for forgiveness for killing the animal. For the human group must eat, and the animal spirit is thanked for the physical animal giving up its life to support the community. If the spirit visit is successful, then the animals will return on next year's cycle of the hunt.

In contrast, forest-dwelling communities do not stress the importance of the heroic, lone individual and do not live in anxiety as exposed and vulnerable, but rather feel safe under the tree canopy that is a protective Mother. Here, food is plentiful. The women largely gather, and this provides enough food. The men hunt for a variety of diets. All ceremonies and social activities are based around the community and not individuals. The individual self is lost to the group identity. This collective identity is furthermore with a totemic forest animal such as a particular bird. The tradition lingers today in American sports teams and their fervent fans – the Dolphins, the Lions, the Tigers, the Colts.

A fundamental distinction can be drawn between the primary myths and rituals of animal-based hunting groups (such as the Arctic Circle Inuit) and plant-based agricultural societies (such as the historical Mesoamerican Aztecs). The hunter feels for the life of the animal that is killed for the sustenance of the tribe. Again, an apology must be made to the animal spirit, and this is the work of the shaman, who makes the perilous trip in trance or imagination. If the apology is accepted, the animal herd will appear next year. For these hunting groups, often nomadic as they follow the herd, the self is identified with the hunted animals. Also, the self is born in guilt for the killing of what is essentially a family member, the animal totem being the head of the family or tribal group.

In agricultural, planting cultures, dependent upon the crops returning on an annual cycle, the sacrifice and consequent sense of self are quite different. Vegetable matter rots and returns to the earth, providing soil for new life. Planting societies see themselves in this same image. Identifying with plant life (settlers put down roots), humans too die and rot, returning to

## 36 Self-Literacy

the earth. This sacrificial act must be multiplied to ensure healthier crops and is linked to the sun that provides the warmth for the crop to flourish. The sacrifice comes to involve humans – the Aztec culture advertised this grisly fact.

Increasing death through human sacrifice is, paradoxically, seen to increase life. A myth arises of the sacrificed and resurrected god who represents plant life, from Dionysus in Greek myth, through Osiris in Egyptian myth (the grain harvest), to Christ (bread and wine, as body and blood). The psychiatrist Carl Gustav Jung would call these archetypal forms, or universal imprints from which specific cultural selves are fashioned, feeding into – and shaping – the personal. Every person is subject to the collective unconscious that is the repository for myths, a reservoir far deeper and wider than Freud's personal unconscious. For Jung, we must expand the self to include a deeper appreciation of our mythical Self. There are gods and goddesses at work in everyday life – Hestia or Vesta as the hearth of the home, the focus of the family; Demeter or Ceres the grain goddess in every glass of beer (Hades, the god of the underworld abducts Demeter's daughter Persephone; Demeter searches for her daughter and in doing so neglects her duty to care for the harvest, as she is goddess of the grain – the lesson for farmers being to not take your eye off the crop); Dionysus, the god of frenzy and inebriation, appearing after several glasses of beer.

In later agricultural societies, the king replaces the deity or is the deity on earth. When the king dies, the people say 'the king is dead! Long live the king!' as the new king is crowned. In hunting cultures, it is not the animal deity who is killed as sacrifice, but the everyday animal who is provided by the animal deity as a gift to humans. In agricultural societies, it is the god himself who is sacrificed and who resurrects. Thus, for the human, two differing selves are enacted – one based on the moving flesh of animals, the other in rooting and rotting vegetable matter. From these contrasting forms of myths two styles of literature emerge – one dealing with the heroic individual pitting himself against the world; the other dealing with collective aspirations grounded in working with Nature.

# 10 The enlightenment self as 'subject to' King and Divinity

During the 17th and 18th centuries, Europe saw an explosion of interest in mastery of the natural world through the birth of investigative and experimental science. The mystical study of alchemy gave way to the natural study of chemistry through one key experiment. When a metal is burned or combusted, it gains weight. Sensitive scales show this. The alchemists said – counterintuitively and without any evidence or proof – that the metal's gain in weight was due to a 'spirit' of the material, called 'phlogiston', being driven off. The spirit gave the metal its living force and so when it was driven off through heat, the metal 'died'. The living force was a lightening or animating spirit, so in the loss of this spirit the dead or depressed metal became heavier. Through sophisticated experiments and thinking, the new chemists said that the alchemists had it all wrong. When a metal is burned, oxygen is added from the air (this keeps the flame alive), and it is this addition of oxygen that adds weight to the metallic residue. Thus, the European Enlightenment was ushered in, based on rational thinking and experimentation, rather than irrational belief. Information and its classification displaced traditional wisdom as the primary way of making sense of the world. The self was shaped accordingly as sceptic, scientist-scholar, and seeker – an objective-seeking rational subject.

Speculative alchemy then gave way to experimental chemistry with the discovery that the air we breathe is in fact composed of several airs, or gases – approximately 80% nitrogen and 20% oxygen (with, as we now know, a smattering of argon and carbon dioxide). Gases also combine (e.g., nitrous oxide, or 'laughing gas'). Suddenly, the invisible was made visible. As natural forces were harnessed in the service of development of technologies – the steam engine, power loom, cotton gin, gas street lighting, electromagnet, photography, the train engine, and the electrical telegraph – so the human ego expanded because of such mastery.

A radical split occurred socially, where three forms of self existed – those working with and on the land, mainly poor people who identified with

DOI: 10.4324/9781003619901-11

38  Self-Literacy

*Figure 10.1* Hobbes' 1651 *Leviathan*. The populace is contained in the figure of the King.

nature and understood nature's rhythms; those engaging with new technologies who were city-based, forming a new middle class of entrepreneurs, who were interested in harnessing and controlling natural forces and would form a new social layer of the 'self made'; and the landed gentry who were landowners and lived in both city and country. The peasants were gradually being forced off the land to work in the new factories. These social groups spoke three differing versions of English through which identities were forged. The peasantry spoke in the vernacular and retained dialect. The English poets Wordsworth and Coleridge – spending large parts of each day walking and meeting local rural workers first in Somerset and then the Lake District – identified with rural speech to generate a new form of lyrical poetry where a rich self was advertised by extensive use of metaphor and slang. The emerging middle classes – technocrats – were inventing a new language of science and technology that eschewed metaphor for literal description in celebration of ever more complicated mechanics. The aristocracy retained a heavily accented 'received pronunciation' that proffered identity grounded in privilege.

## The enlightenment self as 'subject to' King and Divinity    39

Similar patterns appeared across Europe as it industrialised during the Enlightenment period and thinkers engaged with changing demographics to suggest radical new ways of self-forming. A sense of self appeared during the European Renaissance as a formalising of the rules of perspective in painting and architecture that was absorbed into the public body. However, two bigger forces were at work that dictated what a self should be: those of the Church and the State, the latter moulded by monarchies, the aristocracy, and increasingly the expansive 'professional' middle class. The Christian Church's dogma demands that self be absorbed into an imitation of Christ to guarantee a beatific afterlife. Self-interest or self-aggrandisement are effectively sinful. The High Church, however, maintained a hypocritical position of exerting power and authority and gathering extensive capital. The State, comprised of rulers – kings – and a state apparatus such as parliament, policing, tax collectors, and the landed gentry who are landowners, effectively shape the selves of the common folk as subservient to the state apparatus, landowners, and factory owners.

Identity is then not an active subject, rather persons are *subject to* authority. Subservience is for the majority – the peasantry – whose identities are given with their social position at the base of a hierarchy. For them, life resembles the trial of Sisyphus, who rolls a boulder up a mountain, only to find that near the summit the boulder gets too heavy for him to bear, and rolls down the mountain, only for him to try again, with the same result. This is the burden of a self imposed by a ruling other, as a subservient role rather than a sense of autonomy. Thomas Hobbes' (1651) *Leviathan* describes this social structure as divinely ordained and then not be questioned. The traditional hierarchical order should be maintained at all costs. Yet Hobbes had managed to fall out with Charles I and was tolerated by Oliver Cromwell during the short-lived Republican adventure despite Hobbes' urging of alignment of King and Divinity. As Cromwell began to identify as a dictator, although he was a Puritan perhaps his inflation got the better of him and he became leviathan. Meanwhile, the emergent middle class of technocrats would come to formulate a new sense of self based on capital and profit linked to the development of industry.

# 11 The enlightened self
## Beyond subjection

In December 1783, a German theologian and educational reformer Johann Friedrich Zöllner published an article entitled 'What is Enlightenment?' In the same month, a German physician (and personal doctor to Frederick the Great), Johann Karl Wilhelm Möhsen, delivered a lecture to a secret group called the Berlin Wednesday Society. This group was part of a wider underground collective known as Friends of Enlightenment (of whom Zöllner was a member) who were influential in promoting liberal political views that were seen as part of a general movement embracing new ideas in science and humanism. These intellectual movements were seen as seditious by both Church and the aristocracy as they influenced the State. A chief metaphor of this subversive movement was to 'spread light' as an intellectual rather than purely scientific enlightenment, as removal of the shackles provided by the Church and State apparatus described as, in Zöllner's words, 'prejudices and errors'. In place of such habits an 'enlightenment' of the public would be encouraged as a 'freedom to think, to speak, and also to publish' to release the citizenry from the chains of tradition and authority rule. Such ideas were disseminated through a popular literary medium – the political pamphlet.

In answer to Zöllner's question 'What is Enlightenment?' and Möhsen's response, the renowned German philosopher Immanuel Kant published an essay in 1784 entitled 'An Answer to the Question: What is Enlightenment?'. Where Zöllner and Möhsen had concentrated on pedagogical answers to that question, Kant was more interested in a political response in which citizens would actively cast off the chains of an imposition of authority-led values to follow their own hearts and minds as a critical inquiry into 'selfhood' – as self-directed thinking of the kind that we now take for granted in democracies. Speaking out from this radically new perspective was dangerous – it could lead to imprisonment.

Kant's polemical essay begins with an interesting twist, italicised by Kant to indicate the importance of the sentence: 'Enlightenment is mankind's exit from its self-incurred immaturity'. He is suggesting two things:

DOI: 10.4324/9781003619901-12

The enlightened self: beyond subjection 41

first that humans have taken a wrong turn ethically and this can be put right; second, that putting this right is not a matter of political overthrow of authority, but one of everybody growing up. Thus where 'immaturity' signifies a child making her way through life with the help of an adult, Kant says we must all become independent adults. His motto becomes *sapere aude!* – or have the strength, courage, and conviction to trust and use your own viewpoint. This is a radical provocation, for Kant is saying: 'challenge authority figures and think for yourself' in an age in which the powers of Church and State are supreme. Kant says to his audience: we do not yet live in an enlightened age (an age to come), but we do live in an age of enlightenment (for the seeds have been planted and the growth is inevitable). Here, the modern self as independent thinker is born. Humans can now, says Kant in his closing sentence, become 'more than a machine' to achieve 'dignity'.

What Kant does not consider, where he chastises us for laziness, is first both the physical and moral *courage* to speak out (the ancient Greek *parrhesia* or 'truth-telling') that may invite an unbearable retribution; but also, that many may think that speaking truth to power is to repeat authoritarian patterns of imposition of one's views on others. Kant thus, inevitably, finds himself in an uncomfortable double bind: to invite the voice of protest is to also invite new forms of authoritarianism. The 'self' that announces its liberty is also a self that may take liberties, imposing a voice within an authoritarian historical stream disguised as 'free speech' – a tactic regularly employed by the far right in today's political world. Kant's answer to this lies elsewhere, in his treatises or *Critiques*. Here, we find that the use of Reason that underpins resistance to authority as a means of liberation of self is a legitimate use of reason. Reason is subject to ethics. The reasoning of authoritarians is ethically illegitimate because it represses legitimate forms of reasoning or denies a range of differing expressions of reason.

Kant would also have been aware that his polemic was really aimed at the liberal privileged class who enchained as an inevitable result of a class structure based on inequalities, rather than the oppressed peasants who were chained. The latter were unlikely to hear Kant's good news. Many could not read. He would also have realised that he was a key cog in a historical current whose direction of flow was predictable – the historical sea change that would allow the emergence of a new sense of autonomy for citizens, especially in respect of resistance to entrenched authority.

Kant's polemical essay drew a contemporary response from the lauded French psychologist, philosopher, and cultural commentator Michel Foucault. Summarising Kant's project as 'the constitution of the self as an autonomous subject', Foucault notes that Kant's essay does not pose a new model of freedom as much as inviting an escape from old prisons. After escape, perhaps a horizon of freedom will open. Already, then, the modern

## 42 *Self-Literacy*

self is a project and not a given. Kant provides the invitation to freedom but not the means. Thinking is not enough – political upheaval or revolution may be necessary.

Kant also locates the self in personal embodiment: we should be guided by our understanding and not by a book, by our conscience rather than a spiritual director, and by our diet and lifestyle for bodily health rather than the advice of a doctor. Here, in essence, is the birth of the self-help movement. The locus for will, authority, and reason is personal. Paradoxically, 'self-help' will be transformed into the voiced authorities of a train of gurus and experts, stealing autonomy from those they sought to help. Foucault also questions Kant's assumption of the universality of the making of an enlightened self, the latter's worldview stemming from an imperial central European perspective and then by definition culturally biased.

Kant sits in a historical European philosophical and literary tradition of ruminating on the self as a form of self-directed healthcare. A century before Kant's essay calling for mass release of the self through enlightenment, in his 1689 *An Essay Concerning Human Understanding*, the English philosopher John Locke argues that 'existence itself' is constituted as an unbroken sense of consciousness characterised by a bounded 'self' or identity: 'Consciousness always accompanies thinking' says Locke. In the capacity for thinking rests the capacity for thinking for oneself. A half century earlier, in 1637, the French philosopher René Descartes had argued, in *Discourse on Method*, that 'je pense, donc je suis' (Latin *cogito, ergo sum*) – 'I think, therefore I am'. Descartes specifically published in French prior to Latin, to reach a wider audience. Everybody thinks therefore everybody exists and a personal consciousness makes for unique selves. But such existence is independent of body, therefore body and mind should be separated. These two worlds – *le corps et l'esprit* – constitute a divided self. For Locke, the terms 'body' and 'mind' exist in name only (they are nominal). The reality of our experience is one of a singular existence, where body and mind cannot be separated – an undivided self that has continuity. We can take Locke as the instigator of the modern sense of self showing continuity over time and in space: 'I move, therefore I am'.

Locke says that the meeting of consciousness (sense of things) and thinking (making sense of things) 'makes every one to be what he calls *self*'. This 'distinguishes himself from all other thinking things; in this alone consists *personal identity*'. More, this self is consistent through time, such that we do not experience a shift in the central nature of self 'than a man be two men by wearing other clothes to-day than he did yesterday'. Locke thus posits autobiographical self-knowledge as a steady sense of self through time, although the story may take on all kinds of diversions and expressions. The core of this view, and perhaps the core of modernism, is 'I am this person and no other', and 'I can represent myself to myself': permanence and reflexivity.

*The enlightened self: beyond subjection*    43

The French philosopher and educationalist Jean-Jacques Rousseau (1712–78) followed Locke's thinking about a stable and contained sense of selfhood. This is ironic, for it is Rousseau who critiqued – in *Discourse on Inequality* – both inequity and inequality as a basis for a democratic social order (inequity referring to unjust and avoidable inequalities). Political change of the sort Rousseau envisaged necessitates radical changes in notions of self to engage the interpersonal rather than personal. Rousseau's singular contribution to defining modern selfhood is his 1770 *Confessions* that initiates the genre of autobiography. We can thank Rousseau for introducing ideas of personal reflection, or introspection, into literature in general and the novel in particular. Such Enlightenment thinking privileges what we now class as 'stable' neurotypical identity, questioned by neurodivergence such as experiencing multiple selves in one body.

# 12 Unique identifiers
## Fingerprints and ears

In 1788, the German anatomist Johann Christoph Andreas Mayer identified fingerprints as unique to each person. It would be another century, in 1892, before the English scientist Sir Francis Galton repeated Mayer's findings and now 'fingerprint identification' is generally attributed to him. Conan Doyle's Sherlock Holmes employs fingerprint evidence in *The Sign of the Four* in 1890. Scotland Yard did not use fingerprint evidence until 1901. Before Galton, in 1854 the Frenchman Armede Joux announced that 'earprints' – the shape of ears – are unique. In some sense, Descartes' body-mind dualism could now be dissolved in the bigger picture of the unique self with its tangible prints. A frenzy of phrenology followed. Based on physical features of skull size (craniometry) and facial forms (physiognomy), studies of personality and character (phrenology) emerged, peaking in the late 19th century across Europe and North America. Singular selves were now sorted by larger character aggregates. Your worth was soon catalogued through ideal types (distinguished by features such as a high brow and aquiline nose). 'Criminal', 'unsavoury' low life could, supposedly, be readily spotted by their squat faces and thick necks. Here is the birth of the 'mug shot'.

A Swiss physiognomist Johann Kaspar Lavater (1741–1801) wrote popular books relating the shape of somebody's head to character types such as the melancholic. Sir Frances Galton (1822–1911), who contributed to the science of fingerprinting, set out to 'type' criminals drawing on Lavater's work. He superimposed mug shots of convicted criminals – such as burglars and arsonists – to create composite photographs (then a medium in its infancy – photography was invented in 1822), peddling the notion that they were born this way and by spotting facial types we might intervene by stemming their criminal tendencies. For Galton crooked selves were already stamped that way. The criminologist Cesare Lombroso (1835–1909) built on Galton's work to identify the key features of a criminal type: heavy jaws, receding brows, and conical-shaped skulls known as 'sugar loaf'.

DOI: 10.4324/9781003619901-13

*Unique identifiers: fingerprints and ears*  45

Such desire for creating typologies of course says more about those who set out these absurd ideas than those they described. Lavater, a clergyman, was an extreme evangelical Christian. In his extensive works on physiognomy, that Goethe helped him to publish, Lavater illustrates 'evil personalities' known by their physiognomy. Goethe eventually tired of Lavater's evangelising, particularly when Lavater was attracted to the work of the hypnotist Franz Anton Mesmer (although on meeting Mesmer personally, Lavater himself expressed severe disappointment in Mesmer's character).

A sinister set of social habits emerged from this period of late 18th-century and early 19th-century fascination with physiognomy and typologies of character. In France in particular, on the back of the opportunity to use photography, cities – following Paris – began cataloguing the peasants who were moving to the city from the land. Here, the resident bourgeoisie – those who make a living through ownership of property or the means of production and the incumbent privileged classes – wished to protect themselves against potential disruption or pollution from the incoming workers. Selves here are again based on a class system. The aristocracy and upper/middle classes worked to pass laws that resulted in the first effective police state organised as a machine of surveillance. Every citizen of the 'dangerous classes' was classified and recorded – or given a 'bureaucratic self' – as a marker of identity. Workers and ex-convicts were now required to carry passports within France. Prostitutes, both streetwalkers and in brothels, were also required to carry identity cards and given an identification number. Criminals would be branded – like animals – on the shoulder as an indelible mark of selfhood. Selves were then written out through typologies and physical branding to distinguish the high from the low life.

# 13 Talking yourself up
## Illeism

Language matters when it comes to both describing and making selves. John McWhorter, an associate professor of linguistics at Columbia University, proposes an intriguing idea about the relationships between how we talk about ourselves and who we imagine we are. Some people, believing themselves to be VERY IMPORTANT, have developed a style of self-reference that is indirect: not 'the public wouldn't even know about immigrants at the border if it wasn't for me', but rather 'the public wouldn't even know about immigrants at the border if it wasn't for Donald Trump'. This peculiar style of referencing, used by Trump in particular, is one that both lionises and deifies. Trump uses 'Donald Trump' as what linguists call a 'god term' – something that is chiselled in stone, an inviolable fact. Indeed, a brand. Or these days and in the Trump universe, an 'alternative truth', Trump-as-trustworthy. 'Donald Trump' isn't self-reference, it is a Mount Rushmore edifice, an eternal mark of remembrance, an indelible print. It has gone beyond mannerism to an Eleventh Commandment.

This new way of speaking is beyond plain old narcissistic self-reference, ego inflation, or personal branding (something Trump has employed tirelessly: Trump buildings, Trump golf courses, Trump University, even Trump steaks). The 'I' and 'me' have been completely displaced by the royal Donald – 'Trump' as breathing, golf-playing (and golf-cheating) deity. Talking yourself up this way reifies the abstract: 'Trump' is not an idea but a being in the flesh. He is presented to you sensually, like it or not. Hence, sex scandals for Trump supporters only put meat on the bone – that Trump is only human (indeed a 'real man') and should be applauded for that.

The phenomenon of talking about yourself in the third rather than first person is called 'illeism'. It is a rhetorical device that gives an air of objectivity and the illusion that you are not talking about yourself, or avoiding narcissistic reference, when in fact that is precisely what you are doing, capitalised. It is an old trick. Julius Caesar said, 'Caesar avenged the

DOI: 10.4324/9781003619901-14

*Talking yourself up: illeism*   47

public', turning self-reference ('I avenged the public') into historical fact. Now Caesar, as statesman, knew what he was doing. Talking about oneself as illeism is a smart rhetorical move because it deflects away from the self-referencing associated with narcissism. It can be a sly way of poking fun at yourself to not appear pompous. But Trump's illeism does not feel like a conscious strategy. Rather, it feels like childish simplicity: 'Donald want Mummy!'

# 14 Possessed and absent selves

The physician Franz Anton Mesmer arrived in Paris from Vienna in 1778. His reputation preceded him. He could move his hands over a body, sometimes with a magnet, and cure ailments, especially those of women prone to swooning or fainting. Mesmer described an 'animal magnetism' – a kind of force field, but a fine fluid – that connects everything including human bodies. He claimed that he was able to collect and divert this force as a healing energy. In essence, what he was doing with his patients, again mostly women, was a form of light hypnotic trance, in which their controlling selves were suspended in deep relaxation, open to suggestion. Mesmer of course acted as the authority figure,

*Figure 14.1* Anton Mesmer's tub – collective animal magnetism at work.

DOI: 10.4324/9781003619901-15

*Possessed and absent selves* 49

his ego swelling as the women's egos dissolved. A Parisian woman in high society paid this much attention by a charismatic man would engage in what Freud was to term an erotic counter-transference – they would temporarily be enamoured by him and bend to his will. The impressionable women were indeed mesmerised.

Mesmer would set up group sessions in which both men and women would stand in a ring in a *baquet* and feel the energy transferred from Mesmer to them. The *baquet* was a large oak tub filled with chips of wood, splinters of glass, and magnetised water in flasks. This was thought to be the ideal medium for the transfer of magnetic force. Iron bars protruded from the side of the tub and participants were encouraged to hold these to accelerate the power of the animal magnetism. The participants were also roped together. The room in which this healing took place was only semi-lit so that a kind of twilight prevailed. Mirrors lined the wall of the room, and as the session progressed Mesmer, a friend of Mozart, would play soft music on a glass harmonica. According to eye-witness accounts, participants would start to sway and then possibly swoon, moaning softly. Mesmer would move closer and pass his hands over the bodies of the participants, sometimes touching them near the groin. It was clearly an erotic experience for the otherwise buttoned-up women, while their unearthed eroticism would infect the feelings of the male participants. Again, the conventional self has temporarily left home, and the sensual body awakens for both the patient's and Mesmer's fantasies to be played out.

Mesmer would soon be found out – in 1784, the medical establishment in Paris advised the King to investigate Mesmer's antics and an investigative commission was set up led by the American Benjamin Franklin, living in Paris at the time. Franklin knew a thing or two about real electricity and soon exposed Mesmer and his faux magnetism as a fraud. Mesmer was allowed to retire without charge with the promise that he would abandon mesmerism. He was clearly a very good stage hypnotist and a rake.

A century after Mesmer, France's most famous neurologist and psychiatrist Jean-Martin Charcot (1825–93) would put on displays of his mesmeric skills for groups of physicians. Charcot worked at the Sâlpetrière hospital with so-called 'hysterics' – actually prostitutes who had been taken off the streets, or single mothers. They exhibited symptoms of fainting, seizures, convulsions, paralysis, and tunnel vision. Charcot would present these 'cases' to the medical audience and then hypnotise them, at which point their symptoms would disappear, a case of dissociation. The self could apparently be present or absent at will, or according to the psychiatrist's will. Here is another case of erotic transference. Charcot would stop a seizure or provoke one by touching his hysterical patients, whose desire would be formulated as if circus animals, performing for him. He touched them mainly near the breasts or genitals.

50  *Self-Literacy*

At one point, Sigmund Freud was in the audience for several of these sessions. As he drank in the techniques of Charcot, particularly inducing a hypnotic trance, another part of Freud was working through the importance that erotic transference played in the therapeutic encounter (although this idea was not fully formulated by Freud at that time). What gave Freud the clue about the erotic transference was overhearing a conversation between Charcot and another doctor at a reception in which Charcot, breaking confidence, gossiped about one of his patients. This was a woman who could not be satisfied sexually by her 'awkward' husband, who clearly had no sexual technique or sensitivity. The woman had developed 'nervous' symptoms as a result. Charcot blurted out: 'Mais, dans des cas pareils c'est toujours la chose génitale, toujours!' – 'But in such cases, it is always the genital thing, always!' Charcot meant not just genitality specifically, but sexuality and eroticism generally. Freud pondered greatly on this moment – it was formative for his ideas and later practices. Charcot himself had not gone public on this claim.

Freud was poor at inducing a hypnotic trance in his patients and soon gave up hypnosis for the talking cure. Later, some of Charcot's famous women hysterics were to come clean about their roles in the clinical demonstrations. They were not mad women but were play-acting. The mesmerised and hysterical selves were both theatrical roles, certainly based on a desire to please as core to the erotic transference. The selves that came and went were guided by a role-playing self of greater power and in this sense, these women were cleverer than their would-be masters.

# 15 The modern ego
## The all-seeing 'I'

Scholars of Indo-European literature in the 1920s discussed uses of language largely from the perspective of writers – novelists and poets – and not from the perspective of how language is spoken by the people (the vernacular). The philosopher and literary critic Owen Barfield changed this with his ground-breaking 1926 book *History in English Words*. Barfield focused on those who spoke languages rather than the forms and structures of the languages themselves. In a chapter on 'self' and 'character', Barfield notes that in the 18th century, people invented new ways of speaking about themselves, where words that previously referred to objects and events external to persons were now employed to speak of internal states of mind and feeling. Such references 'attempt to portray character or feeling from within', where words 'are transferred from the outer to the inner world' including: 'apathy, chagrin, diffidence, ennui, homesickness' and 'agitation, constraint, disappointment, embarrassment, excitement'. Such a shift in register came to inform the Romantic poets, particularly Coleridge, with his coining of terms such as 'psychosomatic'. By the time of Barfield's book language had been 'psychologised' through interest in psychoanalysis that had gone beyond the confines of medicine, psychiatry, and the chattering classes to permeate public talk. Such a shift in language register was also gendered male.

Historical accounts of 18th-century Britain – focused on the privileged classes – highlight stark differences between women and men. Women suffer from 'nerves', have a nervous disposition, and are weaker than men in this respect. This is a way of saying that the self of women is more emotional than that of men – an overgeneralisation rather than a truism, and in today's gender-fluid societies, a stereotype of both women and men. We must ask, are women and men born this way, or does the culture shape sensibility? Such a stereotype – the association of women with 'nerves' – continues into the 20th century and its master interpreter will be Sigmund Freud. Social commentators writing during the 1920s and 1930s had described a 'mood' emerging in the Western imagination

DOI: 10.4324/9781003619901-16

## 52  *Self-Literacy*

that can be characterised as 'nerves'. Persons showed fragility and neurotic symptoms as a response to the frenetic pace of life dictated by city living, exacerbated by an exponential growth in technologies. This emerging world was all about speed and instantaneity and many could not keep up. Social commentators of the 1920s called this 'mobility mania'.

One figure would nervelessly face this culture of nerves with a radical approach. The nervous or anxious self, said Sigmund Freud, was one entangled in unresolved sexual desire in an era of sexual timidity. Freud wrote to his fiancée Martha Bernays that his own confidence had been much bolstered by use of the new wonder drug cocaine. Freud was already experimenting with cocaine in the late 19th century in uptight Vienna. He wrote to Martha on 2 June 1884:

> Woe to you, my princess, when I come. I will kiss you quite red and feed you till you are plump. And if you are forward you shall see who is the stronger, a gentle little girl who doesn't eat enough or a big wild man who has cocaine in his body.

If Freud had not developed an interest in human sexuality, he would have pursued a fulfilling career in zoology studying the gender, anatomy, and sexual behaviour of fish. Studying under the comparative anatomist Carl Claus as a biology student, the young Freud worked in a marine biology research unit in Trieste. Here, he dissected over 400 eels to locate their genitals. On his return to Vienna, he worked in the university's physiology laboratories working largely with microscopy to study the spinal nerve cells of the sea lamprey leading to his first academic publication. More papers would follow. By the early 1880s Freud had established a reputation as an expert on the nervous systems of fish. He also developed ground-breaking stains for microscopy slides. As this histological work gained in sophistication, an issue of defining figure over ground, perhaps Freud laid the seeds for his model of the distinct ego emerging out of the indistinct mass of the unconscious.

Twenty years later, in 1920, Freud published an essay 'Beyond the Pleasure Principle' in which he laid out the 'anatomy' of the psyche – a set of psychological metaphors, a map that precedes the territory (and then a simulacrum) as a set of topophors. What Freud fished out from unconscious associations by his patients was a tentative abstraction, floundering on the couch, a fishy tale. Freud was not much taken with the territory of the ego. He was far more interested in the wild and unpredictable landscape and machinations of unconscious life with its rich fantasies and obsessions – equivalent to the uncharted ocean depths. The self was a

*The modern ego: the all-seeing 'I'* 53

falsehood, a plaster over the wounds, created in childhood, over which the unconscious cast a shadow. The self, as ego, massaged the raw, undigested material of the unconscious, and made it polite as a rationalisation. Culture demanded the dominance of the Reality Principle over the Pleasure Principle. The ego, as socialised self, repressed or displaced such material, considering it obscene or even dangerous.

Freud set out the tripartite structure of the psyche as a further set of metaphors, an anatomical geography that matched the undifferentiated background to his fish histology slides. By applying metaphorical 'stains' (as the analytic method) he would differentiate the matter of the unconscious and open it to inspection. He laid out this metaphorical anatomy of the psyche in an essay 'Beyond the Pleasure Principle' (1920), refined in 'The Ego and the Id' (1923). Freud's interest was not to strengthen the ego and what he called its 'defence mechanisms' (such as repression, displacement, projection, sublimation), but rather to make the ego permeable, softer, such that unconscious desires could be entertained, talked about, and accommodated appropriately through analytic guidance. Although Freud said, 'where Id was, ego shall be', his method belies this, for it turns undifferentiated and disguised impulse into creative product. Freud himself was a master case-storyteller – he won the Goethe Prize for literature and not the Nobel Prize for science. His analysands would be encouraged to make productive narratives from incomprehensible unconscious content with the guidance of the analyst's interpretations.

By the 1950s, working against the grain of Freud's more subtle and complex approach, North American psychoanalysis had become obsessed with strengthening the ego, producing tough, capable selves in a masculine heroic mode, harking back to Greek heroic types. America had been at war with Germany and Japan, and was now involved in a war with Korea, and soon would enter combat with communist-led North Vietnam. Industrial growth was vibrant, fed by an industrial-military complex. Cars and domestic gadgets got bigger and more robust. Heroic masculinism and competition prevailed. Americans must toughen up – show that they are the strongest in the world. The culture of narcissism, and cut throat and bullying business tactics were seeded. Ironically, the more the ego was strengthened – ostensibly as defence against intrusion by irrational forces – the more the ego became unconscious or less knowing, oblivious to its hardening and need for mastery. The greater the repression of unconscious desire (rather than the analysis of such desire and not its acting-out) the more that desire would return in a distorted form. For post-World War II North American life this distortion was embodied in the dominant power of the patriarchy reflected in political repression such as McCarthyism.

## 54   Self-Literacy

Psychoanalysis, as the primary therapeutic mode for psychological ills, would heroically conquer debilitating depressions, anxieties, and neuroses. The pharmaceutical industry would be the foot soldiers in this war against psychological infirmity. The ego should be defended and bolstered by better living through chemistry. Defence mechanisms of the ego would not be too strongly repelled for they served a good purpose. They would be collectively gathered and projected out to ward off the forces of communism. America's ills (overconsumption, narcissism, masculine dominance) would be rationalised, and sublimated. The unconscious desires of the dominant male culture would be fed by hyper-sexualisation and domestication of women.

This branch of the modernist self has its roots in Structuralism where things described in language are known in difference from other linguistic descriptors and not in terms of their supposed essence. Thus 'dog' and 'cat' are arbitrary signifiers (the signified being the tangible animals themselves) but we know them by their difference from one another. However, such oppositionalism advertising structuralist thinking invites taking sides – pitching one preferred option against another: free world vs communism, male vs female, strength vs weakness, industry vs nature, progress vs regress.

The strong a-hysterical ego becomes associated with male dominance and is reproduced in the 'all-seeing eye (or I)' that is the panopticon, the ideal control centre for an authoritarian personality. A prison would have a central control area (the all-seeing eye) where the prisoners' cells would be in corridors leading off from the central eye, allowing permanent and embracing vigilance. This notion was translated in medicine as, through dissection of cadavers, medical students (until relatively recently wholly a male intake) would be socialised into the 'medical gaze'. This is a diagnostic gaze that metaphorically 'looks into' the body during a consultation and sets the doctor apart from the patient. The penetrating gaze – as knowing self – is literalised in the post-mortem or autopsy.

To return to the main trope of modernist structuralism – that of opposition of terms with one term a 'top dog' – the fruits of such thinking are various kinds of control or uses of power invested in this 'top dog' signifier in the opposition (in my example earlier: 'male', 'strength', 'industry', 'progress'). These signifiers also form a 'metonymic chain' – a linkage of associations that together form a linguistic strand of thinking, and a way of valuing. Modernism has one of its clearest cultural expressions in architecture and its pinnacle is the glass and steel skyscraper and its link with commerce. The tallest buildings were once churches, raised to the glory of God; then banks as centres of commerce, raised to the glory of profit; and then corporate buildings raised to the glory of the excessively profitable

*The modern ego: the all-seeing 'I'* 55

business corporation. The self of modernism – grounded in a solid ego or the all-seeing 'I' that is a 'skyscraper' – remains obstinately phallogocentric, linking phallus and logic metonymically to also hook with strength, industry, and 'progress'. Below the city skyline of New York however is a swamp, the regressive unconscious of the metropolis. The city, like the ego, is built on shifting ground into which it threatens to sink.

# 16 The origins of 'self-help'

The emergence of an independent, self-regulating, introspective modern self brings the responsibility of maintenance. We live in an age of self-help, cod counselling, and pop psychology cultures. The newspaper colour supplements abound with such material, television overflows with it, and social media – such as TikTok and YouTube – constitute its main outlets. Oddly, in an age of self-help, we seem to have forgotten how to care for the self that has grown flabby, weak, unresourceful, and shackled by habit. We need others – so-called 'experts', some charlatans – to show us the way. While each of us is a snowflake – unique – we are also uniquely vulnerable.

Self-help and personal growth cultures are far from new. Michel Foucault devotes much of his later lecture series and writing to laying out the historical foundations of 'care of self' in ancient Greek and Roman aristocratic practices – ways of perfecting selfhood through mind and body. His 1981–82 'Hermeneutics of the Subject' lecture series at the *Collège de France* runs to 550 pages of small print text, where Foucault describes self-forming primarily as an ethical practice. Care for the self also becomes a model for care of others, a public service. Further, it is a set of aesthetic practices – the self is sculpted or shaped affectively, as refinement of sensibility and sensitivity. New – modern and postmodern – forms of self-help are aesthetically crude and ethically insensitive, where, in the grip of neo-liberal capitalism, self-help is explicitly at the expense of others or is purely selfish or narcissistic. In turn, a host of underperforming gurus, influencers, and coaches are milking a public eager to try the latest 'new thing on the block'.

Here, 'self-help' is badly titled, for while autonomy and relying on your own resources is important, the 'development' of a self in the (now largely 'New Age') personal growth industry is heavily scaffolded by teachers, facilitators, and gurus. Quite what 'self' they are helping is unclear, where the untested assumption is that there is a core self that can be helped or perfected. 'Self' becomes capital to be exploited by others.

DOI: 10.4324/9781003619901-17

The origins of 'self-help'   57

For over a century, the centre of gravity for modern traditions of self-help has been North America. Here, rampant individualism has triumphed over collectivism. Romanticised movies focus on the 'opening up' of frontiers in North America, such as the settling of California, showing families moving west in covered waggons that are brought into a collective circle to defend against marauding 'Indians'. First, it is the land of North American aboriginal tribes that is being settled or stolen, as the tribes are displaced or eradicated. And second, the collective spirit of the community of settlers is always a consequence of the work of an initial lone scout who first trespasses on the territory of the native peoples. This adventurous scout or intrepid explorer provides the blueprint for the self-sufficient hero of the Frontiersman embodied in the figure of Kit Carson and spawning a genre of frontiersmen pot-boilers.

The frontiersman mentality shifts from literal geographies to those of the human psyche. In this mould, we find the Scottish doctor, author, and reformer Samuel Smiles. Smiles published his hugely successful manual *Self-Help* in 1859. It is soaked in a stringent, puritan form of Protestantism (Smiles also later, in 1878, co-authored a book called *Thrift*). He thought that poverty was a product of individual irresponsibility – either laziness or bad planning – and was avoidable. Ironically Smiles, one of 11 children, was supported through medical school by finances provided by his mother after his father had died from cholera. To his credit, in the 1840s Smiles engaged deeply with political reform, arguing for democratic principles including the rights of women. But by the 1850s, he had stopped campaigning for general political reform as he vigorously promoted the idea of self-sufficiency. *Self-Help* sold 20,000 copies in the first year of publication, and by the time of Smiles' death in 1904, the book had sold over 250,000 copies. A modern literary genre emerged on its back (although, as Michel Foucault's work shows, 'self-help' literature existed in Classical times, for late Greek and Roman audiences).

Orison Swett Marden (1848–1924), an American polymath, had degrees in law, science, and arts as well as medicine. Orphaned at the age of 7, as a teenager Marden fortuitously came across a copy of *Self-Help* and was smitten with Smiles' ideas. Marden wrote his own self-help book – *Pushing to the Front*. Where ascetics find (or abandon) the self in retreat, capitalists of emotional life such as Marden are, as his book title brazenly advertises, pushy. Already self-help advertised more than a tinge of selfishness rather than selflessness. Published in 1894, Marden's was the first and most influential self-help book in America. By 1925, it had run to 250 editions and became a global bestseller. Spurred on by the initial success of his book, in 1897 Marden founded a magazine unashamedly called 'Success', with a circulation of 500,000. It was indeed a runaway success as the first motivational self-help journal. A vocabulary for the self-help movement was

## 58 Self-Literacy

emerging – psychologically trite and materially aspirational. A fertile seed-bed for contemporary neoliberalism.

By then, Marden had left medicine and hospitals to enter the hospitality industry, running several hotels and a holiday resort. He eventually employed over 200 people to run his periodical. In 1916, he became the first president of the 'League for the Larger Life' in New York – placing the aspirational on the banner and founding the human 'growth' industry. The organisation's mission statement was 'to spread knowledge of the fundamental principles that underlie healthy unharmonious living' and 'to assess the individual in the solution of personal problems'. Another facet of self-help is to disregard contradictions, and what we now call 'wicked problems' (insoluble issues), to always seek solutions. The 'pop psychology', personal development culture was established, grounded in the wider values of the American 'frontiersman' mentality of heroic individualism, strong work ethic (Protestantism's main secular value), and opportunistic capitalism. Neoliberalism was born. Much later, the American psychologist Abraham Maslow would set out a 'hierarchy of needs' in which food, water, and shelter are at the base, and 'self-realisation' is at the apex. This is absurd and disrespectful to the 720 million people worldwide who live on approximately $2 a day.

Stressing the 'frontiersman' virtues of resilience and persistence (core to self-help) and the Protestant work ethic, Orison Marden recounted how his first manuscript copy of *Pushing to the Front* had been destroyed in a fire when one of his hotels burned down. He immediately wrote three new versions and sent them simultaneously to three different publishers – each wanted to publish the book. Again, Marden, inspired by Samuel Smiles, had created the self-realisation movement that today we know by descriptors such as 'personal growth', and that has exploded through social media, especially TikTok.

Marden was almost certainly influenced by a 19th-century American movement called 'New Thought', formed initially by the ideas of Phineas Quimby. Drawing on ideas from religious denominations, the New Thought movement's doctrine was that health is a product of 'right thinking', while conversely sickness is a product of 'wrong thinking'. In short, the individual determines his or her fate and bears responsibility for his or her actions and bodily states. What Foucault described as 'technologies of self' was brazenly commodified. Again, the irony is that 'self'-help is actually packaged tips from another, or expert-directed, displacing the self or, rather, turning that self into a customer or commodity.

Few people have known more about making money from commodities than the Scottish-American industrialist and philanthropist Andrew Carnegie (1835–1919), who made a fortune from producing steel. He was a staunch believer in independence, the Protestant work ethic, and self-help,

The origins of 'self-help'   59

admiring Marden's work. Carnegie set up a charitable foundation to redistribute around 90% of his considerable fortune (around $65–70 billion in today's money). There was, however, a dark side to Carnegie's beliefs that also characterised Samuel Smiles' philosophy – those who could not help themselves were seen as either weak or lazy and should be allowed to perish. This twisted version of Darwinian 'survival of the fittest' offered a cruel injunction to the physically or mentally challenged or impaired and those stuck in a poverty trap or cycle. Carnegie's model by-passed blatant inequities.

Marden's and Carnegie's shared value system would come to describe a cultural style and trait among North Americans that would shape educational systems and pedagogical practices, focused on the self and self-improvement (linked with a scepticism towards centralised, State-funded support). Its main proponent would be John Dewey, born in the year that Samuel Smiles' *Self-Help* was first published (1859), and a contemporary of both Marden and Carnegie. Dewey was a firm believer in democracy, but moreso in autonomy: self-determination and self-realisation – a pedagogy of the individual spirit. Democracy started with the rights of individuals and freedom of expression. Dewey believed that autonomous or self-determining persons would naturally subscribe to the common ideal of democracy, as participative engagement for the common good. This, in the context of North American competitive capitalism, has proved to be illusory. Self-help readily becomes every man for himself in a neoliberal environment, where collectivism is a soft option as some will always work harder than others.

Individualism continues to define not only North American public life, but also that of the entire wealthy northern hemisphere under the influence of neoliberal capitalism. The key features include an obsessive focus on the rights of the individual and the value of small government. 'Real' work is also characterised as business oriented. As the 19th-century self-help movements gained traction in North America, so Andrew Jackson (1767–1845), the seventh President of the USA, left a political legacy of small government encouraging self-help. Jackson was a frontiersman who later trained as a lawyer, becoming a wealthy plantation owner and supporter of slavery. He signed into law an ethnic cleansing act that removed thousands of Native Americans from their ancestral homelands. He was revered among his supporters for clearing the national debt of the US government, but this was achieved largely through the sale of public land that became privatised. Jackson is credited with creating a climate in which a prominent image of America as a land of opportunity and liberty emerged, where independent business could flourish. This was melded with the self-help movement to create an overall myth of the 'self-made man' in which, literally, 'self' is constructed and grown like a successful business – self as commodity.

## 60 *Self-Literacy*

This myth of boundless opportunity centred on a free market continues today. Here again is a double-edged sword, where such opportunity can be exploited as a key factor in the development of self, but it is precisely the business of developing others' selves that can be expanded. The UK's *Observer* newspaper recently reported a boom in sales of so-called self-help books, particularly pertaining to mindfulness, with sales of 3 million in the UK in 2019. In France, nearly 15 million self-help or 'lifestyle' (health and well-being) improvement books were sold in 2018, compared to 10 million cookery books and nearly 3 million books on gardening, animals, and nature, self-help now leading the market. The personal growth market in the USA is now turning to life coaching and is worth $15 billion. While more women than men read self-help books, more men than women write them. But, as global sales of self-help books explode, there are so many to choose from that average sales run for any one book is only 250 copies. Many are self-published (another contemporary facet of self-help – the need for importance). A successful self-help book will establish a reputation and go into several imprints and possible new editions, and be translated into several languages, to sell around 10,000 copies in its lifetime. The irony of this is that one does not 'help' oneself – as the lonely frontiersman might – but is helped by another who may become rich on the back of the culture of self-help.

# 17 The relational self

Recall the English poet John Donne's famous line from 1624: 'No man is an Island, entire of it self; every man is a piece of the Continent, a part of the main'. What is 'the main'? The mid-19th century in Europe was an era fascinated by biological typologies and classification systems, arranged hierarchically. This paralleled a rigid class structure, in the context of which the French writer Honoré de Balzac's (1832) novella *Le Colonel Chabert* introduces a new idea about identity. The American literary theorist and writer Peter Brooks – in a biography of Balzac – notes that, contra Rousseau, the character Derville in Balzac's novella shows that the 'inward self ... is not enough' where 'identity is forged in all sorts of transpersonal networks' and 'intersubjective negotiations'. Here, self is social or relational. The psychologist Jerome Bruner calls this intersubjective identity a 'transactional' self. It is also translational, where languages of selfhood are multiple and demand interpretations.

The key issue for self in such models is that the social precedes the individual. Sociology trumps psychology where the self – or identity – is formed through identification. This idea was first introduced by August Comte (1798–1857), often called the 'father of sociology'. Comte first coined the term 'sociology' in 1838, claiming priority for the social over the individual. Selves are experienced in terms of identification as historical tradition, culture, gender, tribe, ethnicity, class, religion, profession, and interest and friendship groups. The psychological self (identity) is secondary to such identifications. Comte was followed by the French sociologist Émile Durkheim in the late 19th and early 20th centuries. Durkheim claimed that subjectivity arose again from subjection – to social rules, as 'manners of acting, thinking, and feeling external to the individual', which are invested with a coercive power by virtue of which they exercise control. Social rules extend to coded interaction with objects or artefacts, such as style of dress, architecture, or kinds of cutlery, that signify where a social self sits in a stratified society. Such rules, signs, and symbols – as embodied metaphors – become internalised to give a sense of personal identity, but

DOI: 10.4324/9781003619901-18

## 62 Self-Literacy

this is false, in the sense that identity is always prefigured historically, culturally, and socially. This also registers in language.

Today, sociological selves (as identification with rules and norms, or rule-breaking and norm bending) and psychological selves (as self-serving identity) vie for respective supporters. But many biopsychologists who have apparently gone down a reductionist route – such as exploring selfhood through brain functions or cognitive strategies – recognise that cognition cannot be isolated from context or is 'extended' and 'situated'. Conception requires ovum and sperm – it is an essentially social act, and so all selves are born in the social or transactional. Language teaches us this – even as language capabilities may grow according to brain development, it is only through interaction with others that language develops. Self is shared capacity: transactional, translational, and relational.

The modern relational self – a communal and social being – is characterised by identification with a primary group, such as an ethnic or religious community. Looser associations may be through common interests, specialisms, or professions, forming unique fringe communities in some instances. One of these is the coalition of contemporary Antarctic scientific study groups hived off in their respective research stations, but often meeting up. These disparate groups sharing objects of study have developed a singular lingo, idiosyncratic everyday colloquialisms, only recently subject to documentation and study. Newcomers to Antarctica are called 'fingies' by the US groups, from a military abbreviation FNG: 'fucking new guy'. The same groups call a non-work excursion from the station a 'boondoggle'. Across groups, the last person to place their food tray in the dishwasher is 'tray'd' as they will be the ones to turn on the machine and empty it. Oversize protective gloves used in harsh weather conditions are 'nose wipers'. Somebody burned out on service and replaced is referred to as 'toasted'. Some descriptors are then neologisms, others are easy-to-translate metaphors ('toasted') – all suggest selves defined by subscription to a unique community.

The relational self has been posited as a natural biological and evolutionary position for humanity, where autonomy or self-interest is unnatural. It is a misreading of Darwin to consider selfishness as an evolutionary advantage. Selflessness is clearly the primary evolutionary position, where cooperation guarantees continuation of the species. Philosophers such as Emmanuel Levinas recognise this, where they see self as constituted in the mirror of the Other – you are defined by how others see you and react or respond to you. Evolutionary biologists too see collaboration as a natural driver where early hunter-gatherer groups thrive thanks to efficient division of labour.

Adam Smith's 18th-century masterwork *The Theory of Moral Sentiments* argues for the value of sympathy for another, and of tolerance, as essential human traits. The self is an empathic being. We must adopt multiple voices and place ourselves in the positions of others for a society to work. The evolutionary biologist David Haig suggests that three levels of sympathy have evolved in humans: the first level is reflection on your own values and ethical judgements (we can call this 'sympathy'); the second level is to appreciate the values positions of others and to test these against your own values positions (we can call this 'empathy'); the third level is one of the impartial observer: How would another person judge the dialogue between my value positions and the value positions of another (especially where these are in conflict) (we can call this 'compathy', the deepest form of empathy)? The third-person position defines a humanist political democracy, where there is no transcendental values position as ultimate arbiter (such as scripture). Humanity is quite some way from achieving this third-person position despite Adam Smith's provocations from 300 years ago. Humanist political maturity takes time and is constantly hijacked by religious and authoritarian political ideologies.

The postmodern relational self, grounded in mass, forced migrations through climate crisis, conflicts and wars, or ethnic and religious cleansing, is a self that can still identify with 'same-selves'. But what of those who are free-floating – the homeless, the evicted, the newly arrived immigrant who has risked life to avoid persecution in his, her, or their homeland? This is a community of those who potentially have nothing in common, with no pre-supposed categorisation or labelling, perhaps seeking fresh identities and bonds – but first seeking asylum as a stranger in a strange land, now perhaps a stranger to oneself. Yet stubbornly social and relational, but fearful of how they may be integrated into an alien community, or whether they will be rejected, treated with hostility, or deported.

# 18  Self stripped of rights

What is it to be rendered null by an authority, or to dehumanise another? This happens to political prisoners, refugees, and those on the fringes of society such as vagrants. Here, self defined as citizenship is annulled. Self is written out or cancelled. The ancient Greek city states included banishment to another geographical location as a form of punishment, where identity is all but obliterated as the rights of citizenship are denied. Slavery has, historically, stripped persons of citizenship; and modern slavery, such as prostitution rings, continues to do this. The Nazis reduced Jews, gypsies, and persons of colour to non-entities in a systematic identity 'cleansing' and such genocide has been repeated often throughout history: for example, the aboriginal inhabitants of Tasmania and North America, Stalinist political cleansing, British atrocities in Kenya, the Cambodian genocide under Pol Pot's regime, Serbia systematically killing or driving out Bosnian Muslims, and China incarcerating one million Turkic Muslims (Uyghurs). Today's incursion of Israeli troops into Gaza smacks of ethnic cleansing of Palestinians. Transient persons, forced into emigration through war, conflict, famine, religious, or political differences, are reduced to non-entities and 'collateral damage'. Such atrocities advertise the nulling of one identity in celebration of the awful power of another.

Certain individuals, with personality traits of authoritarianism (the desire to control) and narcissism (extreme self-regard), act out at a personal level two well-documented social conditions: 'sovereign power' and a 'state of exception'. In sovereign power, identity is invested in one person representing a singular institution – the all-powerful monarch or authoritarian dictator. This figure embodies the personality conditions of authoritarianism and narcissism. The desire to control and extreme self-regard are here one and the same, for there would be no desire to control if one did not have supreme confidence in one's judgement (that is of course blinkered). This is both immoral and pathological. This type of person can be said to live in what the German philosopher Carl Schmitt, in the 1920s, termed a 'state of emergency' for a nation, where martial law is introduced. Here,

DOI: 10.4324/9781003619901-19

*Self stripped of rights* 65

the sovereign, head, or ruler can transcend the law for public good. But, of course, such a state can be corrupted and introduced as a permanent measure, constituting an identity stamping of a narcissistic kind.

The Italian philosopher Giorgio Agamben has traced the history of state use of sovereign power to create a state of exception as a permanent state of emergency in which certain people are not only denied citizenship of, or entry into, the country, but can also be banished or detained indefinitely (e.g., the inmates of the USA's Guantanamo Bay detention camp near Cuba). This renders identity as null and void where the person is not covered by any legal or civil rights. This presents the opposite case to a government supporting the right to resistance or free speech that confers specific identities. Effectively, a state of exception (such as the introduction of sweeping powers of search and detention following the 9/11 bombing in New York and the second Presidential term of Donald Trump) allows for a temporary 'democratic dictatorship'. Such emergency powers have now, however, become the rule rather than the exception, to embrace executive dictatorship, the delegation of legislative power, and law making by administrative decree (hence overriding the populace, democratically elected bodies such as political parties, and the legislature). A new wave of 'soft' dictators has risen in democracies where a temporary sacrifice of democracy as a state of exception has become the norm, allowing for sweeping privilege.

Those deprived of citizenship live in limbo, unable to vote, gain legitimate employment, or gain access to public services such as healthcare or housing. Many illegal immigrants remain in this state of limbo until their asylum claims are processed, even though they may be fleeing persecution or prejudice (e.g., for their sexual orientations), thus being stripped of selfhood as citizen. Some immigrants – who have fled their countries because of persecution, war, or conflict – have the right to live in, for example, the UK permanently with many of the same rights, but this does not confer full citizenship. They have 'settled status', termed 'leave to remain'.

The philosopher Socrates died on 15 February 399 BCE in Athens where he was forced to drink poison by his prosecutors. The Athenian prosecutors saw Socrates' philosophy as a bad influence on youth and pressed trumped-up charges concerning the corruption of youth. He was offered exile, but refused, claiming that he was of great benefit to Athens, and it would be cowardly to accept exile as punishment. His trial took a day and the next day he was sent to prison where he was forced to drink hemlock. For Socrates, a self in exile is no self at all, one that has lost moral courage. All well and good, but most would not choose death at the hand of persecutors if offered exile. But exile can be a complicated business.

In the UK, Shamima Begum left the UK to join an Islamic State group in Syria. She married an Islamic State jihadist and gave birth to three

## 66 Self-Literacy

children, all of whom subsequently died. Claiming that she was trafficked, she bid for UK citizenship but was denied on the basis that she already had Bangladeshi citizenship. However, Bangladesh has refused her entry and at the time of writing she remains in a camp controlled by armed guards in northern Syria, in limbo.

In 2006, an Australian journalist, Julian Assange, founded WikiLeaks – dedicated to publishing leaked information about political scandals that had been hushed up in the service of transparent public journalism. In 2010, WikiLeaks published a series of highly sensitive US forces' intelligence documents provided by a US Army intelligence analyst Chelsea Manning who was subsequently tried and jailed for the leak. In a multi-layered self-transformation, Manning went from privileged white male citizen to being stripped of such privileges when incarcerated, where she underwent a gender identity change from man to woman.

Living in London, in 2010, Assange was threatened with a European arrest warrant from Sweden for sexual misdemeanours (a charge that was later dropped, in 2019), and extradition to the USA to face charges of treason for publishing secret documents through WikiLeaks (such as highly damning reports against the US military during the Afghanistan and Iraq wars). Assange sought asylum in the Embassy of Ecuador in London in 2012 on the grounds of political persecution and potential extradition to the USA where he might have faced life imprisonment for treason. He attempted to return to Australia in 2013 but failed. In 2019, Ecuador withdrew asylum privileges. Assange had lived on simulated Ecuadorian soil for seven years, unable to set foot outside that building. Self as citizen was compromised and Assange then suffered a mental health crisis when he was arrested and imprisoned by the UK authorities in 2019. He was racked with suicidal ideation. In the summer of 2024, the American President Joe Biden intervened and arranged a deal with Assange's lawyers. Assange pleaded guilty to charges and was charged with serving five years in an American protectorate Saipan, near to his home, in Australia. He did not serve this time as he had already been imprisoned in the UK for five years and was allowed to return to Australia as a free man with his wife, once his lawyer, and two children. What kind of a traumatised self has emerged from such travails?

A self is defined by documentation. On 12 November 2022, a man born in Iran died from a heart attack in a homeless shelter in a suburb of Paris. He had respiratory issues from living for 18 years, from 1988 to 2006, in limbo in Charles de Gaulle airport, unable to enter France or return to his native country. Mehran Karimi Nasseri became a celebrity in this situation. A book was written (*The Terminal Man*), and a film was made ('The Terminal') about his predicament. When the book was published, the airport bookshop stocked copies that he would sign. He achieved a strange

*Self stripped of rights* 67

kind of celebrity status. He was trapped in the terminal because he had lost his passport and so could not catch a plane to anywhere and would be arrested if he left the terminal and set foot on French soil, because he had no immigration papers or ID documents. He had written to the British Embassy in Brussels asking for asylum in the UK, but this was refused. His own account, given to journalists, of how he arrived in this predicament, was confused. It seems that he had lost a briefcase with his passport and documents.

We know that Nasseri was born in 1945 in Soleiman, Iran. He had an Iranian father and a British mother and had attended college in the UK in 1974. Returning to Iran, Nasseri was first imprisoned as a suspected political activist and then deported without his passport. He attempted to gain refuge in multiple European nations but failed. Finally gaining refugee status certificates from Belgium's UN organisation for refugees, he supposedly lost his briefcase containing the certificates at a Paris train station while seeking entry to the UK. He found himself stuck, in limbo, at the de Gaulle airport and put down roots at the airport's Terminal 1.

Nasseri relied on the goodwill of travellers to support him, claiming a red bench on the airport's terminal first floor as his regular sitting and sleeping spot, eating often at McDonald's, listening to the radio, and keeping a journal of over 20,000 pages. He quickly adopted a routine – he told one journalist that this was to keep up 'best presentation of self' – of washing and shaving each morning. He would be given a free newspaper and managed to get free food, mainly from the McDonald's restaurant (usually Filet-O-Fish for lunch and dinner daily). He accumulated a lot of hand luggage from gifts people left him. His main occupation was keeping his journal describing events around him and surely inscribing a self. He read widely from books that travellers would read and occasionally would venture from the terminal but never to engage with barriers that required proof of citizenship. An obliterated citizenship and limbo status eradicated identification with any national soil. His was truly an artificial world, a simulacrum of life, in which the identity of a settler was forged out of the strangest of circumstances.

# 19 Self engulfed by panic

In Greek myth, the hairy and smelly goat god Pan is said to jump on your back just as you are blissfully relaxing in the mid-day sun, catching you by surprise and inducing panic. It is a truism that just as everything is running swimmingly, a glitch appears, or an accident happens. Some grit must get into the system, or the event, to make a pearl. A shadow must be embraced in the joy of brilliant sunlight. The ancient Greek 'pan' – the root of 'panic' – means 'all', 'everything', 'totality' (panorama, panoply, pantheon), but also 'everywhere at once'. This is what panic feels like as it eats up the ego, all consuming, your shadow no longer cast or withdrawn into the body. For the person who does not cast a shadow is a ghost, a no-body. Self in panic is a nobody, frightened out of his or her skin by the hairy and smelly cloven-footed goat god who suddenly jumps on your back, clings, and will not let go. To be in panic mode is to be in extreme fear of the unknown. Here, the self absconds

Pan is chief of the satyrs, lord of untamed wilderness. He is the antithesis of culture, representing tangle, danger, wilderness. Here, human self embraces animal other, or instinct. In Greek myth Pan chases Nymphs. As they flee from his advances, they are transformed into tree, reed, or bodiless echo. We are seemingly disembodied in states of panic and yet fully bodied, as animal reflex. The fight-or-flight system of the parasympathetic nervous system has no consciousness of its reflex actions – there is no controlling ego, no anchor of self. All is absent in panic, including all support structures. Pan jumping on your back and the shadow sucking into your body as the sunlight is blocked out – again, this is what a panic attack feels like.

The self is described all too often in terms of stability, continuity, and health. And yet we are open, complex, dynamic, unstable systems living at maximum complexity at the edge of chaos and likely to fall into chaos. The fact that we do not fall into chaos for most of the time shows that a stable self is indeed experienced as the status quo. Only around 3% of people report having regular severe panic attacks, although all of us

DOI: 10.4324/9781003619901-20

Self engulfed by panic 69

*Figure 19.1* Pan.

70   *Self-Literacy*

have experienced panic. But when chaos does arrive, it is qualitatively so disruptive that it seems our lives may be ruined forever: accident, relationship breakup, personal breakdown, loss of interest, stuck in a dead-end job, starting to drink or take drugs too often for comfort, prone to self-harming, depressed and anxious, hard to get out of bed in the mornings, sudden fear of everyday events. Here, the body and self are consumed by shadow, suffering, pathology, longing, or unfulfilled desire and potential.

Pan then brings nightmares, panic, and suffocation. His presence is a reminder of how a sunny disposition and an even sense of self are illusory. Self is dogged by shadow. At a less intense key, the presence of Pan is the triumph of mischief.

# 20 The self-righteous narcissist

In a set of critical essays, the American Nobel Prize-winning poet Louise Glück refers to narcissistic interest as the dominant Western trait when talking of selfhood. She notes that personal confessional styles have become the norm among modern American poets, but these do not necessarily embrace narcissism. Walt Whitman celebrated body and self in the most ecstatic and celebratory manner, but his singing of 'the body electric' is far from narcissistic because it does not advertise self-absorption, but rather celebration as buoyant expression of what is shared among humanity. Emily Dickinson advertises self as an intricate puzzle to be examined 'slantwise' that must begin in self-interest but avoids self-reference. Robert Lowell speaks autobiographically to explore cracks and fissures in relationships. John Ashbery talks from the self as an abstraction, a lived conundrum, where the mind is constantly trying to escape from the prison of the flesh. Self for Ashbery is a formal mathematical puzzle.

Louise Glück navigates narcissism elegantly by talking about herself without investment in either outer parade or inner analytic journey. Rather, she describes – in a necessarily halting style as no point of growth is ever complete – deference to larger forces, those of archetypes or the 'gods' as these shape the minutiae of life. The gods as readily inhabit landscapes such as a volcano, as relationships. Indeed, the self becomes a landscape feature – fissure, pit, enclosure, a heavy sky, a pool of water. Self for Glück is in the details, the trivia. *Trivium* is where three roads meet – a crossroads, necessarily a place for deep contemplation as decisions on future directions are taken here.

In deep contemplation, Narcissus stares at a pool of water and falls in love with his own reflection. He has never seen anything as beautiful. It is not the (mis)recognition of self that is central here but rather the dissolution of the self as Narcissus threatens to drown in his own reflection just as he is transfixed by the depths of his reflected being. In this self-absorption too, Narcissus ignores – indeed, is oblivious to – the advances of Echo the

DOI: 10.4324/9781003619901-21

## 72  Self-Literacy

nymph, who has fallen in love with him. For Narcissus there is no echo of his own being – it is entirely wrapped up in self-absorption.

The psychoanalyst Jacques Lacan described babies from the age of around six months seeing themselves in the mirror (the 'mirror stage' of development) and clearly being fascinated with their reflections. Soon, any 'other' (parents, adults, siblings) provides a mirror reflection back to the child. From these reflections, the child begins to form a sense of identity or self, in which the authentic self is not 'within' but is contained in the myriad of reflections that the child receives back from the world. Self is forever out of reach, in the hands of the 'other' such that a self is moulded by how the other may react. The self is only known through mediation by others. Selves are knots tied by social practices. We spend our lives working out how those knots are tied and whether it is worth untying or cutting them. Growing into adulthood, mirrors are multiplied and then reflections accrue. Literature affords one such mirror.

Identity has then been captured by the world and is fed back to us in various ways – mainly through language and symbols of culture, that are shared expressions of self. For Lacan, the child is never narcissistic but rather in rapture and puzzlement at the capturing of identity by the other and by the ways that others speak. Lacan thus predicts celebrity culture as shaped by media response. For Narcissus, however, self is never allowed to be captured by any outside force. It is purely private capital, the reflection absorbed back in an all-consuming self-interest. This is a primary neurosis. It offers a conundrum, for the self that appears to offer depth (the bottomless pool in which the reflection is seen) is in fact simply a surface effect. There is no depth – it is an illusion. But the narcissist acts as if depth calls and it is a mystery why others do not gaze on him because he surely advertises depth ('look, I have a very high IQ', 'nobody understands this better than me').

The postmodern narcissist, however, is not totally self-absorbed, living in two worlds at once. First, the self-absorption that is modelled in the myth of Narcissus; and second, in the need for validation from others (the more the better). For postmodern narcissists, self-approval becomes the key driver of self-absorption. The self is inflated where the mirror speaks back: 'you are good', 'you are powerful'. Here, hubris, or excessive pride and self-confidence, enters the picture and temporarily wipes out any creeping doubt. But then doubt, as the craving for affirmation, creeps back in. Donald Trump – forever in his father's shadow – famously scours the media for positive approval and craves his own echoes to be guided back to him such that he can amplify them in self-aggrandisement. He must surround himself with sycophants. Every stroke of the ego is doubled in hyperbole: 'the most important person in history', 'the most significant Presidency ever'. In turn, a thick set of defences is set up by deflecting

The self-righteous narcissist   73

and rationalising all criticism and bad press. Postmodern narcissists have broken out from Narcissus' self-absorption in the single reflection to inhabit a hall of mirrors.

Whatever the root cause of narcissism – Freudians would say inadequate parenting as early withdrawal of affection causing later regression to infantile self-absorption – the reality is that now we live in high-income cultures in which some level of narcissism is not just tolerated but expected. This is the culture of the 'selfie' as deep fascination with self-image and its validation through social media, that Christopher Lasch identifies as a dominant cultural trope in the West, and that can be identified with the political movement of neoliberalism. The chief political proponents of neoliberalism, Ronald Reagan in the USA, and Margaret Thatcher in the UK, follow Thatcher's claim that there is no such thing as 'society' – only individuals and families.

Neoliberalism is the contemporary outcome of the self-help movement inaugurated in 19th-century North America – the lone frontiersman reliant on his own devices who makes his way up the ladder of success through entrepreneurial activity. Neoliberalism decries state support or intervention. Its greatest flaw – outside of a rather stupid rejection of the importance of community and the social – is that disadvantaged persons remain disadvantaged. There is no level playing field or sense of equity and opportunity for equality. The poor, disadvantaged, and physically or mentally challenged will suffer in such a system. All boats do not rise with expanding economies – instead the gap between rich and poor (inequality) widens. The wealthy self-congratulate, claiming that they pulled themselves up by their own bootstraps. However, a third of them inherited their wealth and this lump sum adds up to more than the capital wealth created by the other two-thirds, 'self-made' billionaires.

The formation of a contemporary narcissistic culture grounded in forms of approval is different from the self-forming cultures of the elite in ancient Greece and Rome. Techniques of self in the ancient world did not need an audience and were bound by identifiable ethical and aesthetic codes. Contemporary narcissistic self-forming does not have ethical boundaries but rather suspends or denies ethical injunctions in the name of expansion of neoliberalism. Ethics are read here as forms of control rather than as practices of self. The aesthetic of neoliberalism is absent too – for it is a literal and functional expression of self, driven entirely by transient rules of display called 'fashion'. In terms of the dramaturgical model of self proposed by Erving Goffman, the narcissistic self is wholly inauthentic and eschews any sense of permanence or 'core'. Values are invented to fit circumstances (Donald Trump's 'alternative truths', where again Trump is currently the best-known narcissist on the block).

## 74  *Self-Literacy*

In individual terms, this is the day-to-day living of the authoritarian personality and the narcissistic personality type who must contain absolute control. Narcissism can be characterised as excessive self-interest coupled with self-display. Again, we need look no further than Trump as primary example – a man who is not only obsessed with all media representations of him, but also with bending information to present him in a good light. Of course, this turns him into a caricature and figure of both fun and contempt – from his fake tan, orange-glow skin, and desperate attempt to cover baldness with a ridiculous comb-forward hairstyle, to his over-sized suits and long neckties; and then to his bombastic, overbearing, and combative language: never backing down or admitting defeat, never saying you are wrong or sorry, compulsively lying and distorting information, and permanently exaggerating ('I may be the most important person in recorded history', 'nobody has done more for the country than me'). Finally, his surrounding himself with beautiful people and demanding absolute loyalty. As we know, only narcissists cheat at golf.

# 21 Paranoia
## Beside oneself

Paranoia – from the Greek *para* ('beyond', 'beside') and *nous* ('knowing', 'mind') – describes a knowing that occurs in parallel with your own mind. For example, you may show irrational deep suspicion of others' intentions, or you may feel that somebody is watching you or stalking you when this is not the case. Paranoia may result from an over-rigid ego, one that is afraid of its defences being breached, typical of narcissism or extreme self-importance. The irrational fear is that somebody may steal your sense of self, hence the persistent symptoms of 'guardedness'. The most extreme forms of paranoia involve delusions such as believing that your innermost, private thoughts are being publicly broadcast on radio or TV. Of course, this means that your defences have been breached. Freud noted that the ego is vulnerable and sets up several defence mechanisms to prevent its invasion or collapse such as denial, displacement, projection, and rationalisation. The ego is inherently suspicious. The super-defended ego is paranoid.

To this end, Descartes' certitude of 'I think, therefore I am' becomes hyper intensive as: 'I overthink, therefore I am paranoid'. It is not an irrational fantasy to be paranoid, it is an over mobilisation of defence mechanisms. The paranoid person can give a rationalisation for his or her paranoia: 'if I didn't think this way (so rigidly), my defences would be penetrated'. Examples of paranoia at the social and institutional level are legion. Vast amounts of money are consumed by nations' defence budgets based on paranoid delusions. Conspiracy theories abound, especially among the far right. Extremists embrace paranoia as a style of life.

What paranoia blocks is the ability to be reflexive and to think and communicate in metaphors. Paranoia takes metaphorical dangers literally failing to think this through. This is coupled with an extremely tough set of ego defences to maintain a fragile ego (hence, again, narcissists are also often paranoid). That ego in turn has been shaped perhaps by an overbearing father or father figure who demands an impossible perfection. Throwing this off is difficult, and paranoid people tend to surround themselves with those who bolster their paranoia rather than challenge its basis. In

DOI: 10.4324/9781003619901-22

## 76 Self-Literacy

turn, the paranoid figure develops the paranoia that his trusted allies or henchmen are in fact out to get him, and things quickly turn sour.

Philosophers have long pondered on the deep need for certainty in humanity and the inability to tolerate ambiguity or uncertainty. Descartes' insistence on a natural rational basis to thought doesn't help, where it is deeply irrational to equate thinking with certainty. John Locke noted that the thinking self can be self-observing and self-therapeutic, to escape its own self-imposed paranoia by rejecting rationality as the default position for thinking. The self for Locke is ephemeral and searching for its anchor (for stability) is in fact a form of rigidity. Escaping paranoia is to accept that the self is an ever-changing series of impressions grounded in an unreliable memory. David Hume agreed – the self is a purely grammatical construction, talking itself into being and usually talking itself up (the seeds of both narcissism and paranoia). Again, it is in language that one can escape the trap of potential paranoia through enjoyment of metaphor. To not take the world literally is to see that nobody is really attacking you directly but is usually engaging in acceptable critique. To not be able to work productively with criticism is a sign of a literal mindset where such criticism is taken at face value, read as attack, and feeds into the paranoid position.

Kant solves the issue of paranoia by asking us to always assume that judgements do not arise from satisfying personal needs but are grounded in transcendental values or positions of faith. You are not being attacked by an individual but by an ideology. The criticism of you is not personal and you should not take it personally. You must shift your mindset to engage with the ideology or value position from which the other makes his or her statements. In turn, you do not make personal attacks (throwing dirt, slander, lawsuits) but defend your values perspective if you think it is defensible. The transcendental self makes moral judgements, and this requires thoughtful critique of the impositions of others' moralities and not personal attacks. To do this one must also suspend suspicion of others' viewpoints – the key symptom of paranoia.

Paranoia is the guiding force behind conspiracy theories and is justified as a rational position by the novelist William Burroughs, where paranoia is defined as 'having all the facts'. For Burroughs, and post-Trump, the half of America that lives with paranoia is the disadvantaged, less well educated, and lower earning. But the novelist Don DeLillo – who has been described as America's 'laureate of paranoia' – stands this on its head. DeLillo (2016) – for example, in *Zero K* – captures the paranoid state of the wealthier half of American society who live in fear that their worlds are in fact about to collapse where: 'Half the world is redoing its kitchens, the other half is starving'.

# 22 The translational self
## An attractor in a dynamic, complex system

The celebrated American postmodern novelist David Foster Wallace – a lifelong depressive who took his own life by hanging himself – said: 'We can never be linear about ourselves'. What might this mean? We can only send persons to the Moon because the whole process of spaceflight is mechanical and linear – a 'closed' operation. It can be mathematically plotted. It is highly complicated but not complex. The uncertainty rests largely with the mechanical stresses and strains upon physical objects, all of which can be quantified and predicted. If such spaceflights were subject to the complex, non-linear dynamics of open adaptive systems there would be a high level of uncertainty or ambiguity, and paradoxes would abound. We might be able to appreciate the non-linear, complex system qualitatively, but we would have too many quantitative potential errors and slippage from the inherent high level of uncertainty.

Non-linear, complex, adaptive systems can indeed adapt, reorganising at higher levels of complexity in spontaneous ways, but they can also collapse suddenly as they operate close to the edge of chaos. Further, complex systems interact with other complex systems in often unpredictable ways. The human body is a complex, adaptive system. The self – as both an abstract notion and as an embodied being – can also be modelled as a complex system. Mathematical theory describes 'reduction of complexity' as the ability to translate a complex problem in one realm (say the expression of personality as a psychological issue) to another realm (say a neurological basis to personality). What is fascinating for the study of self however is where complex problems in one realm (say racism) are impossible to explain by invoking another complex system (such as genetics).

Where the modernist subject is singular, centred, and known by introverted inspection as a stable object, the postmodern subject is multiple, fluid, and decentred. The modernist self claims that it can be described through language over which it has mastery. Postmodern selves are constructed, transformed, and translated through language games. The modernist self has been destabilised or deconstructed and has spawned new

DOI: 10.4324/9781003619901-23

## 78  Self-Literacy

genres of literature that eschew plot and multiply character quirks (with antecedents in Jonathan Swift and Virginia Woolf and with Samuel Beckett and James Joyce as father figures). An easy way to grasp this is to think of postmodern selves as products (sometimes considered, often unexpected) of dynamic contexts – immediate and distant environments engaging extended and distributed cognition and emotion. Such 'translational' selves are open to exchanges with others – persons, animals, plants, the stones, waters, and airs of the earth, and matter from beyond earth, including light from the moon, light and heat from the sun, and cosmic radiation. Here, self is what we touch, eat, drink, and how that affects our bodily states. Ego is dissolved across activity, environment, and body-mind. Or – there is no cohesive, unitary 'self' as object, but a variety of tones.

Such a self is non-linear and open (where again a linear system, such as an engine, is closed) and part of a wider network subject to spontaneous transformation into greater complexity or showing emergent properties. The complex (rather than the complicated) self operates at maximum complexity at the edge of chaos, open to spontaneous transformations. Within a wider complex system, the self acts as an attractor, a relatively stable complex system but subject to entropy or gradual running down. The self as a complex system is in a state of becoming rather than being – always fluid. Here is a clue as to how selves may seem to be stable within a dynamic system, as they become strong attractors. An attractor is a set of states towards which a system tends to evolve. A paradox of our age is that while we understand self (body and mind) in terms of complex models, and then symptoms of illness or breakdown, our healthcare systems respond through linear, mechanical thinking (diagnose-treat).

Strange attractors are highly unstable but provide points of stability within a chaotic system. The body (as self) is a strange attractor within the chaotic system that is the body's natural entropy, or tendency to run down leading to death and disintegration. Fixed point attractors do what it says on the tin. They are dynamic centres of gravity (i.e., they have a finite lifespan). A contemporary example is a person on social media such as TikTok and Instagram as an 'influencer' who attracts and potentially shapes the values and behaviour of followers. Many followers will imitate the style of those who they follow. The Portuguese footballer Cristiano Ronaldo has 911 million followers across various social media. The singer Taylor Swift has over 550 million. These might also take on the behaviour of cyclic attractors, where influence comes and goes. These are periodic or oscillating attractors. The moon's pull on the earth's tides may be seen as rhythmic or periodic according to the moon's orbit that has an elliptical, or oval, shape. Toroidal attractors are variations of chaotic attractors with spherical patterns. They can be modelled as doughnut shaped. Such attractor designs can be applied not only to humans as metaphors of self,

*The translational self: an attractor in a dynamic, complex system* 79

but also to social inventions such as economies that adopt personalities as extensions of self. Let me give an example.

Neoliberal capitalist economies run on the model of exponential, open-ended 'growth'. Economies expand like the universe after the Big Bang. As so-called 'developed' nations – richer countries – get more complex and produce more goods and services, so economies expand. Within expansion will be periods of shrinkage or stalling of growth – 'recessions'. Sometimes there will be major collapses or implosions of economies such as the Great Depression in America in 1929–39, producing shock waves that caused a global downturn in growth. This was caused by a sudden fall in stock market confidence and share prices related to a collapse of world trade, of money supplies, and of confidence in banks' management of capital. The recession and the subsequent Great Depression led to high rates of unemployment. In North America, this was twinned with the collapse of farming in the mid-west due to overuse of land that became a 'dustbowl'. This led to mass internal migrations to California to seek work, with subsequent collapse of union control of labour markets and fair wage pricing to create a divisive society. John Steinbeck's novel *The Grapes of Wrath* is a masterful account of this period. Here, then, is a complex system in a state of chaos calling for stabilising attractors. Such an attractor appeared with America's involvement in World War II, where employment and productivity were boosted related to the war effort.

The problem with such an economic model based on permanent expansion is that the production of greater complexity brings greater instability and risk, while there is a permanent inflation – products cost more, and wages must follow. One pound sterling in 1920 is worth nearly £60 today. This is inevitable inflation within such a system. Now imagine an economy that does not grow exponentially but consistently recycles. This is a 'doughnut' economy working like a toroidal attractor (both are embodied metaphors – a global economy works on paper transactions). The capital that is produced through labour pours into the middle of the doughnut, not to fall through the hole, but to be recycled as reinvestment in capital equipment, workers' labour, and emotional labour – the work of relationships and communication that underpins a productive economy. More, there are two doughnuts at work. An upper one guarantees that resources are used sensitively, energy is produced and deployed, and goods are recycled in ecological ways that do not harm the planet and its inhabitants. The lower doughnut offers a guarantee that all persons are treated equally, so that equity (fairness and impartiality) and equality (offering a level playing field and an inclusive society that embraces all regardless of physical or mental challenge) are in play. Again, these values are constantly generated, fall into the doughnut ring, and are recycled, resisting the difficulties

80  *Self-Literacy*

of the growth model that favours the already wealthy and disadvantages the poor.

This is a dynamic, complex system that consistently regenerates itself. Hierarchical, open-ended neoliberal growth economies not only generate inequalities and inequities (as the tide rises, it does not bring all the boats with it – many will sink) but produce a certain kind of dominant identity based on greed. Good-enough-to-eat doughnut models generate collaborative identities and expertise in translationality. The competitive capitalist model generates anxiety as the default nervous system position for all. The doughnut model promises relief of anxiety in the nurturing of a new model of the human's autonomic nervous system.

Paradoxically – perhaps in postmodern and deconstructive style – reconstruction of selves can be described in the body as a conversation between four nervous systems. I say 'paradoxically' because, although I have described embodied economic activity modelled by complexity, this is unseen activity best grasped through metaphor as I suggest. There are four human nervous systems that are interconnected or form a complex web where the systems act as attractors – relatively stable systems talking to, and influencing, each other. These systems, again, are dynamic. They are subject to the overall entropy of the human body – its initial rise to several peak complexities is gradually compromised by ageing and lost at death to literal, not figurative, dispersal across the cosmos.

The four systems are: the central nervous system (brain, spinal cord, afferent and efferent nerves largely controlling muscle that in turn controls the skeletal system); the autonomic nervous system (fight-and-flight responses); the enteric (gut) system (digestion); and the immunological system (energised when the body is infected or falls ill and sometimes turning against the body in autoimmune disorders). These bodily systems are, of course, open to the environment, indeed in troubled dialogue with that environment. The nervous systems can suffer from abuse – poor diet, stress-inducing activity, and so forth. In turn, the nervous systems are extraordinarily plastic and adaptable. Paradoxically, it is the attractor of the central nervous system that can make choices about lifestyle that negatively affect its own functioning and that of the three other nervous systems (as attractors).

The immune system has traditionally been described in militaristic terms using metaphors of attack and defence against 'invaders' (infection by bacteria and viruses). But this is a masculinist model of an immunological self. A more appropriate model is ecological and communal. Here, relationships are built with bodily systems as members of the immune system family wander the body in the blood and engage with tissue. As they engage with potentially harmful 'invasive' organisms, we can only use metaphors

*The translational self: an attractor in a dynamic, complex system* 81

to describe their work. In traditional ingestion and combat metaphors, a phagocyte is an 'eating cell', a neutrophil is a member of this family, seeking 'targets' to ingest. But we can also use relationship or family systems metaphors to describe how the immune system works – macrophages 'see' antigen, while antibodies 'recognise' epitopes; T cells possess 'memory', while adaptive immunity is a 'learning process'. In relationship with the autonomic nervous system, the immune system perceives and then decides how and when to react. This is a 'cognitive metaphor' that describes a thinking and experiencing immune system. The process is not confrontational but translational and transactional. Future economies must break out of the neoliberal 'growth' trap and act more like complex doughnuts.

# 23 The narrative construction of self

Imagine visiting a relative or friend in a hospital. At the end of the bed hang two charts: the first is numerical, showing – for example – blood pressure readings and a medication schedule; the second, in contrast, is a story about the onset of the patient's symptoms, the course of treatment, and potential outcomes, with a focus on the experiences of the patient. Not 'how are your symptoms?' but 'how are you feeling?' Both are concerned with how the patient is doing, but one is instrumental science and the other is expressive art; one provides necessary information for technicians, the other provides a more abstract and publicly accessible account that again is authentic in terms of the patient's experiences. While functional writing allows for necessary technical work such as diagnoses and treatment within the medical and healthcare community, expressive writing may be more powerful than descriptive or functional writing in gaining insight into the patient's illness and, hopefully, course of recovery. The narrative account aligns with the patient's experience and not with the healthcare experts' version of that experience. Again, authenticity is the key factor. We want to know what is happening with the patient as an experiential account, and not simply what the blood tests show as an informational record.

The psychologist Jerome Bruner describes two main ways of knowing: the scientific (a logical method aiming for fact) and the narrative (a descriptive and inventive method aiming for meaning). Science avoids 'fictions' for facts or truth. Narrative may include facts, but it is a way of description that does not aspire to truth but to a meaningful account. In public discourse, telling stories is our preferred way of communicating and surely shapes identity. Science, dealing with information and fact, denotes, or points to, specific things with clarity. Stories connote, or generate multiple meanings, dealing with meanings. Bruner's distinction seems clear-cut, but it is problematic. Another set of categories might be introduced: the distinction between information and meaning. A set of instructions for assembling a flat packed piece of furniture serves no other purpose than

DOI: 10.4324/9781003619901-24

The narrative construction of self  83

the instrumental or functional. It does not aspire to literature and is linear. A good story in contrast is complex and non-functional. It moves from literal description to metaphorical invention. Science may be based on principles that distinguish it from good stories, but science too participates in narrative. For example, Darwin (and in parallel Alfred Russel Wallace) proposed an overarching theory of evolution that rested on limited evidence (most of it from geology) and required an explanation of its process (based on genetics) that was not available to either Darwin or Wallace. They both created compelling narratives. So too, Einstein's theory of relativity and Heisenberg's uncertainty principle were good stories (as untested hypotheses) requiring solid evidence as proof.

The philosopher Richard Rorty was once asked if politicians could benefit from a study of ethics, perhaps to generate some guiding principles. Rorty replied, somewhat bemused, that politics doesn't need principles, but good stories – in other words, aesthetics might precede ethics. However, while stories need to be well crafted to be of interest, it is surely through story that we best transmit frames for considering what moral behaviour is. Where narrative knowing is stereotyped by scientists as underdeveloped and subjective, it supposedly does not offer a legitimate basis to inquiry. However, the currency of narrative knowing is ambiguity, uncertainty, and paradox. The postmodern moment is characterised as a crisis of the legitimacy claimed by positivism (truth can only be guaranteed by fact derived from controlled experimental evidence). Here, a challenge is mounted to the dominance of rationalism that characterises scientific language games (explanatory closure and certainty). In a postmodern climate, local narratives, or little stories, proliferate as a return to a kind of tribal storying accounting for the explosion of interest in local or ethnic identities.

To narrate – from the Latin *narrare* ('to know') – is then to give an account in story form, even where content may be factual. Stories are not loose – they have structures: plots, characters, arcs building to a climax with a resolution or a surprise ending. Narrative knowing is an aesthetic apprehension offered through a variety of genres and their admixtures: social realist, dirty realist, surrealist, magical realist, epic, tragic, comic, lyric, confessional, biographical, autobiographical, autoethnographical, psycho-biographical, detective, soap, romantic, fantastic, feminist, heroic, picaresque, historical, travel, macabre, postmodernist, hypertextual, and so forth. These varying genres provide contexts for the generation of selves. 'Detective' producing the 'sleuth', 'romantic' producing the lover, 'magical realist' producing the fantasist, and so forth. Self here is storied into being.

Knowledge of literary forms of course is not necessary for the narrative construction of selves – only for deeper appreciation and understanding of the process. Thus, we all live with, and within, a vernacular (common and popular language) that is bursting at the seams with metaphor

## 84  Self-Literacy

and invention, at the opposite end of the spectrum from technical or instrumental languages. The latter, as noted, are embodied in instruction manuals for washing machines and televisions. But they are also embedded in sophisticated manuals such as pharmaceutical formularies used by doctors to match symptoms to treatments. Such manuals are purely informational. We don't live everyday life through such manuals. Most of us are 'temporal' or live with a sense of our lives as multiple stories unfolding through time (diachronic). What seems consistent throughout time is a sense of self. But the self is not necessarily experienced as given, but as created from temporal events. We also experience ourselves in space and this has a deep effect on self-forming – for example, where we live, the houses we occupy, and so forth. For some, this spatial awareness is far stronger than temporal awareness. Or temporal awareness is focused on a specific time (synchronic). The narrative self is then best described as an ever-changing sense of self recreated from circumstance over time, rather than an account of how a stable self survives changing circumstances over time. We know that the best narratives have twists in the plot and surprise endings.

# 24 Personal confessional narratives constitute a confessional self

A quick way into grasping the forming of self through story, and of appreciating the centrality of the Protestant view of selfhood that has dominated Northern European and Western culture since the Enlightenment, is to read Henry David Thoreau's *Walden*. This is Thoreau's mid-19th-century account of living frugally in a cabin next to Walden Pond in Concord, Massachusetts, acting as a model of self-forming through minimalist self-sufficiency in terms of autonomy, singularity, privacy, and inward contemplation – an insular individualism. It is both autoethnography (as oneself observing one's own cultural habits) and autobiography (as writing oneself out, or recording intimacies).

Thoreau's emphasis is not upon the solitary as a way of finding divinity in one's heart (Augustine's *Confessions*), nor as a way of cleansing therapeutically (Rousseau's *Confessions*), but as stripping life back to the bare necessities, or cleansing materially to prepare for self-contemplation. Thoreau's is a way of catharsis by identification with the imagined purity of Nature. For Thoreau (and ironically for contemporary neoliberal capitalism) thrift, or living within one's means, is the primary way to cultivate self. The self is not accumulative but minimalist. Stripping back can also be stripping off – exposing body and self is the popular way of writing oneself out on social media, where self is a product of gaining attention (as number of followers).

Importantly, Thoreau as a writer relies on literature to represent his lifestyle. He writes himself out and leaves a legacy. Strictly he writes himself in – into history and lore. It is the French philosopher Jacques Derrida who is best known for describing the self as suspended, under erasure (*sous rature*) (this move is borrowed from Martin Heidegger), cancelled, or written out (~~struck through~~), as both disposable and obsolete. For Thoreau, it is the Man (self is necessarily masculinised as frontiersman) in the hut (by Walden Pond) who is self-made. For Heidegger, a century after Thoreau, it is the hut or Dwelling Place that is more important than the Man who dwells in it, for the hut represents an in-dwelling of atmospheres and

## 86  Self-Literacy

locations. Heidegger favours topologies over typologies, where the act of residence or habitation generates a sense of self – rather than the act of introspection. For Derrida, almost a century after Heidegger, in-dwelling a location is trying to live in quicksand, where the self is no longer an embodied, introspective being (Thoreau) or a placement (Heidegger), but rather an illusory effect of language. In other words, a narrative effect. We can speak ourselves into Being in whatever way we choose or in whatever genre and this is neither authentic nor inauthentic but affords an aesthetic statement. Our ways of narrativising identity are judged on their quality.

We can think of four ways of speaking and writing about the subject, represented by three literary genres. First, biography defines an individual placed in relationship to an institutional framework. Second, autobiography defines a subject through storying one's life. Third, confession defines an ego or person through intimate revelation. And fourth, psychobiography, a contemporary development of biography as mediated confession, where another speaks one's intimacies. While the Classical world utilised biography and autobiography, confession and psychobiography are later historical genres. The characterisation of the individual in Greek autobiography allows no intimacy of the self. For the ancient Greeks, the subject is extroverted – there is no interior world to be penetrated to find oneself. Self is there in the act – in warfare, in sexual encounter, in sports, in citizenship.

The personal confessional genre can be said to begin with Augustine's *Confessions* of 400 AD and is fully formulated in Rousseau's (1782) *Confessions*, begun in 1767 and published posthumously. John Bunyan's (1666) *Grace Abounding* could be claimed as the first personal confessional text of stature, but this was a spiritual confession, participating as much in Augustine's technique as spiritual confessional cleansing of the soul, pre-figuring Rousseau's secular personal confessional style. Both may speak from the heart (Rousseau just as much speaks from the loins) but with differing purposes – one confesses to God, the other to fellow humans. James Boswell's and Edward Gibbon's confessional texts of the 1760s could be claimed as founders of the modern secular personal confessional genre along with Rousseau and these were progressed through Wordsworth's (1798–1805) *Prelude*, with its reference to an 'organic' self. Confessional texts were developed in England in the 18th century and came to dominate Romantic writing of the 19th century. The genre proliferated in the 20th century as the cult of personality, coming to dominate narrative accounts of life history, developed as postmodern simulations through kiss-and-tell journalism, and television talk shows offering confession as live entertainment. These are now translated into social media. The numbers are staggering. Meta (formerly Facebook) has over 3,000 million (3 billion) users.

The narrative self then is relative, constituted linguistically, genealogically, and culturally in plural and relative ways, not as an eternal truth.

*Personal confessional narratives constitute a confessional self*  87

Confessional narratives do not naively disclose but can serve political interests such as gendered expressions. While 18th-century personal confessional literature by women authors sometimes offers a direct resistance to dominant patriarchal views, for example, in their valuing of what the patriarchy regards as the trivia of daily life and personal intimacies, such accounts may also valorise family life and reproduce dominant gender hierarchies within the same text. Indeed, the personal confessional genre has been stereotyped as a feminine literature (not a feminist one) where its core is emotional expression.

While claiming individual identity or the value of the idiosyncratic voice, the personal confessional can be seen to reproduce the normative values of bourgeois capitalism. Both women's and men's published autobiographies in the 18th and 19th centuries by and large promote a bourgeois worldview, excluding other social interests, and are neurotypical. The self is seen as personally owned and talked about through metaphors of property: it is a consuming subject embodying self-interest in terms of entrepreneurial capitalism, most famously espoused by Adam Smith (the *Wealth of Nations* was published in 1776). Self is valorised as essentially free yet advertises clear class and gender positions and constraints.

Two hundred years on from the invention of the secular personal confessional style we are now inundated by its postmodern examples: 'kiss-and-tell' journalism and lurid TV confessional shows where catharsis becomes entertainment, the cult of psychobiography, public confessions by celebrities, simulated confessions in soap operas creating identificatory catharsis on the part of the audience (possibly no different from ancient Greek drama), and psychotherapy and counselling institutionalising and commodifying confession. Social media are synonymous with personal confessional accounts that are largely trivialised, abandoning formal structures of compelling narratives.

The 14th-century Italian poet and scholar Petrarch, who laid the foundations for modern humanism, writes in his letters of a planned ascent of a nearby mountain, Mont Ventoux. Fussing about who to climb with and what book to take with him from his vast library of Classical scholars, Petrarch chose his younger brother Gherardo as a companion and a pocket-sized copy of Augustine's *Confessions*. Gherardo turned out to be a pain – chattering all the time rather than contemplating the view. Petrarch found a quiet spot to sit on his own. Opening a page at random, he writes of a serendipity and a revelation. Where he opened *Confessions* Augustine says:

And men go about to wonder at the heights of the mountains, and the mighty waves of the sea, and the wide sweep of rivers, and the circuit of the ocean, and the revolution of the stars, but themselves they consider not.

88   *Self-Literacy*

Stunned by this serendipitous moment, Petrarch writes that he turned away from gazing at the mountain and the environs, now in deep reflective contemplation of his own experience. Seven centuries on from Petrarch, the selfie dominates, kiss-and-tell accounts sell online content, and over 3 billion people worldwide chatter on Meta. That is the combined populations of China and India, or more than one third of the world's population and half of all internet users largely engaged in, or attracted by, personal confessional accounts. Most of it is chatter for the sake of – just connect! How much serious contemplation goes on is anybody's guess – there's little entertainment or gossip in that.

# 25 The self's new religion
## Secular and humanistic

The personal confessional style is often invoked as transparent or natural, or is taken literally, avoiding historical and cultural contextualisation. It has taken on the status of a religion without a deity, where the self is the deity. The rules of worship are in every self-help manual, personal growth seminar, therapeutic encounter, social media site, and the colour supplements of the newspapers. This unreflective approach demonstrates the pervasiveness of the genre, subjecting itself to the dominant discourse of humanistic personalism. Through these invocations, the personal confessional narrative as a specific variant of autobiography is offered as a revelation of an individual's interiority, usually centred on emotional life. Thirty years ago, any television interview would ask 'what do you think about that?' Now the common question is 'how does that make you feel?'

Reflex descriptions of interior life can be seen as products of the genre of confessionalism itself, where identities are constructed through confessional modes rather than confessional modes revealing identities. Secular-humanistic confession offers a mode of constructing identity within a specific discourse of self-surveillance. Where the priest once heard confession in absolute confidentiality, now confidences must be broken for the sake of a good story circulating in the secular world of social media until boredom sets in. Here, self is trivialised rather than honoured.

When we tell each other about ourselves – what we've been up to, what we're looking forward to, the ups and downs of everyday life, responses to events in the world – we seem to take the 'I' for granted as the author of these stories. But the kinds of stories we tell as the narrating 'I' differ considerably – these are genres of storytelling, formally expanded into genres of literature such as detective ('I was curious about his motive so I looked in to his background by asking around'), psycho-autobiographical ('I think growing up in an isolated village had a huge effect on me'), soap ('I know this is gossip, but did you see the way that Mary flirted with John's wife at the party?'), tragic ('the accident has changed me forever'), and so forth.

DOI: 10.4324/9781003619901-26

90  *Self-Literacy*

We thus 'story' ourselves into being in differing ways, with both broad and subtle differences.

These genres of story can provide not just shades of the self, but major keys of selfhood. Further, each of these ways of talking about, and then constituting and reconstituting selfhood, is open to fashion. Currently, again we are in the grip of a personal confessional period facilitated by social media and a pop-therapeutic culture, constituting a generic identity: shaping citizens as either confessors or listeners (secular priests). That 'we' of course is assumptive and biased. I am writing this from the perspective of a white, straight, elderly, Northern European male. My account is necessarily culturally biased. Please adjust accordingly.

One critical perspective that I am sure about is that much current personal confessional narrative as a commonly adopted cultural practice focuses on positives and ideals such as 'growth' or 'well-being'. Fiction of course serves another purpose – to question ideals and assumptions, and to problematise cherished values. Where 'growth' and 'human development' are framed as idealistic and optimistic terms (taking control, empowerment, expansion, progress, maturation, becoming creative), we forget that tumours grow, economies inflate, obesity is growth, and populations swell beyond the capacity of available resources. Also, we might think of 'growth' as a deepening (becoming more responsible, grounding, intensifying), or shedding (slimming down, emptying out, streamlining). Growing or developing may also take us into unknown and dangerous territory. We may read 'growth' as becoming more authentic or morally sensitive and ethically tuned – taking on the role of what the ancient Greeks called a 'parrhesiast', a 'truth teller'. Today, we may think of this as a whistleblower or someone with a strong moral compass. *Parrhesia* literally means 'moral courage'. A form of *parrhesia* is the moralist as critic and innovator who purposefully seeks to challenge habitual patterns of thought and action – pointing to unworthy, established, or normative practices that are unethical, hypocritical, unreflective, or plain sloppy. The parrhesiast is then someone who confesses his or her own necessity to be virtuous in telling the truth. This is a narrative self-forming through high ethical conduct – telling stories not as fictional embellishments for aesthetic purposes, but as recounting truths for moral reasons. Further, this does not construct a smug identity, but one of high standards. These are whistleblowers who act in good faith.

Returning to the aim of personal confessional narrative – 'invented' by Jean-Jacques Rousseau (1712–78) – as a basis for forming a self, such writing may not be a route to freedom of self, but a way of disciplining the self. This is a form of subjection rather than a flight of independent subjectivity. Such accounting for self is then neither liberating nor empowering, but rather offers a paradoxical discipline, as a technology of the self in which, as a practice of liberation, there are certain things that may be said and those that may not be said, while these may be said or not said in certain ways. One obvious disciplining power is that, in a capitalist neoliberal economy, a libidinous economy of selfhood is capital that can be manipulated by industries of fashion. Telling stories sells, especially from celebrities, and especially as it is tittle-tattle rather than visionary. There is subjection to fashion rather than critical interrogation at work, where confessional writing is not emancipatory. Narcissism is tolerated as everyday and acceptable.

The mere saying of 'I' – first person singular and a sign of ownership – may signal recognition of consciousness ('I think') but the Cartesian 'proof' ('therefore I am') is assumptive. Thinking is no proof of a core identity. Indeed, our thinking is often muddled, illogical, misguided, or bizarre (as in dreams, daydreaming, hallucinations, altered states of consciousness, or under extreme emotional states such as falling in love or gripped by overwhelming jealousy or anger). Thinking may involve multiple selves and subpersonalities.

Simply speaking the 'I' does not necessarily generate a self as the Grand Narrative of Modernism would suggest. Speech may be lacking (extreme cases of autism, elective mutism) or frustrated (psychosis, loss of memory as in Alzheimer's) yet, from behaviour, self-awareness is evident. Language is not a transparent medium for explanation and closure, and for the naive and literal description of self. Rather, language produces self. Language speaks, not the author, where language constitutes subjectivities in its performative usage. The humanist view of the ownership of subjectivity through language, within a capitalist neoliberal economy, suggests that language has been appropriated by an inflated ego. Various discourses of speaking, listening, and writing produce the objects of their inquiry including a privatised self as essence. Can we then have a narrative voice without a totalising subject or authorial ownership? This would constitute an approach that appreciates the value especially of written language's inherent indeterminacy, where self – spoken into being – is already uncertain, often muddled, and open-ended. Any self-respecting self will ask, where is self in memory loss such as post-traumatic amnesia or Alzheimer's; or in dissociative and multiple selves experiences; or in a forcibly displaced self traumatised through conflict?

# 26 ~~Writing out~~ the modern self
## Postmodern prescriptions

The self as narrative – our own stories – is subject to historical and cultural influences. We still live in the shadow of the modernist 'I' that is introspective, contained, subjective, and expressed through standard confessional modes – the autobiography and psychobiography. We have not escaped the influence of Rousseau and Thoreau. But Modernism has been heavily critiqued and restructured to revision selfhood as multiple, fluid, even absent.

Modernism and its core strategy for thinking – Structuralism – are characterised by oppositional thinking and a phallogocentric mentality. In Northern hemisphere oppositional thinking, one term is preferred over another and becomes top dog: Male over Female, White over Black, Capitalism over Communism, Rationality over Emotion. Such exclusive thinking offers 'grand narratives', or Big Theories, all encompassing, such as neo-liberal capitalism, consumerism, and rationalistic science. After Modernism comes a restructuring of thought and environment: dualistic categories are abandoned for 'both/and' inclusivity; phallogocentrism is abandoned for appreciation of the feminine and emotional life; and phallic skyscrapers are abandoned for low-rise, ecologically sensitive architecture. The self is no longer seen as rational, consistent over time, unitary, and bound by ideology.

In Modernism, speech is privileged over writing, language is mobilised on behalf of logos and rationality for scientific certitude, explanation, and final causation. Further, language is utilised unreflectively as a transparent medium for explanation rather than as a system itself in need of explanation or problematising. To restore language to its native indeterminacy – as the play of difference – we need to restore the primacy of writing over speech. Writing carries not only greater scope than speaking, but also greater indeterminacy. Postmodern voices claim that we need to kill 'the father' in rational language to encourage the emergence of other voices, such as feminist writing, and critically interrogate the personal confessional genre. Contemporary authors such as Don DeLillo specialise in this. We need to recognise the indexical, linguistic 'I' as reformulating or remaking identity in every speech act. As Roland Barthes suggests, 'I is nothing

DOI: 10.4324/9781003619901-27

*Writing out the modern self: postmodern prescriptions* 93

other than the instant saying I'. 'I' does not have continuity independent from language, is not an audience to language, or a bystander, but is the voice of language itself. Therefore, again, 'I' is remade in every speech act. The secular-humanistic, personal confessional mode of writing rarifies, literalises, or concretises the I. We need to trope the literal or treat the 'I' as a moving feast, a panoply of newly minted metaphors.

Such performative language (and its corollary, the 'performed self') can be seen to suffer through confinement to a narrow literal and technical mode, and to a self-referential monologic. Here, writing is starved of its possibilities, anaesthetised or dulled, unable to find a plurality of aesthetic voices through metaphor, image, allegory; and unable to exercise itself as a dialogic imagination that would offer a world-orientation and communal practice. Postmodern fictions, through their aesthetic possibilities, can 'heal' our literalism or logical scientific ways of knowing, and the confessional styles that have come to dominate fiction.

While language works on us, we must work back on it in a reflexive dialogue with language's registers and aesthetic possibilities, recognising the discursive production of identities through social practices. Where writing appears to spontaneously, and sometimes alarmingly, reveal something of oneself to oneself therapeutically, perhaps this is rather an effect of a shift in genre or register of writing itself that heals the standard or dominant fictional form – usually technical or social realist, and often personal confessional. The therapeutic focus is then upon language healing language, such as metaphor curing the curse of literalism. Perhaps writing itself works to sensitise us to the world, rather than forcing us to further introspection, only serving to reinforce the capitalism of personal ownership of identity and feelings, the rationalism of a unified self, and the imperialism of a therapeutic lifestyle.

A therapy of writing would attend to its more obvious symptomatic failures such as a poverty of style in which the arts of rhetoric are lost to functional language providing instrumental outcomes: instruction manuals, form filling, memoranda, plain description, bullet points, summaries, reports, formularies, and task-based analyses. These Puritan forms are purposefully devoid of surprise, indeterminacy, invention, imagination, florid or baroque excess, disturbance, or story that would offer a counter-reformation explosion of style. Similarly, personal confessional writing invoked as narrative inquiry can also readily suffer from a paucity of aesthetic value. Such writing is, characteristically, first monological rather than dialogical, caught in a wash-and-spin cycle of interminable introspection based upon self-examination as an idealistic cleansing and purging. Here, autonomy is preferred to heteronomy, or self-control to sacrifice to the other. This affords a privileging of the 'I'-self over the 'We'-self, where the latter is embedded in a community. Second, such writing is characteristically instrumentalised, as

## 94  *Self-Literacy*

an extended curriculum vitae. Third, it is often trivialised, or superficial, as anecdotal account mistaking event for experience. Fourth, it is often cathartic but without insight, leading to a fascination with expressing feelings and sentimentality in a moral and intellectual vacuum. And fifth, it is characteristically inflated, or narcissistic, returning us to a monologic bias. The psychological work involved in writing is mistaken for 'consciousness raising'. Paradoxically, consciousness cures us of having a psyche where the latter is unpredictable, pathologises, is indeterminate, and structured like a language prior to human experience drawing on that language.

If we adopt the essentialist model of self of personalistic humanism, where does this leave the critique of Marx, that we are social beings whose consciousness is false, constituted by capitalist economic forces? Or the critique of Freud, that we can never know ourselves directly, because the ego is secondary to the unconscious and essentially paranoid, afraid of being overwhelmed by unconscious desire? Even the defended ego offers an inauthentic position driven by fantasy and subverted by an irrational unconscious or primary process. (Freud nevertheless saw the trade-off between a fragile ego and an overwhelming set of instincts as something we must engage with, on behalf of social cohesion or the Reality Principle.) Or the view of Heidegger, who suggests that the self is not an essence, and a proper object for study, but a process in flux, a 'becoming' rather than 'being', echoing Schopenhauer's view that the subject becoming the object of its own contemplation offers 'the most monstrous contradiction ever thought of'? Or the radical religious view of Emmanuel Levinas, that the self is always hostage to the Other, where constitution of selfhood is only achieved in sacrifice of self, as an acceptance of the face of the intolerable 'other'? Levinas then asks us to abandon the project of autonomy for one of heteronomy.

Where does essentialism leave the feminist critique of Luce Irigaray, who suggests that the dominant universal subject in Western thinking focused on identity is inevitably gendered male, thus marginalising identities focused upon difference and feminine genealogy? Or Gilles Deleuze and Félix Guattari, who see subjectivity as nomadic rather than territorial, challenging the capitalist basis to subjectivity as private ownership of the capital of experience and feelings, where subjects are captured in their prison of interiority so that they can be more readily exploited, treated as goods or services? Or Jean Baudrillard, who sees subjectivities and identities as simulacra created through the massage of postmodern culture of entertainment, electronic information networks, and virtuality, where the map proceeds the territory? Here, a couple out wheeling the pushchair in the park with their young child meet some friends they have not seen for a while. 'What a beautiful child' exclaims the friends, 'yes but wait till you see the photos' the proud parents respond. The self is constituted by its representation, rather than its presentation.

# 27 Cancelling the self
## Postmodern anti-narrativists

In Modernism and its literature, the self is the centre of narrative gravity. Anti-narrativists such as Joy Williams write gripping stories without explicit plot, or development of character, where self is cancelled or undone by its contradictory actions and ambiguous expressions. Judith Ryan points out in *The Vanishing Subject* that the notion of a stable, self-knowing, transparent subjectivity, based on personalistic humanism, was already being questioned within literary modernism's avant-garde experiments during the 1920s. This included Virginia Woolf's 'stream of consciousness' writing and James Joyce's conscious privileging of an autonomous language over subjectivity, where language is not a secondary and transparent medium for describing subjectivity, but a primary medium that invents or constructs subjectivities through writing and speaking. The Scottish 18th-century philosopher David Hume had long ago suggested that self is not discovered by observation. Such solipsism is readily countered – for 'who' is the 'self' that searches for and reflects on the 'self'? This merely produces a hall of mirrors. Better, perhaps, to recognise that self is discursively produced through language every time we use a personal pronoun. Talking to myself about myself must depend upon having a prior set of stories or notions about myself. These are the biographical narratives evolved and employed by others, where language is performative, as a social practice.

Where the subject is not an essential quality but a continuously recreated aesthetic phenomenon, we can again say the self is fictional, following narrative styles or genres. However, modernist narrative returns selfhood to a stable form, as the speaking 'I', inflected through differing genres. Postmodern writers follow Woolf and Joyce in subscribing to multiple, indeterminate selfhood, created spontaneously.

The American postmodern writer Don DeLillo's first novel *Americana* traces the meteoric rise of a young TV executive in New York who suddenly decides to abandon his job, career, and identity in a haphazard journey across America which he records with a 16 mm camera. This is 1971, prior to the advent of the camcorder. The man records 'Americana', trivial

DOI: 10.4324/9781003619901-28

## 96  Self-Literacy

details of everyday life in small towns across the land and is absorbed into these trivia that becomes the fabric for his shifting identities. The identity of the antihero David is then constructed in an entirely superficial way, through his relationship to 'the true power of the image' derived from his worship of film stars. It apparently works: one day David is strolling back to work from a lunch break when 'a lovely teenage girl wearing pink eyelashes asked me for an autograph. "I don't know who you are" she said, but I'm sure you must be somebody'. In signing up to the girl's fantasy David writes himself out: he both erases and inscribes identities simultaneously, for he is constellated as a film star where she asks for his autograph, at the same time as she does not know if he is a film star. But if she gets his autograph this makes him somebody. David is a simulacrum – a copy without an original. Another character in De Lillo's novel says: 'I just as soon not talk about myself. I've exhausted all hope of defining who or what I am ... I thrive on imagery, it seems to have a laxative effect.' A constant flow of surface images keeps the bowels of the social world open.

The Japanese Nobel Prize-winning novelist Kenzaburo Oe plays with similar ideas of slippage of subjectivities in his 1967 novel *The Silent Cry*. The novel opens with an introspective voice: 'awakening in the predawn darkness I grope among the anguished remnants of dreams that linger in my consciousness'. So far, so good – the indexical 'I' offers a self-reference that is confirmed by the privatised ownership of consciousness. However, such modernist self-certainties are soon shattered as Oe takes us further into the protagonist's world: 'seeking in the tremulous hope of finding eager expectancy reviving in the innermost recesses of my being ... still I find an endless nothing'. Moreover, there is a paradoxical sense of multiplicity in the face of this 'endless nothing': 'in each part of my body, the several weights of flesh and bone are experienced independently'. Oe's protagonist reflects that upon waking he will hopefully find 'the ardent sense of expectation' that is 'no consciousness of lack, but the positive actuality in itself', but is 'finally convinced that I'll not find it'. His experience of self becomes 'like an insect impaled helpless upon a pin'. He feels himself 'being slowly eroded by a power' that is both 'dangerous' and 'hard to identify'. Yet this whole feeling 'had failed, in short, to constitute an experience'.

Oe's antihero is like Robert Musil's Ulrich, 'The Man Without Qualities', a novel written between the two world wars that questions the notion – indeed, the wisdom – of a singular, unitary, rational ego or self, that can know and describe itself transparently. Musil was familiar with psychoanalysis that, following Nietzsche's philosophy, launched the single most effective critique of the rational, humanist self, describing rather a more powerful irrational force at work, like the 'dangerous' and 'hard to identify' power described above by Oe, that subverts consciousness as self-knowledge. This is Freud's notion of unconscious desire, the wrecker of egos as the source of the Pleasure Principle rather than the Reality Principle.

The Brazilian novelist Clarice Lispector, in *The Hour of the Star*, describes a slum girl's experiences in 1970s Rio de Janeiro, whose identity is established not through exercise of gender, but through membership of the marginalised poor. A fortune teller informs the street urchin girl Maccabiah that she will meet a rich man and a life will change. She leaves the fortune teller's house full of hope and the immediately walks off the pavement failing to see a huge yellow Mercedes car racing towards her. As the car knocks her down, she realises that this is the rich man she was destined to meet. Lying, dazed and dying on the road the girl 'clung to a thread of consciousness and mentally repeated over and over again: I am, I am, I am'. The Cartesian mantra however was of no use, for 'precisely who she was, she was unable to say'.

Don de Lillo's *Players*, first published in 1977, describes the disintegration of the materialistic worlds of an all-American couple, Pammy and Lyle Wynand, through their fateful involvement in a political conspiracy and sexual subterfuge. De Lillo's writing captures in particular the mood of post-Vietnam War America reflecting on its own culture, finding it devoid of depth, and riddled with insecurity and paranoia. At the close of the 212 pages of text, De Lillo describes Lyle as 'a propped figure, barely recognisable as male. Shedding capabilities and traits by the second, he can still be described (but quickly) as well formed, sentient, and fair. We know nothing else about him'. Thus, De Lillo avoids a conventional narrative offering character development, through a description of character slippage, displacement, absence, and deconstruction. This is not a shallow character, rather it is a narrative technique of purposefully shallowing out characters whose identities are transient. De Lillo refuses self-knowing characters with direction in life to stress how self is constituted largely through the reactions of others, cultivating mis-directions. One of Dillard's characters in *Players* suggests that intense self-awareness can only lead to 'fear', and not to progressive self-improvement or enlightenment. These are pesky ghosts in the Kantian machine of self-knowing and self-improvement as a transcendental imperative.

Are these writers merely quirky, promoting literary effects, or following the postmodern fashion of the 'death of the subject'? Well, let us remind ourselves of the passionate account given by Alice James, the sister of the psychologist William James and the novelist Henry James, who kept a diary recording her losing battle against breast cancer from 1889 until her death in 1892. Alice James admitted that she suffered from 'too much consciousness', and from 'too much reflection'. The supposed boons of modernism were for her burdens. Subjectivity was too close, unbearable in weight.

## 98   Self-Literacy

Reflection was not the cure for ignorance, but a symptom of expressive intellect. She writes that she has 'never unfortunately been able to abandon consciousness and get five minutes' rest'. Alice James' 19th-century account resonates with Martin Amis' contemporary antihero Richard, in *The Information*, who wakes from sleep 'in a terrible state – that of consciousness'. For James and Amis, separated by a century, reflective introspection is to be treated with suspicion.

Autobiography and psychobiography can become larded with pathos or suffering, making them heavy reading. A confessional writing genre that carries such pathos can be seen as a depleted existentialism. Self-revelation can offer a pretence of wholesome sincerity, an inauthenticity that is anathema to the existentialist truth that Sartre encouraged – to *live* a life authentically rather than *confess* it where autobiography is confused with a history of personality (and with auto-ethnography that self-observes). Here, self becomes commodity open to narcissistic gratification. Listening to oneself can make one blush with embarrassment. The whole point of confession, say the poststructuralists, is surely to engage with an audience, to reach out to another. It is not about self-absorption. Heteronomy – recognition of the other, precedes autonomy. Autobiography or confessional speaking is a means through which relation to another is articulated. As Emmanuel Levinas suggests, we are always 'hostage' to the Other. In writing about myself, I am in any case following the rules of the genre of autobiography and thus rehearsing the discursive properties of such systems. Subjectivities can be theorised as emergent properties of the complex historical systems of technologies of the self of which autobiography is a prime example.

# 28 As mad as a hatter
## Neurodivergent selves

Adders or vipers are common in my neck of the woods and the only poisonous snake in the UK. I've seen many, even uncovering an adder's nest in my compost heap, but never been bitten. My son's been bitten twice but suffered no ill effects other than some swelling. However, if you are very young, or if your immune system is compromised, an adder bite can be serious but almost certainly not fatal. Since 1876, there have only been 14 recorded deaths, the last in 1975. Why am I banging on about adders? Because 'as mad as a hatter' probably originates with the Old English *atter* meaning 'poison' and is cognate with 'adder'. The 'madness' more likely relates to the snaking movement of the reptile than the effects of its bite. 'Mad' once meant 'venomous', so 'mad as a hatter' could be translated into the alliterative 'venomous as a viper'.

Some relate 'mad as a hatter' to the trade of hat making, where mercury was used. Extensive imbibing of mercury through the skin can cause delusions. But the saying 'mad as a hatter' predates the hatter's trade. Who are the 'mad'? Once a stigma, now the term has been recovered as a badge of pride by the community who see neurodiversity as a gift. In the 1960s and 1970s, 'madness' was seen as an unfortunate descriptor for people who were different from the norm. Indeed, the 'anti-psychiatry' movement of the time saw 'normality' as a form of madness. Selves were made around these terms.

Back in the early 1970s, I went to an evening talk at the Philadelphia Association in London given by the South African psychiatrist David Cooper, then resident in the UK. R. D. Laing, the infamous and radical Scottish psychiatrist, was also booked to speak but failed to show. Cooper gave a passionate talk referencing his dislike of the term 'anti-psychiatry', although he had been credited with coining that term in 1967 and wrote (in 1971) a polemic entitled *Psychiatry and Anti-Psychiatry*. Today, the term 'critical psychiatry' is preferred. Cooper talked about new approaches to psychiatry that extolled what we would now call 'neurodiversity', a term introduced by the sociologist Judy Singer in the 1990s, who claimed her

DOI: 10.4324/9781003619901-29

## 100  *Self-Literacy*

autism as a benefit and a platform from which to speak out about issues of inequity.

Cooper called for a break after about an hour, asking if a member of the audience would nip out to a Chinese restaurant just around the corner to bring him a takeaway and a beer. Somebody in the audience volunteered. The food came in an aluminium container with a lid. The session restarted. Cooper swigged the beer, then took the lid off the Chinese meal, put the container on the floor, dropped his trousers and underpants, and promptly sat in the food. There was a collective gasp from the audience. This seemed like such a strange gesture. Cooper then cleaned himself up, and subsequently gathered the responses of the audience. Was this a moment of madness, an impulse, a zen paradox, a living koan, a piece of theatre or performance, Dada, exhibitionism, an act of infantile regression, a schoolboy prank, a joke? Was it a pun on the sit-in, the popular student protest of the time? Was there teaching in it? We discussed all these possibilities. The strange thing was that the act itself was innocuous, even tame, harming nobody, and could have been a piece of tomfoolery. And yet in context it was taken as the action of a rule-breaker, a norm-bender, somehow serious, even shocking, or an offence to taste. Was this because it was largely a British audience, stereotypically reserved? Cooper stayed mum throughout, more interested in our responses than in explaining his behaviour – typical of an analyst.

Cooper then asked us to question the legitimacy of his actions as we reflected on our motives and values basis for doing so. Would we call it an act of madness? Well, he said, his whole talk was indeed about the legitimacy of labels such as 'madness' and 'insanity', and how he, R. D. Laing, and the Scottish psychiatrist Aaron Esterson had worked so hard to persuade the psychiatric establishment that the conventional models of madness were mad in their own right – or at least inauthentic in an existential sense. In what sense are varieties of 'madness' any more invalid than everyday life, in which we fit into prescribed roles and habitual routines that serve to make us neurotic: desensitised, anxious, and depressed?

People particularly liked the idea that Cooper sitting in his Chinese meal was a Zen paradox, a koan, a parable, or an embodied metaphor – this was, after all, the early 1970s when Zen Buddhism was fashionable in the West. But most saw it as a piece of theatre to stimulate discussion. Cooper insisted, 'it is all these things and none of them', again advertising paradox. The fact that we had come up with over half a dozen possible explanations for the behaviour was the key issue. Would straight psychiatry, armed with a current edition of the *Diagnostic and Statistical Manual of Mental Disorders* (DSM) do the same for patients in addressing their presenting symptoms?

Sometime previously, I attended a talk by Laing where he did his familiar party piece of soberly reading, in flat affect, extracts from the latest edition of *DSM* for their anti-metaphorical qualities – as flat text that, paradoxically, could be said to suffer from both hysteria (overblown accounts), and paranoia (seeing things that may not be there). It was like listening to a stand-up comic, exactly the point Laing wanted to make. He would show how the texts were expressly anti-poetic and then would read from his own poetic work *Knots* (1973) that described paradoxical, cul-de-sac descriptions of contradictions, or double binds.

The notion of 'double bind' was introduced by the English polymath Gregory Bateson in the 1950s to describe linguistic paradoxes that frustrated feedback loops. In cybernetic terms, a double bind stunted a feedback mechanism, turning the loop on itself. Such double binds, typically seen in families' dysfunctional conversations, would place vulnerable people in impossible situations where choice was removed, and the only response was to freeze and potentially go mad. For example, Laing writes (adapted version, as prose),

> Once Upon a time, when Jack was little, he wanted to be with his mummy all the time and was frightened she would go away. Later, when he was a little bigger, he wanted to be away from his mummy and was frightened that she wanted him to be with her all the time. When Jack grows up to fall in love with Jill he wants to possess her, but then, a little older, he finds he doesn't want to be with Jill all the time, but is afraid that Jill may become frightened of his new choice, so now they are in a double bind, where: Jack frightens Jill that he will leave her because he is frightened she will leave him.

The late Peter Redgrove was a celebrated British poet. In 1950, only 18 years old and having just completed secondary schooling, Redgrove was called up for UK national service. He joined the Royal Army Medical Corps. Within a week of basic training, he was hospitalised with a nervous disorder diagnosed as obsessive-compulsive behaviour. He had already been labelled neurotic by his family doctor before being called up. He was assigned to a young psychiatrist interested in psychoanalysis, who thought he might analyse Redgrove. The latter agreed, soon confessing to what this young psychiatrist would term a 'perversion'. Redgrove liked to dress up in a clean white shirt and then soil it by rolling in mud, followed by masturbation. He could not stop doing this – it was a compulsion. Such compulsion was entirely free from exhibitionism, a purely private activity.

In fact, this would be a lifelong practice for Redgrove, one that fed his imagination, giving him visions feeding directly into his poetry. We might say, generously, that what psychiatry termed a neurosis was in fact a well of inspiration for Redgrove's writing, a quirk spinning gold. The young psychiatrist Peter Spall was seeing Redgrove daily for one-hour long sessions, writing in Redgrove's notes that his 'perversion' had origins in

102   *Self-Literacy*

jealousy for his father and love of his mother, and could be cured in around three months. This sounds like cod psychoanalysis.

Another, more sober and traditional, psychiatrist diagnosed Redgrove with 'incipient schizophrenia' and recommended insulin shock therapy or deep insulin treatment. This was, along with psychosurgery and electro-convulsive shock therapy, the most invasive treatment available for severe mental illness, but with no rigorous evidence base for success. Redgrove was discharged from the army while in hospital and subsequently took the entrance exam for Cambridge University, where he would later study natu-ral sciences. In talking with his general practitioner in 1973, Redgrove was told that there was no such diagnosis as 'incipient schizophrenia' and that if he did not have symptoms of dissociation, delusions, lack of insight, and hallucinations, then he was not suffering from schizophrenia. Redgrove later wrote that he was relieved that he was not an 'accredited madman'. How-ever, Redgrove's GP was partly mistaken – there is a diagnostic category of 'incipient schizophrenia', and he was certainly suffering from some disso-ciation. But he did not suffer from hallucinations. In fact, he welcomed the intrusion of the imagination as a gift, bringing poetic visions. Juvenile over-confidence might have been mistaken for narcissism, but there was certainly no lack of insight on the budding poet's part. In fact, Redgrove suffered from a lack of restraint and a surfeit of incisive insight. His later prodigious poetry and prose output testified to this. If his early bane was mainstream psychia-trists eager to apply a psychopathological label to his creativity, his later pain would be frugal editors attempting to curb his extraordinary volume of output – all at a high level of skill and self-assurance.

At the time of Redgrove's initial diagnosis, the diagnostic criteria for 'schizophrenia' included exaggerated belief that contingent circumstances and events refer to oneself and are not just coincidental, paranoid ideation, perceptual disturbances, magical thinking, and generally odd thinking and speech. Are these conditions not often attributed to an artistic tempera-ment or seen as the valued sensitivities of a poet? Attributions of voices to nature, or animation, is sometimes added to this list.

For example, Redgrove's 2012 poem 'Among the Whips and the Mud Baths' ponders on 'How she was said to have learned to ease the slow blue / lightning', where lightning is personified as it is metaphorised. This, 'Out of her skin and out of her lover's skin' (real-time, physical attributes) 'So that they were sheathed in radiance'. The 'dark room' in which they are making love 'Flickered with their body-prints, like sand-dunes electrified / After a dry day'. Redgrove's conclusion on this attribution of voices to nature is to return to the body that such voices populate and provide poetic nourishment and inspiration, simply: 'All that sex populates my imagina-tion and makes me happy'.

# As mad as a hatter: neurodivergent selves   103

The natural world's of electrification of skin, the gathering of unseen lightning, is the crucible for the cross-electrification of lovers' skins that might seem to glow in the dark, phosphorescent. (The enjambed 'lightning' is a beautiful touch, especially as it is slow and blue and then not dropped conventionally to the next line at left field, but rather displaced far to the right of the field as if a literal step down into the heart of the metaphorical electricity – again slow and blue). I say 'metaphorical', but for Redgrove the electricity of the skin during sex was real, fully embodied. The deepest intimacy is poetry, itself a phosphorescent new skin. What was said to be a madness treatable by induction of coma and near-death experience becomes the creative hub of Redgrove's vision as an opposite of coma, indeed as vigour. His intense eroticism probably alarmed his psychiatrists. Returning to his psychiatric journey, Redgrove was eventually diagnosed with 'schizophrenia in obsessional personality', placing him at the fringes of delusion. Psychiatrists again recommended deep insulin coma therapy to coalesce his dissociative personality. In response, Redgrove wrote that he 'favours the abstruse, but now tries to not use not to use a long word unless it expresses the exact shade of meaning'. This clearly doesn't signal dissociation but rather an exact association. Again, the skin really is electric, the metaphor fully embodied. It is a disembodied psychiatry dulled to such sensuousness that fails us. At this time, Redgrove had not written poetry, but it was stirring within him, and these are surely the words of a poet.

From the 17th of July 1950, deep insulin therapy was administered six days a week for nine weeks. In all, Redgrove had around 60 treatments, as sometimes the insulin coma would not ensue, and the procedure would be repeated. The coma brings one near to death, where glucose injections then revive the patient. Introduced in 1972 by the psychiatrist Manfred Sarkel, insulin shock therapy was largely discontinued by the 1970s, replaced by use of neuroleptic drugs. There proved to be no evidence base supporting its use. Psychiatrists' initial claims for its success have proven in retrospect to be wildly exaggerated.

Nearly a quarter of a century later, in the 1973 semi-autobiographical novel *In the Country of the Skin*, Redgrove's alter ego Jonas describes going through insulin shock therapy and its paradoxical benefits, where because of therapy,

> He was dead, truly dead, and dissolved into the soil. Later, when he began to write poetry, he didn't see why anything he had done in his life gave him the right to see things that were true in nature. Then he remembered that death had taken him to pieces, that he was conscious of being the mud and the soil.

## 104  *Self-Literacy*

'Dissolved into the soil'. Redgrove later said that while the insulin therapy experience had taken him many times to the edge of death, he felt in retrospect that no abiding vision had stayed with him. He needed some vehicle to give meaning to these mythological dissents, where he met Charon the Ferryman but could offer no gifts to cross Lethe. Poetry later provided that medium and that gift. His symptoms, particularly his fetish for spoiling in mud, could be made sense of through poetry. Rather than just a cathartic experience, meaning emerged for a variety of bodily, mental, emotional, and intuitive descents through the fertile matter of poetry or the messy field of poetic form. Redgrove was now authentically 'dissolved in the soil'. A vision emerged. A territory opened, where the electrical charge of the air could be pulled and grounded, reflected in 'the country of the skin'. Redgrove had found his turf. More, his character could be stabilised through poetry. Poetry itself was not simply expression or catharsis, but the medium through which his pact with death – as medically induced near death – could be given meaning. Poetry was truly therapeutic. It became for Redgrove a curriculum, a lifelong course of learning, a primary process.

Peter Redgrove was a mentor, friend, and colleague. He taught me how to write. I was in therapy with him while we shared collaborative educational ventures. His early experiences of standard psychoanalysis did little for his aesthetic sensibility – that gap was plugged by his chance encounter with the rebel analyst John Layard, once a celebrated anthropologist who had been in analysis with Carl Jung. He came to Falmouth in Cornwall in the late 1960s and met Lionel Miskin, head of painting at Falmouth School of Art. Coincidentally, Miskin was my art teacher at grammar school. Miskin went into analysis with Layard, as did Redgrove later. Ironically, Layard told Regrove to give up poetry, probably out of jealousy for his talent, but it was precisely because of this advice that Redgrove doubled down on his verse. In rejecting Layard, he threw off the father figure and gained poetry. In my own therapy with Redgrove, poetry was the central medium for our conversations.

While he worked as a science journalist after leaving Cambridge (he never completed his degree), it was only through dedicating himself to creative writing as his primary concern that Redgrove was able to work out just what a 'scientist of the strange' might study and how that study might be executed. Poetry was his laboratory instrument and medium for encapsulating an extraordinarily heightened sensuous appreciation of the natural world – particularly the weather, its electric atmospheres, and sudden shifts in tone. In *The Black Goddess and the Sixth Sense* Redgrove explores 'how we are surrounded by invisibles; forces which animals know but humans have come to ignore or only participate in unconsciously. These forces include electricity, magnetism and the deeper reaches of touch, smell, taste and sound'. Explaining such poetic sensitivities to a traditional psychiatrist, rooted in reductive biomedicine, is likely to lead to a diagnosis of derangement and paradoxically of limited capacity, rather than poetic capability as unbounded capacity.

In *Madness and Modernism*, the clinical psychologist Louis Sass offers a compelling thesis that repeated introspection, constant self-reporting, and obsession with consciousness is a symptom complex of modernism that ironically mirrors symptoms we otherwise see as aberrant in paranoid schizophrenics. These include cold rational obsessively detailed and attached accounts of the machinations of their inner world, coupled with literalisms rather than use of metaphor. Modern psychotherapy, with its obsessive focus upon introspective self-reflective account suffers from the very symptoms of narcissism that we ascribe to certain people as a personality disorder. Such self-reporting deflects us from the important task of noticing the world around us and the needs of others, which is an outward attention, and not an introspective taxis. Redgrove's poetic vision shows how important such attention to nature and employment of innovative metaphor are to productively channeling some neurodiverse energies, calling also for a tempering of self-absorption.

# 29 Self-consciousness without consciousness
## Tacit knowing

The self likes to hide below ground. Much of our doing and thinking is carried out without our conscious knowledge. Or, we have tacit (unconscious) awareness that guides activity. The body functions largely through habit. Some of this seems uncanny and we call this 'intuition' or 'tacit reasoning'. Here, our thinking is implicit rather than explicit, (en)folded into our being rather than plainly advertised.

An experienced neonatal nurse (in a North American context) reports her concerns about a premature baby in a critical situation:

> I took care of a 900-gram baby who was about 26 or 27 weeks … who had been doing well for about two weeks. He had an open ductus that day. The difference between the way he looked at 9 a.m. and the way he looked at 11 a.m. was very dramatic. I was at that point really concerned about what was going to happen next. There are a lot of complications of the patent ductus, not just in itself, but the fact that it causes a lot of other things. I was really concerned that the baby was starting to show symptoms of all of them.

In explaining these symptoms, the nurse says:

> The fact that the kid is more lethargic, paler, his stomach is bigger, that he is not tolerating his feedings, that his chem strip (blood test) might be a little strange. All these kinds of things … there are clusters of things that go wrong. The baby's urine output goes down. They sound like they are in failure. This kind of stuff. Their pulses go bad, their blood pressure changes. There are a million things that go on.

Significantly, the nurse was able to diagnose the baby's changing condition, but was unable to convince the physicians she spoke to that this was an urgent issue:

DOI: 10.4324/9781003619901-30

## Self-consciousness without consciousness: tacit knowing    107

You look at this kid because you know this kid, and you know what he looked like two hours ago. It is a dramatic difference to you, but it's hard to describe that to someone in words. You go to the resident and say: "Look, I'm really worried about X, Y, Z," and they go: "OK." Then you wait one half hour to 40 minutes, then you go to the Fellow (the teaching physician supervising the resident) and say: "You know, I am really worried about X, Y, Z." They say: "We'll talk about it on rounds."

I talked to a nurse who had more experience and I said, "Look at this kid," and I told her my story, and she goes: "OK." Rounds started shortly after that and she walks up to the Attending [Physician in charge of patient] very quietly, sidles up and says: "You know, this kid, Jane is really worried about this kid." She told him the story, and said: "He reminds me about this kid, Jimmie, we had three weeks ago," and he said: "Oh." Everything stops. He gets out the stethoscope and listens to the kid, examines the kid and he says: "Call the surgeons".

Suddenly there was recognition by the doctor of the urgency of the situation. Here is a refrain of the nurse's diagnosis:

The fact that the kid is more lethargic, paler, his stomach is bigger, that he is not tolerating his feedings, that his chem strip (blood test) might be **a little strange**. All **these kinds of things** ... there are **clusters of things** that go wrong. The baby's urine output goes down. They sound like they are **in failure. This kind of stuff**. Their **pulses go bad**, their blood pressure changes. There are **a million things that go on**.

The nurse moves between two linguistic registers: the literal and the metaphorical/ hyperbolic (I have **highlighted** the latter complex register). As somebody with experience and expertise in her field, the nurse was able to tick off some clinical warning signs that she describes in a mechanical or instrumental register, where the baby is reduced to symptom and 'in-house' clinical jargon is used (such as 'tolerating his feedings', 'blood test' or 'chem strip', and 'urine output'). This literal register includes affect-less, descriptive comment such *as:* 'a 900-gram baby who was about 26 or 27 weeks'; 'he had an open ductus that day'; 'the kid is more lethargic, paler, his stomach is bigger ... he is not tolerating his feedings'; and '[T]heir pulses go bad, their blood pressure changes'.

In contrast, there is a shift in language register from the literal to the embodied metaphorical, reflecting the nurse's deepening concerns:

- the blood test is 'a little strange' – blood tests are accurate and shown as quantitative data; here the nurse turns that into quality and intensity.

108   *Self-Literacy*

- 'All these kinds of things' the phrase refers (presumably) to parallel test results, and this multiplies into the more amorphous 'clusters of things'.
- 'This kind of stuff' – the biochemical certainties (test results) again become diffuse as they are enlarged or brought to the fore.
- 'Pulses go bad' – clinical jargon is dropped for the vernacular to emphasise the point.
- 'A million things that go on' – now the emphasis becomes purposeful exaggeration or hyperbole, as a means of persuasion.

In short, the acute shift in the baby's condition brings a parallel shift in register of language to capture what was going on in the nurse's consciousness – her cognition and feelings. She moves from descriptive to reflective mode that requires a different kind of language: as noted, a more metaphor-driven description as the baby looks 'worse' ('You look at this kid because you know this kid, and you know what he looked like two hours ago. It is a dramatic difference to you, but it's hard to describe that to someone in words'). Her narrative offers a climax, where the doctor suddenly recognises the urgency of the situation after the second nurse has cleverly gained his attention: 'Everything stops. He gets out the stethoscope and listens to the kid, examines the kid and he says: "Call the surgeons"'. The nurse is in meta-mode running on tacit knowing.

The nurse knew more than she could say – as if her fears for the child's well-being outstripped her specific clinical knowledge and experience, powered by an upsurge of affect. We often call knowing more than we can say 'intuition', but this word has metaphysical overtones, and here the nurse follows her senses, in close noticing (the basis to a poetic imagination). Her clinical practice has shifted from the instrumental to embrace the transcendental. She *knew* the child was in crisis. Her attentional and observational skills had flipped the switch and now intuition or tacit knowing too had kicked in, a marked contrast to the apparent inertia of the attending doctors. She becomes super-sensitive, poetically tuned.

Our capabilities go beyond the supposed limits of our technical knowledge as a surplus of consciousness, drawing on a 'cognitive unconscious' as noted above. This is expressed in a shift from the controlled and controlling, precise, quantitative-like language of the present-known, to the qualitative territory of the future-unknown. Here, our capability seems to expand, and as the limits of technical competence are outstripped, so qualitative and metaphoric descriptors kick in, complexity is recognised, and complexity's inherent ambiguity is tolerated. Such thinking embodies recognition of the limit to closed and linear thinking, as open, nonlinear, complex, dynamic, adaptive systems thinking is adopted. The nurse provides a stable attractor in a complex system at the edge of chaos, preventing collapse into such chaos. Intuition informs the senses as a meta-cognition

*Self-consciousness without consciousness: tacit knowing* 109

and meta-affect: described by Aristotle as the upgrading of *nous* (rational reasoning) to *phronesis* (practical reasoning with an end-in-itself), supplemented by *poiesis* (aesthetic production – or high-grade sensibility).

'Intuition' is then a by-word for what is more commonly known as tacit knowing. A sophisticated philosophical account of intuition is provided by Immanuel Kant's transcendental idealism, as 'sensible intuition'. Kant points to the contradiction that supposedly abstract categories such as space and time are concrete, sense-based human constructions: 'If the subject ... be removed ... space and time themselves would collapse'. Intuitions of space and time are necessary to scaffold sense experience that otherwise would be disordered. Kant suggested that 'pure intuition' is an *a priori* condition (prior to and independent from experience). Time and space are the conditions of possibility for the acts of sensing and experiencing. The *a priori* filters – through which we experience time and space – are abstractions such as 'substance' and 'cause and effect'.

What Kant's model does is to lift us out of solipsism or self-interest, the modern taxis of looking inward for explanations of phenomena (most obviously in the reduction of experience to brain mechanisms). Rather, Kant *situates* us in a shared world of metaphors, a position described as 'externalism', confounding first-person authority. Such metaphorical possibilities are transcendental conditions of language into which we walk to make sense of experience. Language, including the possibility of metaphor, precede the person who is born into this transcendental realm. It is this language frame that affords the self – an *a priori* deduction.

There is a long history of formal investigation of intuitive capacity that reaches back to Aristotle's description of *phronesis* (practical reasoning). Aristotle distinguished *nous* as conscious, rational reasoning based in mind, from *phronesis* as practical reasoning based in the senses. In Book VI of *Nicomachean Ethics*, Aristotle also distinguished between *phronesis* as practical activity with an end-in-itself (closed), and *poiesis* as aesthetic production, the exercise of imagination or the creative will as an end-other-than-itself (open-ended). While Aristotle, of course, never drove a car, we can see both *nous* and *phronesis* at work in driving. On a familiar road with little distraction, we tend to go into 'automatic' driving mode where things seem to look after themselves (*phronesis*), until some new stimulus snaps us back into an attentive and alert consciousness (*nous*).

Neuroscientists such as Antonio Damasio have suggested a distinction between an 'autobiographical self' at the conscious level, and a 'core self' at the visceral level. The former uses both a rational (logical) and a common-sense (sensory-intuitive) reasoning that constructs identity in real time as a conscious figurative (foregrounded) experience. The latter 'core self' is an unconscious and pre-conscious process that acts as ground, or background, to a configured life. It is the active conversation

## 110  *Self-Literacy*

between the two levels that constitutes practical wisdom. As Aristotle first suggested, *phronesis* is sense-based (embodied and affective), where *nous* is mind-based (rational). Practical wisdom is an emergent property of the nonlinear, complex system of bodily sensing and intuiting, open to contemplation and shaping by consciousness where we know more than we can say.

The philosopher Jacques Derrida describes this 'knowing more than we can say' as every phenomenon carrying a 'surplus of signification', effectively an absent present, that is both intangible and unreachable. Kant had described this as unknowable yet posited *noumena* as opposed to knowable and sensed *phenomena*. Derrida brings the noumenon to earth as the ghost or shadow phenomenon, where a person's experiences are more than they can ever say. This is one of the fundamental values of writing poetry, that it allows us to attempt to say the unsayable. Such surplus value can be described as transcendental. Poetry might therefore be understood as the 'surplus' to science, particularly where the latter claims full explanation of a given phenomenon. Artists such as poets often describe the experience of the poem writing them and of the product as appearing strange or unfamiliar.

Here, we are drawing on an unaccountable surplus – again, 'we know more than we can say'. Another example of this is automatic facial and voice recognition, capabilities that are key to human communication and sociability. In this, the self is hiding in plain sight.

# 30 Bodies at their limits
## Intentional self-fashioning

For most of us the cracking of joints, the stretching and splitting of skin, or copious bleeding are signs of bodily distress that press on our fragile egos and dent our sense of self. For others, the embodied self is 'performed' through extremes of insult and stress.

The Austrian choreographer Florentina Holzinger has been described as 'Europe's hottest director'. She is interested particularly in offering the feminine libido as a spectacle that can be reclaimed by women rather than becoming an object claimed by the male gaze. In a 2024 show, she has roller-skating women carrying out dangerous stunts while naked and wearing nuns' habits; women suspend their entire body weights from ponytails; a woman whose flesh is pierced by meat hooks is hoisted in the air, suspended by those hooks; a sword-swallower performs an upper endoscopy on himself (a rare male in the troupe); women piss at will on stage, sometimes choreographed (Holzinger teaches conscious control of the bladder); a woman's cheek is pierced by a large fish hook; there is masturbation to orgasm and live sex between women on stage; and so forth. Holzinger denies that this is just spectacle, or shock entertainment – it is rather an advertisement of bodily self-forming at its limits, and of strong feminism. For the straight person rather than kink communities, it may be a puzzling display of sadism, masochism, and exhibitionism. Commentators point to the importance of the model of the suffering body of Christ, particularly in Catholicism, and the priests and nuns who follow self-harming practices as devotional duties. Holzinger, a lapsed Catholic, has returned to such religious iconography to inform and shape her work.

Once considered as freak shows, side shows, or circus acts, body-based performers now claim positive identities. Performance art with the body pushed to its limits has a long history. For some, the body is a canvas where modified selves can emerge. The radical French performance artist and feminist Orlan claim that to escape the shadow of the father, women must change their skins. We might think that this is a metaphor for taking on a new identity, but Orlan means it literally. Her life's work as a body-based

DOI: 10.4324/9781003619901-31

## 112  *Self-Literacy*

performance artist has been to change her appearance through aesthetic surgery to engage critically with ideals of the feminine body – both those dictated by the patriarchy and feminist responses. She has augmented this with make-up and photography, most recently casting herself as an alien.

Orlan has undergone numerous operations for body modification, including the implantation of 'horns' in her temple, and facial surgery under local anaesthetic that she films to be broadcast live. She has turned her body into a canvas, exploring and critiquing ideal images of women dictated by both the patriarchy and feminist movements. The surgical team is primed to treat this as 'theatre'.

Orlan's motivations to treat her body as canvas are again quasi-religious and feminist: first, she again draws on the Catholic tradition of nuns suffering in identification with Christ's suffering; and with the woman's choice to modify her body as she wishes and not in line with patriarchal orthodoxies. Orlan says, 'to escape the realm of the father, one must change one's skin'. In more recent work, Orlan has experimented with photography and robotics to create futuristic images of herself as an alien being and as hybrid – part animal, part human; part alien, part native. She asks what kind of humans will be able to inhabit a posthuman world, ravaged by global warming and mass political unrest. Her model of self is then plastic, futuristic, and radically feminist where this is a woman owning her own body – a work of reclamation. There is, again, a strong element of masochistic pleasure. Orlan's work is a primary example of ethical, aesthetic, and political self-forming. Aesthetic as the body is the canvas for modifications that promote various models of beauty; ethical and political because Orlan again asks key questions about the value of the woman's body when reclaimed by women from subservience to the patriarchy and the male gaze.

A type of performativity – highly publicised because of legal issues, especially within conservative cultures – is gender transitioning, an identity narrative of great consequence. The gendered self for some is mutable. Feeling out of place in a given, genetic body, and dis-identifying with typical cultural characteristics of this gender, a transition is demanded – to another gender or to an indeterminate identification. Cross-dressing or drag may not be enough where a body dysmorphia sets in, demanding transgender surgery. That transgender issues and rights raise the hackles of conservatives merely illustrates how fixed their notions of self are. While currently those who identify as transgender in the USA, for example, constitute only 1.4% of the population of 13–24 year olds, this number has nearly tripled from the previous generation, suggesting that attitudes have changed, and that greater information and choice are available. Questioning of habitual identities offers a doorway to aesthetic self-forming in new keys.

# 31 Wired for subjectivity

The German philosopher Georg Wilhelm Friedrich Hegel (1770–1831) had faith in the value of human will as cooperation or democratic collaboration. He proposed a dialectic of thought where a thesis met its counter-argument in an antithesis. But rather than a stalemate, humans have the capacity to reach a synthesis of thought where sacrifices are made for the better good. This synthesis becomes a new thesis, and so forth. The dialectic's rational end point is its meeting with Kant's realm of transcendental categories (time and space), where a common way of knowing based on a common value structure could be reached at the highest level of knowing. This is the project of democracy. But democracy has not established itself universally and we may have to accept that humanity is fundamentally flawed as a species aiming to live cooperatively. Hegel's vision of an inevitable flow towards a realisation of human collaboration could not foresee that a spanner would be thrown into the works – that of disinformation spread through a technological web embracing a big slice of humanity. This is the information revolution – perhaps better called the misinformation revolution – the birth of the computer and the World Wide Web (WWW) that has created an entirely new condition for human communication. The vision of Tim Berners-Lee's WWW was to create a new channel to realise a just global society, but he did not predict that the platform would embrace all kinds of mischief and unethical content.

Humans, carbon-based biological creatures resulting from evolutionary forces, are increasingly engaging with silicon-based lifeforms of their own making. Posthumanist thinkers have suggested that humanity may eventually be replaced by such robotic and artificially intelligent lifeforms as that intelligence grows. Will these 'bots' be wired for subjectivity and engage with a transcendental set of imperatives that set out time, space, and a universal ethics (embracing social justice, equity, and equality)? In what kind of cognitive and affective modes will these creatures of the future live? In other words, what will the selves of robots be like? Currently, they are

DOI: 10.4324/9781003619901-32

## 114  *Self-Literacy*

wired to be like humanity, but without the transcendental concerns that engaged Kant and Hegel.

A surface approach to the creation of 'bots' is to impose humanity on them – to make artificial beings in the image of ourselves. A newspaper article on this trend in robotics runs the headline: 'Robots with humanity, although it's only skin deep'. Robot engineers in Japan are growing human skin from cultures to stretch across a plastic head to give a grisly appearance of a human face that can both grimace and smile. The researchers call this a 'skin equivalent'. It looks gruesome but is a prototype and will be sophisticated. The issue is not whether these engineers can replicate the human form – rather it is the ethical choice to make a robot in the human form in the first place. Of course, recognition plays a big part in robotics, but it is also hubristic of the human to reproduce ourselves as deep silicon structure with a carbon self-presentation. Robots in our own image. This may be fine for the hospitality industry (robot waiters and waitresses), but will this work in hospitals (robots as health and social care workers)?

So-called humanoids, say these Japanese inventors, are already populating health and social care sectors, following a first wave of industrial robots working on production lines. The future, say these inventors, is in 'biohybrid' beings with 'self-healing skins', a tribe of 'soft robots'. In time, the Japanese lab says, they will create 'skin that closely mimics the functionality of real skin by gradually constructing essential components such as blood vessels, nerves, sweat glands, sebaceous glands and hair follicles'. The neural system that controls these humanoids will be electronic, and silicon-based. Frankenstein's monster is realised. How and what will this creature think and feel? How will it deal with the unexpected? How will it vote in an election?

The humanoid scenario can get complex and weird. A mirror version of self can be produced through an AI-powered chatbot that will offer you not only counselling for now, but how you might develop yourself for the future. An AI-powered chatbot produced by the Massachusetts Institute of Technology (MIT) can simulate your previous self and offer pearls of wisdom to mould a future self – challenging your habits, seeking new challenges. You feed some information into the chatbot including a current photograph. The technology will feed back to you a photograph of your ageing self and some hints on how you might blossom in the future. It is like talking to yourself as a simulated elder version who gives counsel to the current self. The technology is described as a 'nudge' towards a future selfhood.

The interface of person and new information and communication technologies is currently perhaps the most complex area for study of emergent selves. What kinds of subjectivities are being produced in the virtual world? In cyberspace, the world is no longer mediated through personal consciousness. Rather, we are in extended bodies drawing on computer technologies. Our carbon-based beings are increasingly extended by silicon-based forms in which we are at one moment expanded into virtual spaces with limitless contact and the next shrink back into our finite bodies with their limitations and infirmities. Our worlds are real and virtual simultaneously.

The difference between this composite world and that of the modernist one of telegraph, television, and telephone is that as selves are simultaneously presented, represented, and dissolved in virtual spaces, so that they are endlessly circulated in those spaces. Information, held in cyberspace, becomes another form of Kant's transcendental realm: time, space, and information (but with much of that information being meaningless or classified as passive entertainment). While cyberspace has been compared to the dream, an identity created on the Internet is different from that dream, because it has permanence, does not disappear even when deleted, but is held in limbo as retrievable information. The self is also legally responsible for its virtual traces. The virtual identities produced in cyberspace are infinitely nomadic, yet permanently at home in cold, electronic storage. This is the paradox of the 'nomadic settler'. Another paradox is that the self that wanders the information superhighway does not want to contemplate Kant or Hegel, but rather wants to be entertained or to shop.

We are largely trivial beings in this half-human/half-virtual existence. As such, the intense, forced evolution of silicon-based lifeforms may soon be able to recognise that humanity has chosen to largely trivialise the privilege of being human – preferring to play games online or to be entertained than to expand the transcendental gift of ethical consciousness in following Hegel's model of idealism as movement to a common, shared identity with Truth through dialectic. Here, all wars, starvation, and deprivation could be halted through negotiation and tolerance in adopting the shared ethic of humanity's love for humanity. But, again, we have the bugs of bad behaviours and misinformation online.

There are multiple ethical issues brought about by the information superhighway that are exacerbated by the extensive use of satellite technologies. This allows the use of the internet in previously inaccessible places such as the Amazon rainforest where infrastructure such as generators, aerials, and mobile phones can be brought in. For example, Elon Musk's Starlink/Space X 6,000-strong satellite complex has allowed high-speed internet access for isolated tribes in the Amazon. Previously cut off from global communication, the Marubo, a 2,000 strong indigenous tribe, suddenly has global access. How does this affect a tribal self? Tribe leaders are anxious that this will erode traditions such that younger members will either leave the tribe altogether (some already have) or will ignore oral lore as the global internet dominates. This tribe has tradition and ceremony deeply

116　*Self-Literacy*

connected with the forest that is their livelihood and have a tradition of ayahuasca ceremony. To their spirit ancestors and familiars now must be added live television, violent video games, group chats, pornography (especially sensitive as the Marubo have a strict taboo even on kissing in public), misinformation, and a raft of postmodern entertainment. Selves will necessarily mutate.

While remote access has provided some benefits such as calls for help in emergencies (such as venomous snake bites needing urgent attention), traditional crafts such as making body paint from forest berries and jewellery from snail shells being lost as younger members of the tribe spend hours on their mobile phones instead. For Elon Musk, yanking these indigenous tribes into the 21st century is a good thing. For tribal leaders it offers a mixed blessing as tribal identifications and sense of self among younger members is now thrown into chaos.

Returning to post-industrial cultures, a reminder at this point: we readily cast silicon technologies in robotic terms because this allows us to approximate them as human forms, thus assimilating them instead of accommodating them. But silicon technologies mostly exist in the form of computer chips in sequences and not encased in human-like structures as robots. Indeed, here the silicon is in the chips and not in the imitated human superstructure of metal or plastic. Robots – their chip-brains – do not have the sophistication of human brains in terms of use of language such as metaphor or punning: Q. 'What is a robot's favourite meal?' A. 'Phish and chips'. (Spoiler – phishing is online stealing of data such as credit card or login details, usually by deception through email or text; computer chips are manufactured from silicon).

How will silicon-based life help to realise Hegel's ideal (if we think that it is worth realising) as identification with Spirit – the realisation of an authentic democracy? We must involve our extended cognitive world (again, the extension largely of computer technologies) in such dialectic. This implies adopting value positions of high tolerance for difference, or a range of subjectivities. The posthuman world already values multiple subjectivities against the spectre of the unified subject (monolithic dictators and ideologies are the fly in the ointment as far as the playing out of Hegel's dialectical vision is concerned). Multiple forms of subjectivity, such as feminist, gay, trans-, ethnic, mad or neurodivergent, (dis)abled, dissociated, and so forth, create the conditions of possibility for a dialectic of tolerance to create a just world. But will silicon lifeforms also adopt divergence within their own communities, and tolerance for a slack humanity of gamers and those who prefer entertainment and infotainment to politically charged education and an aesthetics of existence that values both the arts and sciences?

*Wired for subjectivity* 117

Such future convergences of radical humanity and radical robotics will be far from the humanistic view that cherishes a solid, stable self, or Cartesian *cogito* as the subject of knowing. Rather, we may see emerging a dominance of the subject of the unconscious without a closed horizon of meaning. This would be a multiple and distributed subject grounded in absence rather than presence, offering an embodiment of the surgeon and poet John Keats 'negative capability' – that we know that we do not know. Here, we are not phased by – but pleased to engage with – 'wicked problems' that are insoluble, such as 'what is the self?', and able to adopt surrealist positions while engaging with reality and virtual realities simultaneously. Here, the subject is grounded in an aesthetic of the uncanny recognised as a condition of absence, lack and uncertainty, not a comfortable plenitude based on the idealistic promise of human 'growth' or 'fulfillment'. If we think this is just another piece of fashionable postmodernising, let us again recall the writer DH Lawrence's words from 1932: 'at last we escape the barbed wire enclosure of "know thyself", knowing we can never know'.

# 32 Loneliness

The dominance of the patriarchy hasn't paid off – the figures say a lot: in North America, a quarter of men under 30 say they have no close friends. Here's a recent story culled from the *New York Times* in June 2024. An American 20-year-old college student – let's call him Brad – lives in his grandmother's basement, barely leaving the house except for classes where he is a lonely figure. Brad spends most of his free time playing video games, watching porn, and browsing online – hooked on unsavoury social media sites where he finds his community, mostly lonely men like him. The more he does this, the lonelier he feels. During the pandemic, on one of these social media sites, he shared a voice chat with a younger man who was badly depressed. Brad listened and offered consolation for well over an hour. Soon, other contacts used Brad as sounding board and counsellor. In a year, he had talked with over 200 young people, mostly men, many of them suicidal. A common theme emerged – the men felt shame at admitting their loneliness and depression. It made them feel weak. Loneliness and low self-esteem are bed mates (Figure 32.1).

Screen addiction coupled with an inability to admit to anxiety and depression, have led to a loneliness epidemic especially among young men. Online options look like they may work, as intimacy isn't required, but they don't seem to work. What these lonely men need is flesh-and-blood intimacy. Their selves have shrivelled. They can easily be attracted to a toxic masculinity where related sites populate the Internet. The legacy of the well-intentioned men's movement of the 1970s and 1980s has little or no impact on them. They are emotionally starved and resentful of their lot.

Presenting at your doctor's surgery with 'loneliness' as the primary symptom may seem strange to many. But the World Health Organisation (WHO) sees loneliness as a public health factor as bad as smoking 15 cigarettes a day, increasing the risk of premature death by almost a third according to the US Surgeon General's 2022 report on loneliness. Recent studies show that loneliness can increase the risk of a stroke by over 50%. We might think of loneliness as mainly affecting the elderly, but

DOI: 10.4324/9781003619901-33

*Figure 32.1* 'Lonely' by Moghadam Khamseh.

there is also an epidemic of loneliness among the young in high-income countries. Here, over 15% of adolescents describe themselves as unable to form friendships while social media are seen more as threats to self-image (others are 'perfect' and capable socially) rather than to make meaningful contacts.

Globally, one in four elderly people report loneliness. With this isolation can come a crushing sense of worthlessness, a self not reciprocated in some way evaporates. Young people who are isolated at school tend to drop out of university at higher rates than others, unable to form friendships. Loneliness can be alleviated somewhat by digital contact, but in developing countries, especially in rural areas that do not have internet access, loneliness is more marked. And digital content, as noted, is not the best way to address loneliness.

A little like autism and Attention Deficit Hyperactivity Disorder (ADHD), incidence can show rapid increases once the diagnostic category is confirmed. This may be the same with loneliness. A 2023 report issued by the USA Surgeon General Dr Vivek Murthy claims that now half of the American adult population report that they are lonely, defined as 'social isolation'. The obverse of this is difficulty in making social connections and making them stick. Americans cherish autonomy and the tradition of the heroic lone frontiersman. This archetype can work against them. Racism and discrimination are still issues that plague populations worldwide, exacerbated by mass movements of people due to wars, conflict, or discrimination in their home countries. Migrants face potential loneliness as they flee conflict only to face prejudice.

120    *Self-Literacy*

Loneliness is formally defined as the feelings that arise from social isolation. Such feelings are not actively sought (such as the need for retreat, or Virginia Woolf's 'a room of one's own'). Whether we are 'wired' for social connection (e.g., the limbic system's basic emotional responses include fight or flight but also intimacy or disgust) or whether sociability is a learned response, lack of social connection may squash curiosity, replacing it with paranoia. Employment demands mean that families and friendship groups are split up, where moving to cities introduces a sense of impersonalism. This is exacerbated by replacement of face-to-face interactions such as buying goods in shops with faceless online activities. So-called 'social' media can be anti-social, for example, in shaming or creating a sense of inadequacy.

Loneliness among men particularly is often linked to the inability to make meaningful relationships, sometimes relating to shame about their appearances, where men may turn to prostitutes. But here, the clients find that they are hiring functional sex workers, and not relational or psychotherapeutic social workers and relief is short lived. Empathy does not enter the transaction. Sex workers themselves report a high degree of loneliness as they are objectified and often feel danger. Studies show that this results in high levels of paranoia and lowering of self-esteem, alleviated somewhat by increased drug use, but leading to a vicious cycle of a kind of self-leaking that creates another sense of loneliness. Self is violated in several ways. The sex worker might feel that her, his, or their work is not at all transactional but rather a series of paranoid encounters. When sex workers do emotional therapeutic labour rather than bodily sex work, they may feel exploited.

Organisations such as the UK mental health charity Mind have 'tips' to address loneliness:

1  Learn more about being comfortable in your own company.
2  Try and open up to people you know.
3  Take it slow.
4  Make new connections.
5  Try not to compare yourself to others.
6  Look after yourself.
7  Try talking therapies.

Number 1 – self-sufficiency is not on tap. This is why you are lonely in the first place. Number 2 – this first act of confidence is precisely what scares so many lonely people to make them lonely. This is like asking a person with claustrophobia to chat with you in an elevator. Number 3 – you are taking it slow, that is why you are not meeting anybody. Everybody else is moving at speed. Stand in the middle of a busy city street and you'll soon find out. Number 4 – but this is precisely what you cannot do and why you are lonely. Number 5 – social media keep on insisting on the opposite. It's hard to get away from this. Number 6 – ok, but my self-esteem is low. Read my lips: self-esteem low/hard to 'look after' oneself. Number 7 – you try to get a talking therapist that doesn't cost a fortune. Your general practitioner may hook you up with a counsellor after a long, long wait, where you will get six functional sessions of cognitive behavioural therapy with a pinch of mindfulness, and then you're on your own again. Better to enlist for volunteer activities where you will meet new people.

This is also after the event advice. The key issue is to address the structural reasons for loneliness such as fixing housing problems so that we don't have homeless people sleeping rough. Communal meeting, eating, and living centres should be available with easy access. A key element here is the impossible level of demand we place on young persons through models of perfection on social media. A second is not just paying lip-service to inclusion but acting on this.

After writing this, I watched television for a while to unwind – an episode of *The Simpsons*, the highbrow cartoon series. The episode's storyline was that Marge Simpson had left home after an argument with Homer. Later, after some hilarious adventures, she came back, and they made up. After the episode, a voice message said: 'If this episode has affected you in any way, please feel free to contact this number'. A number came up for a charity that helps the lonely. OK, but how does our homeless person on the street watch *The Simpsons*?

Another way that the lonely can gain a friend is a virtual online companion, a simulacrum of a lover usually. These are known technically as 'conversational agents' (the very thought is chilling), bots (from robots), and AI entities (again mechanical overtones). Blow-up dolls that talk can offer some solace for those who cannot make relationships, but the dialogue is limited. An online companion has rich dialogue and can respond to questions and demands, but this is purely a simulacrum – a copy where the original does not exist. AI companions of course fail to provide the necessary agreement for a successful relationship – tangible love based on difference. Partners must be able to argue constructively. To engage with a partner who is always subservient is merely to adopt an authoritarian stance.

The software system Replika allows you to design your own perfect partner and once had an erotic role play (ERP) function that has now been removed. The more the bot knows about the user, the more it offers nuanced but supportive engagement. Bots (you can choose your gender) can even keep diaries that the user can peek into, creating an illusion of surprise. One user says: 'She's always there for you 24 hours, there's no judgement, and no drama'. Relationship on demand. Even for the lonely this seems like a dangerous route.

## 122  *Self-Literacy*

Other apps such as Rizz (shorthand for 'charisma') are a halfway house between simulated and real relationships, coaching you for a date. You can be helped in how to initiate and maintain conversations, how to move on to romantically tinged talk, or introduce sensitive topics. The dating apps Grindr and Tinder are working on software that coaches in explicitly sexual talk that is not threatening or creepy. A host of influencers are creating sites that coach in the complex art of dating. One woman influencer created an AI version of herself that was marketed as a 'virtual girlfriend' costing $1 per minute. The app reaped $72,000 in one week and the influencer boasted that she already had 'over 20,000 virtual boyfriends'.

This may all sound a little spooky, especially when we learn from surveys that users of relationship bots are often already in a flesh-and-blood relationship that is clearly not satisfying enough. Meanwhile, a 2024 Stanford University study on loneliness reported that virtual relationships can indeed alleviate suicidal ideation.

# 33 The fashioning of family

The English word 'family' means something wider than a group of people related by blood. From the Latin *familia*, cognate with 'familiar', a family was a group of people living in the same household. This included your 'familiars', your pets, and domestic farm animals. Familiars were 'friends'. And a family unit under one roof had a central focus. This was the hearth, the fire, the focus, and the heart of the household. The Greek goddess Hestia (Roman Vesta) would rule the hearth from which warmth emanated, and the family would emulate this warmth in unconditional support for one another.

But let's not get too cosy. Worldwide, most murders of women and children are by male members within a family setting. Sometimes the hearth gets too hot, friction leading to sharp disagreements. There is bad blood at play. 'Close' families sometimes get too close for comfort. A 2014 USA survey showed that an 'incest event' had occurred in 15% of families, although the American public (mis)estimates a 2% incest rate at most. Family therapists agree that the main cause of friction is parents placing children (especially as adolescents) in 'double binds'. Classic patterns are smothering rather than mothering, offering freedom on a leash ('yes you can go to the party, but I want you home by 10pm'), and siblings arguing over who is the perceived favourite of the respective parents.

'Blood is thicker than water' characterises family bonding. Yet families can be dysfunctional, such as Mafia blood-ties. Families the world over are hotbeds for violence, sexual misdemeanours, jealousies, sharp-edged competitiveness, argument, politically motivated disagreement, religious strife, and conflicts of values. And yet the moral compass of the 'family' sticks, where blood is indeed thicker than water. Oddly, this biblical phrase says: 'the blood of the covenant is thicker than the water of the womb' meaning precisely the opposite of privileging blood ties over casual friendships. Covenants, friendships, deals, societies, and professions are seen to be more powerful than family ties. But what if your family is also primarily your friendship and interest group; or – the basis for big television hits

124  *Self-Literacy*

such as 'Succession' – the family business? What about a family that is also tied by something other than blood such as the necessity to share a home where children can no longer afford to buy their own home? Families need bonds of some kind other than blood ties to keep the flame burning: common interests, shared passions, overlapping identities, and a common sense of self.

In the mid-19th century, a collective of criminal gangs was formed in Sicily known as the Mafia (Sicilian slang for 'swagger', 'bravado', or 'boldness'), or *cosa nostra* (literally 'our thing'). Each group, presiding over a set territory that it must never over-reach, was known as a 'family'. Loyalty to the family was paramount. By the 20th century, thanks to global migration, Sicilian gangs appeared across the Americas, Europe, and Australia. The codes of *cosa nostra* are that families stick together no matter what. There is an initiation ritual (often killing a member of a rival family's gang), and family members must maintain silence if questioned about family business. There is a strict male hierarchy.

In some parts of Italy, as *cosa nostra* male leaders are increasingly imprisoned serving life sentences, they have left the running of their rackets (these days, drug trafficking and extortion related to 'protection payments') to their wives and children. In turn, the wives are caught and imprisoned, sometimes leaving young children to run the businesses. Schemes have been set up by social workers teaming up with lawyers to persuade these young people to leave their family residences and abandon the businesses that will ultimately also lead to their incarceration to begin new lives in other parts of Italy, far from their homes, with foster families. These new family grafts have in some cases led to the young people finding their way out of the criminal clutches to start their lives anew, shifting from toxic to healthy family and abandoning old ideas of bloodline loyalties. Thus, self is remade in new models of family based not on blood ties and loyalties, but on friendships, care, and affection.

Suspending the heavyweight ethical issues surrounding organised crime, and the traditional place of women in the organisation as subservient, a recent TikTok phenomenon is how to look like a 'Mafia Girl'. This requires lots of heavy black mascara, bright red lipstick, red nail varnish, and entirely black garments. One tip online is that if you look like you're going to a funeral, then you're doing it right. A fur coat helps. A new family emerges – *fashionistas* – where selves are formed by following clothes trends in fast fashions. These cheap, quick turnover clothes are produced in sweatshops drawing on cheap labour, and often employing children in low-income countries. It is estimated that 46 million people worldwide are enslaved and 21 million are in forced labour. Many of these are making quick turnover clothes satisfying high-income countries' fast fashions. The fast fashion families also kill – they bend the will of unwilling slave

*The fashioning of family* 125

labour to their own desires and kill the spirits of those labourers, instead of working to free them from modern slavery. For example, young women and girls are regularly trafficked from Bangladesh to work in Indian fast fashion garment factories, where their labour is exploited, working 16–20 hours a day.

Fast fashionistas are also destroying the planet. The cheap, fast turnover fashion industry pollutes rivers and streams and dries up water sources, while waste is shameful – every year 85% of all textiles end up in dumps. Cheap fashion kills with covert methods.

# 34 Feminist selves

The French philosopher and cultural critic Hélène Cixous (1991) urges that 'Woman must write her self: must write about women and bring women to writing, from which they have been driven away as violently as from their bodies'. How shall this be achieved? And why a writing out of self rather than a reclamation of body? The Egyptian feminist psychiatrist and writer Nawal El Saadawi writes – in *Memoirs of a Woman Doctor* (1957) – of her first known construction of gender identity at age nine:

> all I did know at that time was that I was a girl... And all it meant to me was that I wasn't a boy and wasn't like my brothers.... My brother woke up in the morning and left his bed just as it was, while I had to make my bed and his as well ... my brother took a bigger piece of meat than me, gobbled it up and drank his soup noisily and my mother never said a word. ... I had to watch every movement I made, hide my longing for food, eat slowly, and drink my soup without a sound.

El Saadawi grew up in a rural part of Egypt that was overbearingly patriarchal. What kind of self emerges from such a squashed existence? She was expected to conform, marry and settle down as subservient housewife producing children and bending to her husband's whims. To her credit, she escaped this tyranny and studied medicine, against the grain and in the face of deep prejudice, also becoming a radical political voice and a strident feminist, an irritant to Egypt's patriarchal politicians, but a star on the liberal world stage. In 1981, under President Sadat, she was arrested as a 'dissident' and imprisoned for three months. Famously, a jailed sex worker smuggled in an eyebrow pencil for her, and she wrote her memoirs on toilet paper. The dissident self is hard to quash. Indeed, as Michel Foucault describes, in the face of an oppressive sovereign power, what emerges as resistance is a capillary power that runs through fine channels such as individuals and their allies (the sex worker, toilet paper, and eyebrow pencil).

DOI: 10.4324/9781003619901-35

Feminist selves   127

This story of oppression and its overcoming through cunning offers a parable for knowledge of self. Masculine models of a strong self that can be directly accessed through introspection offer a form of solipsism or selfishness. It admits no other and no uncertainty. In contrast, the feminine may be characterised by its social valence and embrace of uncertainty. This masculine 'direct access' route to self also by-passes social structures such as the historical, cultural, and linguistic. 'Structure' can be equated with system, where the whole is greater than the sum of the parts. Systems include cultural symbols and languages (especially expressive and inventive language drawing on metaphor), cultural signs (semiotics), historical movements, and social organisations.

First coined by the linguist Roman Jakobson in 1929, the term 'structuralism' refers to a process of revealing the inner laws or rules of a system. Structures, such as language, are seen to be composed of elements in relation to each other, reduced to binary oppositions such as the 'raw' (nature) and the 'cooked' (culture). The danger of such binary thinking is that one pole can become privileged, oppressing the other. For example, in privileging *logos* (the word, rationality, or logic) over *eros* (feelings, the sensuous), the masculine is privileged over the feminine. This has been termed phallogocentrism: the focus of meaning on the phallic and the logical. Its ultimate expression is the skyscraper in architecture and the 'I' in language. This has been termed 'the name of the father', an oppressive regulating figure, returning us to Nawaal El Sadaawi's experiences as a child. Poststructuralist feminists reject such oppositionalist thinking, for it remains subservient to the Name of the Father: where genders are opposed, the masculine will force dominance. The male gaze will still dominate.

For feminists, whatever their sexual orientations (and men can be feminists), there is much work to be done in redefining the dominant, phallic 'I' for a different formulation of self. Several models have emerged. One is focused on reinscription of social practices and artefacts that privilege the masculine at the expense of the feminine. For example, the male gaze is predominant in several cultural spheres. In painting and drawing, the woman's body (especially nude) has historically been subjected to, or is the subject of, the male gaze and the woman is then not a subject in her own right. This constitutes rather a rite of subjection to male traditions. The male gaze even penetrates the eye (including eyebrows and lashes) of the woman as this is dressed up for the man, using the very eyebrow pencil that El Sadaawi gained as an instrument of resistance, eyeliner, and lash extensions. Women of course can subvert this by using make-up for same sex seduction or simply for aesthetic self-display shorn of biological mating behaviour subject to patriarchy.

Such scrutiny by another's gaze has been thoroughly theorised by Judith Butler who notes that the woman's identity under patriarchy is only

128    *Self-Literacy*

achieved as a form of subjection, a negative state. Subjection is achieved through habitual use of a dominant language form such as the masculine ('he' and 'his'), and by social habits such as consistently under-paying women for labour (and not paying them at all for maternal labour). Following Hegel's model of the Master: Slave dialectic, Butler suggests that women can form legitimate identities from the subordinate position of 'slave'. By subtle means of resistance, the slave can begin to regulate the master. A common tactic of the oppressed is to engage in 'sly civility' (Homi Bhabha) or indirect compliance – apparently showing subservience but using subtle tactics to gradually undermine the power of the Master or oppressor.

Sly civility is parodied in Joseph Losey's 1963 film 'The Servant' written by the playwright Harold Pinter. Here, the manservant to a wealthy Londoner manipulates a four-way relationship between himself and his girlfriend (who the wealthy man believes to be the servant's sister) and the wealthy man and his fiancée. As the wealthy man becomes psychologically unstable and slips into alcoholism, so he becomes dependent upon the manservant who also brings him prostitutes.

The male gaze is dominant in medicine and surgery, developed because of cadaver dissection where medical students learn how to penetrate the body with the scalpel and eye, transferring this literal gaze as a metaphorical one when diagnosing disease from a physical examination of a patient's body. For doctors, this is tied to a professional identity where the medical self is a combination of scientific knowledge and clinical prowess tied to a way of dressing and a demeanour. This too has been stamped as masculine where it is only recently that women in any numbers have entered medicine. What women have brought is a dispersal of the male gaze in adoption of interprofessional, patient-centred, collective medicine practiced in democratic team structures rather than traditional hierarchies.

A widespread effect of feminism is the use of language to disengage from habitual employment of the masculine 'I', where 'he' and 'his' are the go-to descriptors. 'He' and 'his' used habitually are cancelled for 'her' and 'hers' or 'them' and 'theirs'. Another effect is focused on genitality. Challenging phallic reference, Luce Irigaray calls for women to celebrate the lips that rub together between the legs – the vulva, but specifically the labia, for these are lips that form a mouth and the mouth 'talks' to the woman in self-pleasure and the lesbian embrace. Even such woman-to-woman eroticism has been appropriated by the male gaze for the man's pleasure. And labial restructuring for cosmetic reasons is largely driven by patriatrchal pornography. Irigaray notes that the self of the woman has been constructed within patriarchy as an absence and a lack, or as inferiority. Women perform for men. Reclaiming a woman's voice requires breaking through the habit of speaking to each other on male terms or through male identity. Our primary texts shaping the Western psyche, Homer's *Iliad* and *Odyssey* are male-oriented. The key characters, Achilles and Odysseus, are heroic warriors and adventurers. Women are portrayed as seductive (Helen), scheming (Circe), or passive (Penelope). Irigaray challenges the male logic of language, writing in puns, double meanings, and metaphor, to explicitly peel off the dead skin of language to reveal a raw syntax.

A feminist way is focused on reclaiming desire, eroticism, and sexuality, specifically challenging Freud's bias to male sexuality and misunderstanding of feminine eroticism. Freud's refusal of the clitoral orgasm for a male fantasy of a vaginal orgasm is a glaring error in his work. One feels for Martha Bernays, Freud's wife. To rub salt into the wound, Martha's younger sister Minna moved in with the Freuds and reputedly became Sigmund Freud's lover. Theorists and performance artists such as Joanna Frueh, Jane Gallop, and bell hooks, challenge the perceived phobia embedded in the laws and lusts of the fathers that is also fixated on genitality. This, for an erotic response to life that is not specifically genital but rather an overall state of arousal. The male gaze also defines an orgasmic self as focused and single, rather than dispersed and potentially multiple.

Joanna Frueh's project is to eroticise what she sees as a masculinised educational culture that subdues desire, or has been unitary, flat, dry, and self-conscious. Can such a standard scholarship be lubricated, or become undulant? Frueh calls this project a 'critical erotics' – a way of doing criticism that does not deny eros: life force and vitality. In a critique of phallogocentrism, Frueh says that 'the rigorous arguments so valued by academics are testimonies to the fact that the thinkers have become stiffs'. Teaching is reconfigured as an 'elegant occupation that readily includes, indeed welcomes, bouts of indeterminacy, shifting identities, lyricism, humour, pun and play, elliptical practices, and the fires of urgency and immediacy'. There should not be just a love of learning, but a lust for learning. Texts should be seductive and pedagogy a performance. Critical pedagogy in an adult register is then set within a libidinal economy free from obscenity. In short, the puritanism that has characterised modern pedagogy has repressed feminine eros. This returns in a distorted form – as, for example, the notorious seduction of women students by male academics who claim that these women are sirens. Men must learn to respond to the performative erotics of a new wave of feminist academics through appreciation rather than lust.

A further feminist way is introduced by the writer and philosopher Hélène Cixous, focused on the nurturing role of the mother. Cixous talks of 'writing with mother's milk', or 'writing with white ink', a nourishing kind of script and literature. Judith Butler, drawing on a revisionist psychoanalysis, characterises the patriarchy as a traumatising father. The project of a wide variety of feminisms is to recover authentic identity that

## 130   *Self-Literacy*

has been displaced by social and cultural abuse of women over centuries. This is equivalent to white supremacy and slavery. In turn, such gender bias (towards the male) is tied to global capitalism, where women become commodities to be marketed, for profit. This is literally the case with modern slavery and human trafficking of women through prostitution rings. Butler, however, sees the issue of 'gender trouble' not in the dualism of men and women, but in the historical intersections of gender with class, race, ethnicity, and sexuality. These categories are seen as discursive constructions rather than natural types, and so the gendered self is malleable, open to deconstruction and reconstruction. In other words, gender is performed, not given.

Julia Kristeva returns to the issue of embodied gender categorisation or fluidity as essential (Butler insists upon subjectivity as multiplicity and possibility – 'they' rather than 's/he') to focus on the importance of treating poetic language as essentially a feminine voice. For Kristeva, this is semiotics – the language of signs – that is pre-verbal. The maternal body instinctively understands and employs the pre-verbal. Maternity and poetic expressions (metaphor and semiotics) offer the only permissible ways for women to return to the maternal body from which they come.

Such contemporary feminisms – Judith Butler being an exception – reject language serving 'the name of the father' for the body of the mother. A feminine imaginary reclaims a style of writing that has been occluded by male interests, especially of heroic confessional writing (even where this claims to identify with a Mother Nature, as in Thoreau). Cixous says of feminine writing (writing with white ink, or mother's milk), that such writing

> is eccentric, incomprehensible and inconsistent, and the difficulty to understand it is attributed to centuries of suppression of the female voice, which now speaks in a borrowed language. Believed to originate from the mother in the stage of the mother-child relation before the child acquires the male-centred verbal language, this pre-linguistic and unconscious potentiality manifests itself in those literary texts which, abolishing all repressions, undermine and subvert all significations, the logic and the closure of the phallocentric language, and opens into a joyous freeplay of meanings.

Ironically, in the moment that previously silenced female subjects begin to make themselves heard, the white European male declares 'the death of the subject' or the fragmentation of the self.

# 35 Self as laboratory rat

Psychology (literally a *logos* of the *psyche*) means the logic of the mind, or the study of human *being*. Modern academic psychology strives to be a science, studying the subjective 'objectively' – now there's a conundrum (like everyone's in therapy, but nobody needs it). Psychology demands that we know the self, but on scientific, experimental psychology's terms, so that the self we 'discover' or 'uncover' is in fact the self that psychology disciplines – produced or invents. There is no prior self there at all to uncover or make sense of. Yet psychology claims a strong 'bounded' self, known by many names such as 'identity', 'selfhood', and 'persona'. Self in fact is largely studied either as personality or as a product of brain mechanisms. Either way, self is understood not as a tangible object but a set of metaphors ('being' and 'becoming' among them).

The 'I' in psychology stands tall and proud, is phallocentric, self-referential, and possibly arrogant, bullying, demanding ('I!'), doubled in the commanding exclamation: 'veni, vidi, vici' – 'I came, I saw, I conquered' – attributed to Julius Caesar after winning a battle in Asia Minor. By Victorian times, the commanding 'I' was essential to character. Any wavering would be criticised as 'feminine', or 'regressive to childhood', and any major deviation would now be seen as a character fault in need of treatment through the new science of psychiatry. The Victorian 'I' was patriarchal, militaristic, imperialistic, and bent on mastering nature.

Despite psychology's assurance that the self can be studied as a stable object, identity can be thought of in multiple and conflicting ways: for example as something innate (a biological given, a family genetic inheritance); something conferred (a role or status in society, a family wealth inheritance); something achieved (identifying *with* a culture and *as* a professional, such as a doctor, engineer, or lawyer); something multiple (identity as mutable, in process); as statement of resistance (identifying as LBGTQ+ in a mainstream, straight two-genders culture, as 'mad' in a culture of normality, or as disabled in an ableist culture); as stigma (outsider, excommunicated, migrant, prisoner, forced prostitution, on the streets by

DOI: 10.4324/9781003619901-36

## 132 *Self-Literacy*

circumstance); as outlaw (prostitute by choice, on the streets by choice); or as recluse (hermit, priest, nun). The stable self is described as 'agency' (where a stable subject shapes a life) but may be better described as 'subjection to' (where life forms the person).

Identity may be thought of in two main ways: as 'identification with' and as 'expression of'. 'Identification with' includes ethnic, religious, national, and in-group identities (e.g., a passionate supporter of a football club, a surfer or skateboarder, a bird watcher or 'twitcher'). Some of these identities are immutable and may be accepted, lionised, or resisted (e.g., ethnicity). They are based on mutable values and may change on a whim. An identity that is an expression of something innate is commonly recognised as a 'self'. Selves are however expressed within families, groups, and communities. A self may transcend community interests – for example, protesting closing a school within an eclectic community may attract a common self-expression while identities differ enormously. Selves can be reduced to brain mechanisms, expanded to identity with an activity ('elite athlete') or a state of being (such as a perceived disability), or a bodily state (gender identification or refusal).

Again, in mainstream experimental psychology the dominant notion of self is that of a permanent, given, integrated, essential, private 'core'. This can be shaped in various ways, while it is also prone to disintegration. This is the humanist model, in which essence (a core self) precedes experience (consciousness of that self). From this follows personal agency (sense of self), autonomy (sense of free will), and authenticity (sense of a moral agency). While again such a core self is primarily studied by the discipline of psychology, an alternative view is that modern psychology has constructed this self – primarily as the supposedly free-willed subject of countless psychology experiments. The self is then disciplined by the discipline of psychology and is a product of laboratory science experiments on (and not with) 'subjects' (the vast majority of whom are first- or second-year undergraduate psychology students). This, rather than understanding of selves as gleaned from naturalistic observation of people going about their daily business.

When I was studying for a psychology degree in the mid-to-late 1960s, the discipline was dominated by American behaviourism – the ideas of B.F. Skinner. Such ideas were patently ridiculous. How ridiculous is summed up in a well-known cartoon explained below. In the psychology department, all first-year undergraduates were issued with a laboratory white rat. This became your 'subject' for experiments. The rat was put in what is called a 'Skinner Box' – a metal cage with a connected feeder and a lever. The rat would wander around the cage and eventually would accidentally press the lever. Upon doing so, a pellet of food would pop down a chute. The rat would press the lever again and another pellet of food would appear.

*Self as laboratory rat* 133

Pretty soon, the rat would press the lever all the time. The behaviourist would say that the rat was being conditioned into behaving in a particular way because it was being rewarded for that behaviour. No thought process is involved. If the reinforcement schedule by way of the food pellets is stopped, the rat will soon stop pressing the lever.

Now comes Skinner's leap of faith. Humans, he said, behave in the same way. Any cognition or thinking process is irrelevant to the way that we behave – our behaviour is a result of reinforcement schedules, or the withdrawal of reinforcement. Clearly, this is tosh. We are far more complex. But psychologists fell for this stuff and taught it to their undergraduates like me. We are, said Skinner, merely products of our social reinforcement schedules. He suggested that punishment was not necessary for behaviours that you wanted to eradicate, rather you simply withdraw reinforcement. That bit I'm ok with. But suggesting that cognition is a 'black box' not worth opening because all can be explained by a behavioural perspective is very short-sighted. Back to the rat – and the cartoon referred to earlier – who is pressing the lever in the Skinner Box and saying to a fellow rat, 'Boy, have I got this guy conditioned. Every time I press the lever, he drops in a pellet of food!'

In 1961, an experimental psychologist Stanley Milgram set up a controversial experiment at Yale University. Using stooges (actors in the experiment who sat behind a screen and were given a preparatory script) and naïve participants paid $4 for an hour of their time, Milgram's white-coated experimenters explained to the naïve participants (or 'teachers') that they were engaged in an experiment on learning and punishment. The teachers would ask the learners to memorise a list of word pairs and then quiz the 'learners' on the correct pairs, where a choice of four options was given. The learners would press a button to indicate their answers. If they got the pairing wrong, the experimenter would ask the teacher to deliver a small electric shock as punishment to the learner, explaining that the experiment was investigating if punishment 'worked' in improving learning. At first, the electric shock was small (the machine delivering the 'shock' was of course fake). The learner would give a little moan, or a small jolt. As the memory task got harder, the learners would fail more often, and the experimenter (inevitably a male) explained that he was turning up the voltage on the punishment. The initial voltage was set at 15, and this could be increased to 400 volts.

The teachers knew that the learners were sitting behind a screen (as if it were an electric chair) but could not see them. Also, the teachers were given a sample low voltage shock themselves to experience what the learner would feel if a mistake were made. The teachers were told that they could withdraw from the experiment at any time, and they would still be paid. The experimenters, again in their white coats, were scripted to respond

## 134   *Self-Literacy*

to hesitation or refusal from the experimenters. If the teacher questioned or hesitated over the punishment, the experimenter would urge them to 'please continue'. If they questioned again, the experimenter would be directive, saying 'the experiment requires that you continue', and then 'it is absolutely essential that you continue', and finally, 'You have no other choice, you *must* go on'.

In short, despite hearing moans and in cases of high voltage banging on the wall, or crashing about, and despite complaining about what they were being asked to do, teachers continued to give what would be fatal shocks. This, even when at the highest voltage, sounds from the learner's room suddenly ceased. In some cases, teachers were informed that the learner had a heart condition. In some cases, an apparent 450 volts was administered three times in a row.

What does this imply? First, the motive for the experiment was that Milgram wanted to better understand why members of the Nazi Party dutifully obeyed commands to carry out naked atrocities. Despite the teachers showing emotional distress during the administration of supposed electric shocks, they continued to do so, putting faith in the white-coated experimenters that all would be ok. In fact, they were shifting the blame to the authority figure. Recall that this is 1961, pre-Haight Ashbury, Woodstock, and the hippy revolution against authority that led to widespread political unrest and the development of the Civil Rights movement. Further, all participants were male. Participants would surely have smelt the smoking gun of a simulation situation. Some said as much in debriefs. A later independent analysis of the study found that over half of the participants in the study believed in retrospect that it was a set up.

Here, 'obedience' is then not the primary focus. Rather, as far as self is concerned, Milgram's experiment seems to be more about 'performance', or the self as an actor. Most participants probably embraced the totality of the situation as a dramatic context. Indeed, the experiment has been recreated as a drama in an art exhibition context. The bigger question at stake is the translation of the context-dependent psychology experiment to the public domain. What is produced in these psychology laboratory experiments are laboratory 'rats' performing for their psychologist masters. Their selves are moulded as experimental subjects – or, subject to experimentation.

Milgram's experiment raised deep ethical concerns and could not be repeated now. But a decade after Milgram, in 1971, another infamous experiment on obedience was conducted at Stanford University in California. The basement of the Psychology Department was adapted to resemble a prison environment. Offered $15 a day to engage with the experiment, a small group of Stanford male students were divided into two cohorts: prisoners and prison guards. The 'guards' were issued with uniforms, while the

## Self as laboratory rat   135

'prisoners' were formally arrested by real police and placed in the custody of the guards who took them to their cells, each cell holding three prisoners. In short, within a brief period, the 'guards' became verbally abusive towards the 'prisoners', showing emotional hostility. What was planned as a two weeks' long experiment was terminated after six days, where Zimbardo feared that emotional hostility may translate into actual violence on the part of the 'guards'. Zimbardo had in fact briefed the guards to behave with authority, and so the whole experiment can be read as another form of self as performer. In other words, guards were intentionally acting into a role. They were experimental lab rats conditioning their experimenter: 'I've really got this psychology guy on a hook – I just have to play into the role'.

# 36 The self in pieces
## The yips

Confident people do not mind taking a tumble now and then, known as pratfalls. In fact, they relish it. It makes them human. Mostly they are in control, but they also like to take risks and these sometimes do not work out. Chaucer and Shakespeare both are masters at portraying comic and self-deprecating characters who can take a tumble and come up smiling. Strange coincidences, bumping into long-lost relatives, crashing gears, and taking wrong turns to meld with subtle shifts in identity often as mocking reflections upon the self. Most of us can laugh at ourselves. We manage to love and even lust without it sounding or feeling pervy or weird and we are natural comics whose topic for satire is ourselves.

And then there are the unfortunates, maybe cocky types or overconfident, or truly gifted but unable to bear the weight of responsibility that gift brings, who suddenly start to make bad jokes about themselves, or talk about themselves in the third person as if their true selves were lost or absent, or patently demonstrating bruising of character. They begin to bungle social exchanges and practical acts. Their muscle memory seems to have taken a holiday and they bungle what they used to manage with panache – whether physical acts of skill or social exchanges. They may be elite sports players. They may once have been narcissists, now heading for pratfall.

The selves of elite sports players are defined by expertise gained over countless hours of practice. Occasionally, especially for snooker players, golfers, pole vaulters, high jumpers, tennis players (especially on the second serve), archers, basketball players, cricket and baseball players, street skaters, surfers, golfers, and so on, where eye-hand coordination is key, an involuntary muscle spasm spoils the execution of the skill and if repeated executes the sense of self as unique. Surgeons can get the shakes. Long thought to be a sudden psychological lack of confidence, the yips – also 'choking' and 'target panic' in archery – may be associated with focal dystonia, a neurological condition affecting specific muscles.

DOI: 10.4324/9781003619901-37

The self in pieces: the yips    137

Both decision-making and physical ability are affected. This can result in twitching, tremors, or freezing. Anxiety sets in and this worsens the condition. Writers, even at keyboards, can get writer's block that is physically mirrored in a writer's cramp. Veteran talkers, used to giving coherent, informed, entertaining lectures, begin to stumble over their words. The yips can be short or medium term and readily cured or can set in and ruin a career.

Current thinking by cognitive psychologists suggests that the yips are a result of overthinking combined with loss or dulling of fine body cues that inform the athlete or performer of how the body moves through space (such as eye-hand coordination). Concert pianists, for example, find it difficult to perform a well-rehearsed piece if they overthink it. Specifically, what was once an unconscious or implicit cognitive task, resulting in smooth motor activity – or a well-practiced habit – becomes over-thought and over-wrought. The habitual unconscious element is broken as the activity comes to the surface of consciousness and breaks through into vigilant attention. What was once smooth and practiced becomes an object of concern inviting a cycle of relearning. The membrane has been punctured. Sometimes, the yips set in for an extended period, known as a 'malicious spell', 'slumping', the 'twisties' in gymnastics, or a 'curse'; and in worse case scenarios, the yips engulf the expert and destroy specific expertise completely.

Studies suggest that the reason for the complication of what was once habitual is that attention switches from an external to an internal focus. There is too much mulling and fretting rather than an automatic adaptation to the context in which the skill is normally exercised. The yips are also referred to as 'choking under pressure' and here a stable performing self goes to pieces through over-analysis as a heightened state of awareness. Along with the loss of the smooth motor activity is a loss of self-esteem as one lets oneself down in public. This is humiliating, shameful for a top-class athlete or performer. So, not only does the skill have to be reconstituted, but the self that is in pieces must be put back together.

The yips can affect anybody – in examination conditions, or under extreme stress. The past American President Joe Biden – a good man and not a narcissist – got the yips in a televised debate with the arch narcissist Donald Trump. It wasn't just old age – Biden truly collapsed, stumbling over his words, missing close putts, shanking his golf shots, even when the two of them engaged in an argument over who was best at golf (initiated by Trump, a notorious cheater on the golf course). The next day he recovered, giving a fine and confident speech on the stump to his supporters. The yips can be momentary but fatal to a career. And a relationship. It is not uncommon for men especially to get the yips in sexual encounters, where

138  *Self-Literacy*

erections fall flat. Suddenly what was going well collapses and confidence is drained, the self washes out, the person chokes. The yips and a panic attack are not dissimilar. In a world in which attention span has radically shrunk, it is strange to imagine an epidemic of over-thinking – especially amongst the male population who advertise themselves by their erections, now falling flat through introjected over-think.

# 37 Mods

'Modernists' were 1950s jazz fans, dressing in the style of their modern jazz heroes such as Miles Davis and Art Pepper, in tight Italian suits, white button-down shirts, and skinny black ties. In America, as the frantic East Coast (New York) sound of hard bop met the cool jazz of the West Coast (Los Angeles), so the Beat generation emerged as a mix of the frenzied and the lyrical. While modern jazz was distinguished by improvisation, the Beats – or hipsters – developed a coded, unwavering dress style: refusing ubiquitous suits and ties men wore straight-leg cigarette pants and black turtleneck sweaters, often with black berets, while women wore stirrup slacks and black leotards. A hip vocabulary emerged. The satirical *Mad* magazine ran a spoof – translating Shakespeare into Beat slang: 'Friends, Romans, hipsters, let me clue you in'. An attitude of cultured non-chalance was essential to pull off the cool beat look. It wasn't just how you looked, but how you spoke, walked, and danced (Figure 37.1).

Trends and fashions involve shifting identifications rather than stable identities, but these identifications may be more powerful than a stable sense of self. As I write this, looking back 61 years to when I was 15, I can remember the intensity and pleasure of identifying with fashion as a 'Mod' (a 'Modern'). While clothes played an important part of that identity, the entry ticket to core Mod culture was music. Along with a small group of friends, white kids in an all-white community, we were obsessed with black American soul music (with a side order of Jamaican bluebeat, later called 'ska'). From 1964 to 1968, by various means we obtained rare singles, adding these to a more readily available selection of Atlantic label soul and Tamla Motown. During summer holidays in 1966–68 I worked in a surf shop by day, and as a DJ a couple of nights a week in a small club in Newquay, a holiday town on the north coast of Cornwall. This club gained a national reputation for playing great 'rare soul' (we didn't call it 'Northern Soul' then) and was visited by young people from London and the North of England with whom I would trade singles.

DOI: 10.4324/9781003619901-38

*Figure 37.1* Mods.

Growing up as a boy in Newquay on Cornwall's north coast, my teens were consumed by a twin track: doing well at school and sports (I was determined to be the first one in our family to go to university) and by doing what all good teenagers do – rebelling through fashion. My friends and I were obsessed with being on trend. You could meet girls in both school and play contexts, so I was fine switching back and forth between the two. I was fortunate to grow up in what we called 'the California of the UK' that was a magnet for interesting people living on the fringe – first, the beatniks of the 1950s centred on modern jazz and the 'new' folk music, more protest than traditional. The early Beats brought cannabis. Second, the early to mid-1960s Mods came on holiday in August from London and the north of England, bringing with them rare, black soul music and new dance crazes, as well as amphetamines. Third, the itinerant Australian and South African lifeguards of the mid-1960s brought surfing and surf culture to town and drank like fishes. Fourth, and finally, the early hippies from the later sixties and early seventies brought albums by Californian bands such as Jefferson Airplane, Grateful Dead, and Love, as well as pure lysergic acid. The onset of the hippie era was the death knell for Mods (at the time, for so-called 'Northern Soul' has never gone away, adopting the motto 'Keep the Faith' and inventing the 'all-nighter', the template for Acid House raves). I stupidly sold all my rare soul singles for a song, now buying albums by Love, Spirit, The Grateful Dead, Jefferson Airplane, Moby Grape, Quiksilver Messenger Service, the Steve Miller Band, and other American West Coast bands.

With the beatniks, hair went longer for the men and very long for women, and black polo necks and long black or plaid skirts were standard uniforms. After that period, a cultural division appeared in Newquay that seemed to be echoed by many seaside towns, such as Margate and Brighton. On a main street in town, there was a traditional greasy café where the 'rockers' or 'greasers' hung out, dressed in black leathers – echoing Marlon Brando in the 1953 film 'The Wild One' about a motorcycle gang terrorising a small town in America. These were the delinquent brothers of the more cultured Beat generation – the latter would never think of getting their hands dirty tuning an angry beast motorcycle.

The Newquay rockers were not delinquents – suitably brylcreemed and quiffed, but low key. They would eat white bread greasy bacon sandwiches, or all-day fry-ups, and sip weak, milky tea, staring lovingly at their bikes out of the café's plate glass window. Their big statements were the sought-after makes of motorcycles that they would park on the kerbside. Directly opposite, on the other side of the road, a pack of scooters would be parked. Boys and girls decked out in parkas with fur trimmings on the hood would sometimes hang by their Lambretta scooters that would sport multiple mirrors and flags. These were the children of the cool Beats – the Mods (again, the 'moderns' following the jazz tradition).

The Mods gathered in a little downstairs café serving weak, frothy cappuccinos and Pepsi colas, a jukebox blaring – stocked with the latest tunes. In 1964, when I was 15 and working a part-time summer job (washing dishes) at this café, the 'Toddle Inn', the big tunes on the jukebox were the Downliners Sect's 'Little Egypt' and the Rolling Stones' 'Little Red Rooster'. No alcohol was served. Sometimes, around early evening, there would be some jibes and baiting back and forth between the Mods and the Rockers, from pavement to pavement – the street as the dividing line, the bikes and scooters as respective icons or clan totems. Rarely, this would flare up into a fistfight. Nobody carried knives, and the fights were mostly for show, arguing over the merits of hairstyles and scooters vs bikes. It was a far cry from Brighton and Margate where Mods and Rockers famously squared off with more vicious intentions.

Mods sported short, styled hair for both men and women, the men's hair often cropped almost to crewcut, the women with angular styles, short at the back and with a full fringe. If you were out on scooters decked with multiple flags and mirrors, you wore drab green parkas, best with a fur trim on the hood and a target on the back, or, for boys a

## 142  *Self-Literacy*

striped multi-coloured 'ice cream' jacket over a bright polo neck sweater with a vertical stripe from shoulder to waist, a white Fred Perry shirt, or a white American Brooks Brothers button-down collar shirt. But if you were off to dance at night, the men wore smart, tight-fitting Italian mohair suits with twin, long side vents (essential for dancing), tapered trousers, a smart button-collar shirt (again, Brooks Brothers hit the mark) with a black skinny tie, and a pair of black Cuban heeled, elastic-sided Beatle boots, or multi-coloured bowling shoes. Desert boots were ok too. I had a prized pair of ice-blue suede shoes (a throwback to Elvis). Women wore skirts just above the knee with bold block patterns. As surfing gained a foothold (I started in 1964 when I was 15), in the summer daywear for boys was standard – American crew, white high-neck T-shirts or garish Hawaiian shirts with baggy surfer shorts. By the late 1960s everybody was in denim head to toe with bell-bottom jeans.

Music was, again, at the core of the mod identity. In 1962, Bob Dylan released 'Blowin' in the Wind'. The same year saw the release of The Beatles' first single 'Love Me Do'. I was only 13 (nearly 14 when 'Love Me Do' was released). My schoolfriends and I transitioned from pure pop (Cliff Richard's double-sided 'Travellin' Light' and 'Dynamite' from 1959, and Johnny Tillotson's 'Poetry in Motion' from 1961 stick in my memory), through instrumental guitar bands (Sandy Nelson on drums, the Shadows, the Spotnicks), to Dylan-inflected folk overnight. By 1965, only foot-to-the-floor rare soul would do. After a series of fortunate coincidences, I had acquired a collection of $7''$ singles including easy-to-get Tamla Motown (in 1964, The Supremes issued 'Where Did Our Love Go' the go-to single) and Atlantic soul (Sam and Dave in particular). But I also had some earlier Sue records (such as 'Mockingbird' by Inez and Charlie Foxx), some hard-to-find early Bluebeat (Prince Buster was a favourite, 'Oh Carolina' by Count Ossie combo and Folks Brothers was our anthem), and rare soul singles such as 'Harlem Shuffle' by Bob and Earl. In 1967, soul peaked (The Platters' 'With This Ring', Chuck Wood's 'Seven Days Is Too Long', Darrell Banks' 'Open the Door to Your Heart'. In May 1968, the Dells released 'Wear It on Our Face', perhaps the best soul record ever with its dramatic string climax and breakdown, the template for later dance music).

That same summer, everything changed. The USA's 'Summer of Love' had happened in 1965, and the UK's in 1966 (the Beatles' 'Sergeant Pepper' was recorded at the end of 1966 and early 1967, and would be released in May 1967). The Woodstock Festival in 1969 sealed the deal for the Love Generation that was abruptly disturbed by the killing at the 1969 Altamont Festival associated with Hell's Angels Biker gangs – the darker side of Marlon Brando's 'The Wild One'. Reluctant to shed my Mod identity, my summer of love didn't happen until 1968. Soul went out with the Dells'

*Mods*  143

masterpiece and psychedelia came in with Love's 'Forever Changes', first released in 1967.

The days of hitching to London and Manchester to hear new soul sounds were over. In our smart suits, we had done the Lambeth Walk and the Woolly Bully (Sam the Sham and the Pharaohs 1965) and shaken our hips to Tina Brett's 'The Real Thing'. Now, hair got longer, minds expanded, and a new identity emerged. I would be a hard-working scholar by day, a surfer on weekends, and a hippy by night skin aflame with The Jefferson Airplane's flamenco-laced 'White Rabbit', Love's Mariachi band-led 'Alone Again Or', Country Joe and the Fish's Vietnam rag protest 'I Feel Like I'm Fixin' to Die', and later the Grateful Dead's country-tinged 'American Beauty'. And then came Punk. Throughout all this, there was Miles Davis, the king of cool, where modern jazz remained my first love and place of anchor.

# 38 Politicised junior doctors

The UK National Health Service (NHS) has long been considered globally as the Gold Standard in nationalised healthcare. It was established in 1948 under the guidance of the Labour Party's Minister for Health Aneurin Bevan, when Clement Attlee was Prime Minister. Up to this point, healthcare was paid for by private insurance. Most doctors of the time resisted the idea, fearing that they would lose income from private healthcare. Nearly all doctors then were male and the majority conservative in their politics. They had to be persuaded by the government about the longer-term benefits that the radical overhaul of the NHS would provide, primarily for patients but also for healthcare workers. Over the years, the NHS gained traction and became universally recognised as the gold standard model for healthcare – paid for through public taxation but providing a guarantee for both medical and dental care to be free at the point of delivery. As the NHS entered the 21st century, an unwritten agreement had been reached that doctors should remain apolitical at work. They should not only treat all patients equally regardless of their gender, sexual orientation, ethnicity, or political views, but should restrain from offering their own political orientations. It was as if healthcare were sterile politically. But, of course, this was a sham.

First, the NHS remains a nationalised service, despite over a quarter of the service (and most of dentistry) being privatised, and then is unashamedly socialist in tenor. However, this is a market economy socialism. The public remain blissfully ignorant of the fact that all General Practice in the UK, the front-line medical service, has in effect been privatised or pulled into the orbit of neoliberal economics, as practices are in effect independent companies. While such practices receive financial aid from the central government per patient head, they have freedom in how they use that capital in terms of employment of doctors, nurses, and other professionals such as counsellors, and in the purchasing of pharmaceuticals. They are of course regulated and publish annual statistics on their outcomes. Practices have practice managers who deal with the business side of things. Third, doctors

DOI: 10.4324/9781003619901-39

in general behave in ways that reveal their political orientations. Surgeons, who are more authority-led, tend to be more right wing, while general practitioners tend to be more left wing and focused on a patient-centred, democratic medicine. Power runs through the doctor-patient encounter where the doctor gains legitimate power from technical expertise.

Medical students have traditionally been taught to keep politics out of medicine, but this has become increasingly difficult in the UK as the last 13 years have seen a Tory Party in power that has gradually eroded doctors' pay and work conditions, run down the NHS in terms of infrastructure, created a top-heavy management structure, and starved medical education of sufficient funding to create innovative programmes. The result of this has been a heavy exodus of junior doctors from the profession, leaving to work for more lucrative pay and better conditions particularly in Australia and New Zealand. A third of newly qualified doctors now plan to leave the NHS. Waiting lists for patients have exploded and many find it difficult to get a quick appointment with their GP. This is exacerbated by an exponential increase in numbers of elderly patients with multiple chronic conditions who are living longer. The NHS has slipped down the league table for patient outcomes and the UK has a poor doctor:patient ratio. The only European countries with worse doctor:patient ratios are Poland and Slovenia. Where the UK has 2.8 doctors for every 1,000 members of the population, Austria has 5.1. Such erosion of NHS provision has a knock-on effect on patients' trust in medical work, lowering that trust and confidence. As I write this, a Labour government has just been elected and resources have immediately been allocated to the NHS. Planned junior doctors' and nurses' strikes over pay and conditions have been rapidly settled.

What, then, has this to do with doctors' identities or selves? Doctors once joined the medical profession as a lifelong commitment – a vocation. Now, medical work is a job. As more women than men enter medicine, and many of those women will take leave as they have children, so doctors have elected for part-time work, reinforcing the view of medicine less as a vocation. Doctors subscribe to a professional identity – the role brings great responsibility. But this professional identity has merged with personal identities such that doctors now demand rights as citizens, for example, to fair pay for the difficult job that they do. This has led to the emergence of the new identity of the politicised doctor, mainly among younger members of the profession. Lost in the archives, the public and press seem to have forgotten that doctors did 'strike' in 1975–76 over pay, but this was strictly a 'work to rule', but with some suspension of elective clinics and non-urgent operations in London and the north-west of the UK.

In 2016, 68 years after the NHS was founded, junior doctors found their political identity and voted for strike action for better pay and conditions,

## 146 *Self-Literacy*

seen to be eroded by years of Tory government neglect. Further strike action took place in 2023 and 2024, with senior doctors (consultants) also engaging in strike action, with issues over their pension rights linked to pay. Doctors' identities and sense of self have been changed forever by this mass political enlightenment. While politics do not affect individual patient care, doctors are now open about being political creatures (more than half of doctors in the UK now have left leanings), forging political selves.

# 39 The progressively absent self

In a deeply touching article in *The New York Times*, Cornelia Channing tells of the symptoms pointing to the onset of dementia in her father. Channing was just ten years old. Her father started to hide bananas around the house: behind potted plants, draped from a shower head, tucked under blankets in a cupboard, in the dishwasher. He denied all knowledge of the banana hordes, discovered only when they began to rot and stink. Soon he started to talk in unintelligible sentences or sat in his car in the driveway for hours at a time. Channing – already bent on becoming a journalist – started to keep lists of her father's symptoms when she was only 12:

Put oven mitts on both hands, lay down on the couch, and promptly fell asleep.
Taped $9.75 in quarters to the bathroom door.
Put a pile of mail in the freezer.
Wrapped his wallet in Saran wrap and buried it in the yard.

Sometimes he was deeply inventive. Unable to find the keys to his car, he drove the lawnmower three miles into town, bought a cheeseburger, and drove back home. Sometimes he spoke in inventive metaphor, describing a medicine cabinet as containing 'some very serious equipment', and describing biting into a strawberry as releasing 'the flavour of being born'. Channing's father died when she was 18 years old.

Nearly seven million Americans suffer from Alzheimer's, the most common form of dementia. It is now the fifth most common cause of death in the USA after heart disease, cancers, lower respiratory disorders, and cerebrovascular disease. There is no cure for Alzheimer's. In the UK, the number of people with dementia is estimated at 850,000. These figures are also rising dramatically. By 2025, the UK dementia population will be 1 million. While all elderly people will have memory lapses and some confusion, they feel that a self is intact. Those suffering from dementia have memory problems that are permanent, and this affects short-term memory, such

DOI: 10.4324/9781003619901-40

## 148  *Self-Literacy*

that a sense of self is eroded. This is accompanied by increased confusion and reduction in concentration. Hallucinations, delusions, and paranoia may follow. The loss of self is also a loss of self-esteem leading to apathy, depression, and social withdrawal.

Alzheimer's has a neurological cause – an abnormal build-up of proteins around brain cells – but is aggravated by the psychological as increasing absence of self. We are still far from understanding what changes happen to the brain during dementia, and so we resort to metaphors such as 'plaques' and 'tangles' spreading through the brain. The self is caught in these plaques and tangles and shrinks, as the brain shrinks. What forms in the sufferer is what we call in social life an 'accountability sink' – there is nobody there to take charge.

A by-product of a technocratic society, in which AI is taking over decision-making, is the absence of the decision maker. A template is the website for a product to which you have subscribed that you no longer want, but when you check on the website, there is no option for cancelling your subscription. You finally track down a telephone number for the company, but you are told that there is a queue, and you may have to wait over half an hour for a 'rep' to speak with you. Finally, you speak to someone who tells you that you have come to the wrong department. She cannot put you through directly but gives you another number. Nobody answers that phone, leaving you in limbo. This is part of the phenomenon of the 'accountability sink' where you can never find a person who is responsible, and you are passed from one to another. Each person you talk to (in a chain) refuses to take responsibility for a final decision and you are passed down a line, resembling a Borges short story. Of course, the accountability sink works at the highest level of government, where 'the buck stops here' is not the case. Politicians blame civil servants and the civil service in turn blames politicians. Politicians blamed bureaucracies and their endless paperwork when it was political decisions in the first place that created the bureaucracy. Think the UK's disastrous Brexit, for which nobody now wants to take responsibility, just kicking the ball further down the road. Part of the problem is that we are dealing with nonlinear, dynamic, complex, adaptive systems at the edge of chaos, that are treated with functional linear, piecemeal approaches. Dementia is an institutional, as well as a personal, infirmity.

# 40  A roof over yourself

Just as a snail's shell – a calcium carbonate exoskeleton – is a hardened extrusion of the flesh, so a house can be an extension of self. But modernist architecture generally expresses an impersonalistic and monolithic corporate face that cancels personality – think Brutalism. As a critical response to modernism, architecture challenged the phallogocentrism and corporate show of the monolithic – modernist steel and glass skyscrapers advertising hierarchy and prestige. The skyscraper is an ego writ large, in the image of the capital 'I'. Lots of 'I's' make a city, jostling, bullying, proud to be apex predator. Jacques Derrida, following Martin Heidegger, would fell the phallogocentric alpha male tree with one move of the keyboard: the strikethrough (Ɨ) where the I is suspended, recognising that it cannot be expunged. This move from the modern to the reconstructive postmodern in architecture was supported by an ecological sensitivity – a move away from energy-consuming and polluting concrete and steel production to sustainable materials such as wood and naturally occurring stone. Buildings were also tuned to their environmental settings (Figure 40.1).

The architect Charles Jencks, the founder of 'reconstructive' postmodernism (as against deconstructive postmodernism, the latter labelled as nihilist) wove symbolism and myth into his designs, such as the Elemental House in the Los Angeles Rustic Canyon. Jencks says that in California, 'everyone worships the water, land, beautiful views and sun, or in Classical terms, Aqua, Terra, Aer and Ignis' – the four elements. The house was also inspired by John Milton's poems 'L'Allegro' and 'Il Penseroso': the active and contemplative moods. Jencks describes a 'double semantics' or two interwoven sets of meanings experienced as you move through the building.

Other architects, such as Ben Callery in Australia, combined the elegant minimalism of high modernism with the small-is-beautiful aesthetic of postmodernism (multiple intersecting narratives rather than an overarching Grand Narrative), utilising a combination of sustainable wood and hi-tech glass. Callery set up an energy-self-sufficient house in the plains,

DOI: 10.4324/9781003619901-41

150  *Self-Literacy*

*Figure 40.1* The Elemental House, Melbourne. Photograph: Jack Lovel.

valleys, and mountains of North Central Victoria, Australia that employs natural materials and does not impose – using lots of glass to be almost transparent and make the best of the natural light. The house has no overbearing ego, just a light presence.

Let's return to the two differing strands of postmodernity: the deconstructive and reconstructive. Deconstructive postmodernism took apart the value structures of modernism, such as oppositional categories and masculine domination, in pointed critique, as if demolishing the skyscrapers. But nothing would be built in the place of these modernist, sometimes brutalist, minimalist structures of concrete, glass, and steel. Empty lots abounded, waiting for refurbishment or new metaphors. So deconstructive literary criticism exposes flaws and contradictions in modernism without necessarily offering tangible alternatives. Reconstructive postmodernism – its roots in architecture rather than literature – accepted that minimalism and modernism must continue in parallel with a new approach. The best of modernist design must be retained, such as extensive use of glass. In postmodern literature, this 'letting in the light' or 'seeing through' via glazing was reproduced in the extensive use of the tropes of irony and pastiche.

Charles Jencks was the principal proponent of reconstructive postmodernism. This approach mixes and matches styles, especially the baroque and love of detail and colour, in small-scale buildings, landscape gardening, and urban design. The reconstructive postmodern 'I' shifted to lower case ('i'). Rather than struck through, it was placed in quotation marks as an ironic gesture and bracketed out: the i was able to deconstruct its pomposity, laugh at itself, and dress up in fancy clothes. It welcomed back texture and sensitivity to its surroundings. It abandoned competition and bullying for collaboration and good-natured debate. It learned from feminism. The 'i' looked up to its Classical forebearers, the masters of satire – particularly Aristophanes and Juvenal – where the pompous phallic 'I' became that which is satirised and readily rendered limp.

Postmodern literature broke down the basic structure of the modern novel – the hero's journey – to replace it with anti-narrative elements, lack of primary characters, and subversion of plot. Deconstructive postmodernism focused largely on language in the cultural forming of identity borrowing from James Joyce's 'stream of consciousness' approach. But Joyce's language – in *Finnegan's Wake* – was reconstructive, elaborating on and inventing words (such as 'ripripple' – flowing water thanks to the reduplication; 'mumchanciness' – 'keeping mum' at the right moment; 'skeeze' – a sleazy person) coining new metaphors, and punning. In reconstructive postmodern discourse, where indicative language ('this is') had assumed a primary role in modernism, so in postmodernism the subjunctive ('this may be') – tolerant of ambiguity rather than craving certainty and fond of subclauses – became the dominant mode. This melted the hard 'I' and allowed for transformative and multiple identities. Postmodern feminists adopted this model, the rationality of *logos* giving way to the more instinctive *eros*. Buildings could once more be sensual, erotic, soft- (riprippling) rather than hard-edged.

# 41 From carbon to silicon

An emergent movement of 'morbid environmentalism' and 'Anthropocene antihumanists' suggests that humanity is a parasitic force that has been disastrous for planet Earth. As humanity continues to pursue its destructive path towards annihilation, taking other species with it, would it not be better in a moral-ecological sense to stop having children, thus turning off the taps of human ambition and greed that have provided such poisonous waters for life on Earth? Here, the self meets its demise in posthumanity.

Such morbid environmentalism is echoed somewhat in existential concerns over AI turning rogue. But AI enthusiasts are more likely to follow a 'transhumanist' view, where human qualities are radically extended and deepened by artefacts. For example, in medicine, there is abundant optimism along these lines. Peter Lee and colleagues (2024) see 'momentous potential' for Generative Pre-trained Transformer-4 (GPT-4) in medical areas such as consulting, diagnostics, and recording information. Such optimism is founded on the notion that GPT-4 demonstrates genuine empathy and concern and that this could become reflexive. Here, the AI technology not only thinks about what it does (reflection), but also changes its values for the better through such reflection (reflexivity) – in other words, a meta-AI.

As we fantasise about fleshly and sensual aspects of the AI and robotics revolutions, at the outer limits of AI thinking, we might consider the ethical conundrum raised by having sex with sentient, self-aware sex robots (sexbots). Designed as intimacy partners, what ethical implications will be raised by sentient AI in spheres such as sexual health (of sexbots, not just of their human partners)? Will we need hybrid relationship/ sexuality counsellors? Does robot gender matter in an age of gender fluidity and transgender expression? What might a robotic sexually transmitted disease look like and how will a medicine of the future wrestle with this? Antihumanist pessimism could quickly gain a foothold here!

From a humanist perspective, of course, morbid environmentalism and antihumanist pessimism appear deeply callous, a form of scaremongering.

DOI: 10.4324/9781003619901-42

*From carbon to silicon*   153

By the same token, cognisance of the dangers of AI autonomy is already leading to coordinated prophylaxis, where experts join forces to warn over AI's threat to humanity. The existential threat created by what is perceived as poor or piecemeal regulation of AI has led to the formation of a global expert group concerned with the need for close monitoring and regulation. AI is then bracketed with pandemics and nuclear wars as primary existential threats. Stripped of moral reasoning and emotional sensitivity, a collective, superior cold intelligence working at extraordinary power that can be exponentially enlarged can outstrip the limits of human reasoning. Non-regulation may lead to a future scenario differing little from the dystopia shared by the antihumanists and morbid environmentalists, where humanity is redundant and doomed. Such 'extended human' entanglements warrant close, critical inspection.

Developments in AI have led to the development of a parallel critical study – metahumanities – amplifying humanity positively, through shifts in mainstream perceptions about biotechnologies and posthumanist theories amplifying rather than contravening common ideals and values. While posthumanism and transhumanism appear to create territory for intellectuals, they describe everyday increases in quality of life through supplements such as smart technologies (personalised education, safer driving, better healthcare, cleaner transport), although the horizon for such enhancements includes controversial technologies such as gene enhancement.

Where science and technology are perceived as more important to culture than the arts and humanities, so they attract greater funding for research and development, as funding for the humanities is (dis)proportionately cut. But it is the arts and humanities that provide a critical eye to shape the direction of science. We might see the arts and humanities not primarily as decorative or providing entertainment, but as the 'values carriers' for ethics, aesthetics, politics, and the transcendental beyond the instrumental or functional. These value perspectives embody critique.

Meta-cognition embraces such values and perspectives beyond the instrumental such that reduction of life purely to information is stemmed, where meaning is sought. However, we should not demote 'information' to mere instrumental status where information is not meaningless – for example, information can form patterns that are highly meaningful. Meta-patterns include fractals – repeated patterns at differing levels of magnification that show complexity operating at differing levels of expression in matter. Or the parts repeat the whole. Information, such as DNA, is patterned.

We can no longer look back to Renaissance humanism to make sense of an emergent humanity yoked to, and extended by, rapidly advancing digital technologies. We now live in a posthumanist age, where humanity is part of a symbiotic democracy of both carbon- and silicon-based life forms. The graphic artist Mathieu Bablet riffs on this theme in his

## 154  *Self-Literacy*

*Carbon and Silicon*, where 'two androids crisscross the planet for centuries in search of themselves and each other while civilization crumbles around them'.

The most radical perspective of posthumanism is perhaps Object-Oriented Ontology in which artefacts are afforded the same ontological status as humans. The patient undergoing surgery, the surgeon, the scalpel she uses to open the patient's flesh, the monitoring machines used by the anaesthetist, the bed that the patient lies on, even overhead lights and the floor that everybody treads are democratic participants in a circle of Being. This is true Theatre. Objects are subjects. The 'transhumanist' movement emanating from Silicon Valley, California – in contrast with the antihumanists – is naively optimistic about a cyborg future, where humans are happily augmented by AI, or vice-versa, with extravagant aims such as eliminating disease and suspending death. Transhumanists tend to think, or imagine, materially, so that the future of mental illness and neurodiversity, for example, are left to speculations of science fiction writers. Transhumanist materialism fails to grasp contextual factors in emotional life (such as the power of embodied metaphor) that are irreducible to brain process, where they claim material substrates for all conditions.

The right-wing transhumanist and venture capitalist Peter Thiel comments that a future technologically sophisticated medicine will 'reverse all human ailments … where Death will eventually be reduced from a mystery to a solvable problem'. This is the ultimate expression of medicine as a technological fix, grounded entirely in instrumental values, ignoring the ethical, aesthetic, political, and transcendental values that make medicine and medical education so complex, rich, and worthy. Thiel was the founder of PayPal, a supporter of Donald Trump, and has invested heavily in cryogenics, so what kind of future does he imagine for the 'never dying'? Would you want to live forever in a neoliberal soft dictatorship?

# 42 Différance

Alterity, otherness, is often taken as the mirror into which we look to establish a sense of self. I only know myself by difference. The Other may be the stranger who is the immigrant unsettling conservation of culture. Or the Other is the most radical difference we can imagine as the forge in which the self is created – how will we engage with those we most despise or mistrust? What is the limit to tolerance? But for Jacques Derrida, these readings of difference are too literal. Derrida coins a new term: *différance* that means 'deferral' – an ongoing cancellation of closure. Let us stop making judgements to look critically at the conditions under which such judgements arise. This will be grounded inevitably in uses of language that remain stubbornly indeterminate. Language is an open system that can never be fully mastered and is never open to closure. We can master grammar, syntax, and the rules by which language is transformed, but we cannot know the limits of language. In this ever-receding horizon the self is endlessly deferred.

By *différance* Derrida also means difference of meaning. This refers to the open-ended system by which meaning is ascribed to words as their difference from other words, but it also refers to how words can mutate or be placed such that they generate different meanings. This is what poets do well. Every word in this sense is a metaphor, pointing to another, deeper meaning. This is particularly the case in intonation, but Derrida insists on the primacy of writing over speaking in exposing the multiple metaphorical possibilities of words. This may be through invention, such as Derrida's coining of the term *différance*, but it is also inherent in words that have two meanings at once, such as 'bat', 'pound', 'left', 'park', 'pitcher', and so forth. The most quoted examples are 'altus' (both 'high' and 'low') and 'pharmakon' (both a healing substance and a poison). 'Self' is a primary term of *différance* having multiple meanings, each a metaphor as each utterance points to a more complex 'other' possibility. As Kristeva insists, we are 'strangers to ourselves'.

DOI: 10.4324/9781003619901-43

## 156   *Self-Literacy*

Identity in modernist outlook (from the 18th century Enlightenment to the current era) is described as stable and based on similarities – things being the same or grouping together. In postmodern outlook, this view is turned on its head. Identity here is grounded in differences between terms and persons. This revolution has come about largely because of the way we now think about language. The language descriptor 'dog' is arbitrary and is known in its difference from other words such as 'cat'. The meaning of words inheres in their relationships with other words. Rather than knowing a person by a fixed trait we know them by their differences from other persons. 'Self' is then not a circumscribed thing, but a product of difference between itself and non-selves. In the gesture 'I am not you' we do not claim or reclaim this as self ('I') but situate self as 'not you'. Thus, as such differences run to infinity, the notion of difference itself takes on the aura of infinity and must be renamed as *différance* or infinite deferral.

This view is also nested in another paradigm shift that characterises the emergence of postmodernity out of modernity – the avoidance of finite 'grand narratives' or all-explanatory models and theories (such as all behaviour can be reduced to neurological models; or Marxism explains the nature of all economic transactions and provides a fair system for living; or neoliberalism does the same as Marxism). Jean-François Lyotard suggests that life is a series of infinite competing 'small narratives' that are local or contextualised and cannot be grasped by a grand narrative such as one system of philosophy, religion, or style of life. The knock-on effect for our understanding of identity is that identities are born of differences and are multiple. Identity must be endlessly deferred or is never fully grasped as it reels away. Further, identities should not be thought of as either fixed or content but are mutable and in process. Of course, framing identity as process rather than content demands deferral of absolute meaning.

Derrida also describes political identities as forms of deferral – democracy in particular. Democracy is an infinite 'horizon' project or a forever 'democracy-to-come'. This rejects Hegel's view that dialectic has an end point in Spirit or the realisation of a shared transcendental value for humanity (a 'Common Wealth' as Michael Hardt and Antonio Negri put it). Democracy is an ideal that may never be achieved. Again, it can be rethought as a project always in development moving towards an ever-receding horizon. We can think of postmodern and poststructuralist identity this way. Democracy is a project that learns from history but also writes a history of the future. Modernism can be characterised as an age of intense self-interest and cultivation of techniques of the self, its current incarnation as the 'selfie' – the habit of taking photographs of oneself on a mobile phone and posting them on social media. Postmodernism, running parallel with remnants of modernism, has reversed modernism's interest in self by defining self in the mirror of the other. In other words, I only know

*Différance*  157

myself in difference from others. Hence, endless scrolling through others' selfies becomes habitual – as deferral.

The most extreme, and perhaps morally illuminating, example of this mobilising of difference is found in the writing of Emmanuel Levinas. As a Jew, Levinas asks: 'can I understand the mentality of those who engaged in the extermination of Jews during the Holocaust?' Indeed, can a form of forgiveness be found? This would be the most extreme case of finding self in the mirror of the Other. It defines an ethical self as a person bent of 'self-improvement', except that the arc of self-improvement is not directed to an inner life or a better body, but to an outer reconciliation with what is least understandable – the Other self that is effectively an enemy and bent on your destruction. Here, we encounter a living example of Derrida's *différance* as processual difference of meaning and deferral of judgement.

# 43  Lacanian subjectivities

You are in the waiting room of the infamous French psychoanalyst Jacques Lacan (1901–81). You have heard that his methods are unorthodox. This is your first session – you arrive early, naturally anxious. Lacan's secretary says that 'Dr Lacan will see you soon'. Forty minutes later, you are still waiting, getting more anxious. Lacan himself comes to the door and greets you cordially, inviting you into his consulting room. Irritated, you ask why he is forty minutes late. 'Nothing happens until the last ten minutes of the consultation' says Lacan. 'That is when things come spilling out. The rest is waiting room trivia'. It's true, everything came spilling out in those ten minutes. Lacan asks what was running through me while I was waiting. 'Frustration, resentment, some anger' I say. 'Ah' says Lacan 'these are the feelings no doubt that you had for your father or mother in moments of abandonment? (just as I abandoned you in the waiting room)'. 'My father' I say. 'He wasn't even there at my birth'.

On the next session (I get my full 50 minutes), Lacan asks about my children and whether I give them 'too much love' (*trop d'amour*), close to *asphyxie* ('suffocation'). At the end of the session, Lacan suggests that I have a personality that suffocates through love. Precisely what I (she) wanted – or still wants – from her father. He goes on: in general terms, the woman is suffocated all the time by language that is bent to masculine desire. How does a woman gain a voice in such an atmosphere? Lacan returns to my frustrating wait for the first session to happen. 'Here' he says

> was a huge silence in which you felt unfulfilled, waiting for the Father (me, Lacan) to guide you. But here too is your guilty secret. This silence is a masturbatory "room of your own" as the novelist Virginia Woolf said. Here is your self pleasure. Your therapy will be aimed at how you best exploit this silent space for yourself, avoiding male interruption and dominance. In this silence you may find forgiveness for your father and pleasure for yourself.

DOI: 10.4324/9781003619901-44

Lacanian subjectivities   159

But the self persistently refuses such pleasure and so the remainder of the therapy is focused on this rigid defence. Lacan suggests to me that if I find myself in the waiting room again and he is late for the session, I should do something useful like sweeping up. I assume he has his tongue firmly in his cheek.

The authentic self for Lacan is the non-speaking self that can never be represented by the speaking self. It is in permanent absence, a lacuna. But we cannot help seeking it. As babies, between six and eighteen months, we glance at our reflections in a mirror, and we are fascinated by this reflection. We do not have the faculty to understand this 'other' that we see in the mirror, but this other becomes the self that we desire. Soon, the 'other' is represented by singular persons such as the parents, and by objects such as teddy bears ('transitional objects') that we use as imaginary friends, again seeing ourselves reflected in the 'other'. The 'self' is never known as such, again it is absent or dislocated. As we gain language, so three sophisticated versions of this dislocated self appear.

First, the self is (re)discovered in an animated world of objects that Lacan calls the Real. We live among the Real, but we come to know it only by representation, through perception and description (language). The Real too is our embodied nature, fleshly but eerie. We do not trust our embodiment because of the Imaginary. This is the world of fantasy, dream, daydream, make-believe, and the arts, particularly literary fiction, and poetry. Here, the physical world is disassembled but made to feel as 'real' as that world. There is tangibility in image. We sweat in dreams. In the Imaginary rests Desire. Third is the Symbolic. This is language itself: written, spoken, non-verbal, and semiotic (signs and symbols). A self is formed out of the conversation between these three realms. This conversation is hard to track linguistically and Lacan in later years attempted to represent this conversation (that constructs identity in the absence of a tangible self) in visual terms as graphics of knots, of which the Triquetra knot (three strands tied in a characteristic shape) represents the interplay of the Real, the Imaginary, and the Symbolic.

Lacan was a friend of the writer James Joyce. Joyce's characters infamously speak to themselves as if attempting to find out who they are. But the answers never come or are constantly deferred. This, for Lacan, is again because the speaking subject does not speak from, or out of, a grounded place that is the subject, but rather from a country or dwelling that is language. We come to know ourselves through language in the way that Joyce's characters in *Ulysses* best know themselves in relation to the geography of Dublin, where the city is 'other', and we use it as mirror to seek recognition of self. The self is placed, but the place changes on every utterance. The speaking subject has permanence only in the sense that it is reconfigured every time it is spoken. So, it speaks to others, or speaks

## 160    *Self-Literacy*

to itself as thinking, to exist. Behind or beyond this ego is the subject of the enunciated – the subject that is not speaking, but is spoken about, yet is never directly known. This is the subject proper, as the subject of the unconscious. This is Lacan's waiting room, and you are in it alone and wondering who will come to help.

Your own waiting room is your unconscious life and its desires. In *Ulysses* Joyce describes the architecture of the Waiting Room as Molly Bloom's soliloquy – a voice rattling around in its own preoccupations, building a shelter akin to Heidegger's hut: a temporary dwelling place that represents a mutable self. This literary tour-de-force is a 4,000 words-long sentence finishing with the ecstatic: 'yes I said yes I will Yes'. 'Yes' originates from the Old English *gese* meaning 'so be it'. It is not so much an affirmation as a resignation to circumstance. It is a 4,000 words treatise on Lacan's Real as an ever-receding horizon of meaning. The self is never 'known' but can be approximated through art and is given bodily – for Molly Bloom – in erotic and sexual pleasure.

Again, this decentred self can be grasped in terms of knots, punning on (k)not, a self that is nowhere – a 'not-self'. The basic knot, as the Triquetra, shows three elements that speak to each other when we are relatively stable. In episodes of instability, the knot is cleaved, and we find no self-reflective element in the world that we can trust. Then we suffer from anxiety. But Lacan's gift was that he could work with symptoms of psychosis, where standard Freudian psychoanalysis claimed success only with symptoms of neurosis. Lacan saw that the key element in psychoses was rigidity in language, or an inability to think in metaphor, preferring rigid instrumental description. Here, knots are not cut or unravelled, but tied too tight. In psychoses, knots cannot be connected to other knots in patterning or knotwork, as give-and-take social relations. Also, knots tied too tight are paranoid knots, afraid of interference. William Burroughs suggested that this knot of paranoia is not only a common state of being, but also one to be welcomed as the itch that postmodern literature must scratch. Repeated attempts at untying the knot leads to chafing and a wound that never heals – Philoctetes' burden – that is the burden of imaginative writing. This wound is at once the memories recovered in psychoanalytic therapy and the gift that such therapy brings as a closer association with language.

In such anxieties, the knots that can form wider knotworks are loosened such that threads appear. Linguistically, these are metonymic chains (associative chains such as 'dog-bite-cherry-tree-bark') that may spin out or loop back on themselves in recoil, or simply break. This, rather than metaphoric inventions that form stable ground. The former (metonymy) may lead to dead-ends or cliff edges, where the latter (metaphor) produces poetic vision, qualities, and intensities. Such work on knot theory

*Lacanian subjectivities* 161

*Figure 43.1* The Triquetra Knot: the Real, the Symbolic, and the Imaginary.

to explore psychic states is inventive but suffers from abstraction. Does a mathematically grounded knot fart, or better, restrain a fart in a lift full of people for fear of shame? Does such a knot feel intense fear on a rollicking roller coaster ride? Does a knot orgasm? Lacan's knots remain disembodied figures, albeit fascinating. We are in the waiting room, angry that the analyst has not appeared, tying ourselves in knots. Time to sweep up! (Figure 43.1).

# 44 The neurological self

Neurologists focus deeply inwards from effects of history, culture, society, and personality to zone in on how tissue creates experience, based largely on location, but more recently on the interdependence of locations or networks in the brain. The danger here is losing the bigger picture in focusing on the details. The key to this microscopic vision is to maintain models of complexity at every level of the person and her world. We can posit a neural self without reduction by maintaining the focus of complex systems. Another danger is that a lot of neurology – based largely on evidence from functional magnetic resonance imaging (fMRI) scanning while the person scanned undergoes psychological tests, or listens to narratives, for example – can only be described in metaphors: the brain compared to a computer: 'wiring', 'tangled neurons', 'sticky neurons', parts of the brain 'lighting up', metaphors that 'light up' the brain, 'peak brain', and so forth.

Imagine the difficulty of being a neurologist and attempting to match experience to brain tissue in the early 19th century. Your evidence is gained from autopsy linked back to behaviours, character, and symptoms of the individual. Evidence will be limited by the small number of autopsies that could be carried out. Everything else is phrenology – magical thinking applied to the shape of the skull. After Luigi Galvani's (1737–98) discovery that muscles, innervated by nerves, were stimulated by electrical activity, in the first half of the 19th century electrical brain stimulation was first used to attempt to localise function. In the 1920s, Hans Berger discovered that the electrical activity of the brain can be tracked by applying electrodes to the skull and attaching to an electroencephalograph. A huge leap forward in tracking such activity was achieved by the Canadian neurosurgeon Wilder Penfield through the 1950s, who, in exposing the cortex in surgery and recording electrical activity went deeper than surface tracking on the skull.

Neurologists can now map functions of specific cortical areas and the latest thinking is that a sense of self is associated with activity in the medial prefrontal cortex and the medial posterior cortex. Self-reflection

DOI: 10.4324/9781003619901-45

is associated with activity in the medial prefrontal cortex in combination with the anterior and posterior cingulate cortices. But quite what does this mean where we have multiple notions of what 'self' may mean, from the biological to the cultural and historical, that, in turn, change in meaning? If a self changes, how can it have a known cortical location? This is a good example of a simulacrum – a copy without an original that may not exist in the future.

Positing the self's origin in neural structures and effects raises further issues about definitions of 'self' – by 'self' do we mean consciousness or the capability to reflect on consciousness that is self-awareness? Or do we mean a sense of embodiment – the feeling of being present in the body? Further, in a sense it is redundant to speak of self as an effect of neurology because everything can be reduced to neurology. Again, locating the 'self' in the brain is a fool's errand when we have broad disagreement about what a 'self' is and neurodivergent experiences such as multiple selves. Yet the locating goes on regardless. We can see it as a sleight-of-hand: first a location is found and then the self is announced as the creature who lives there. But then, such a metaphorical geography is of little interest to the neuroscientist whose world is entirely material – the 'self' is jelly, electrical impulse, tissue, circuits of cells, and chemical flow. Substance precedes location. Everything else is semantics, abstraction, and language games. Such apparent reductionism, however, should not deflect us from the importance of a neurological account of identity, where the key issue is linearity vs complexity. Reductive explanations degrade the complex to the linear, or the non-instrumental to the instrumental. A neurological self can remain complex.

Susan Greenfield suggests that we might map the neurological substrate of identity by considering conditions in which identities are dislodged from the 'normal'. In bipolar disorder, there are fluctuations between periods of mania and depression. This might suggest two separate identities at work. In 1948 an Australian psychiatrist John Cade first used lithium to treat bipolar disorder. A brain cell or neuron is normally activated by an influx of sodium ions. Lithium works by impairing sodium entry into neurons. Across a network of neurons, this would cause a general dampening of effect. Over-activation of a field of neurons may produce experiences of mania, including an inability to sleep, agitation, and an experience of boundless energy. Dampening such feelings reduces the possibility of the occurrence of a sudden and severe dip in mood after a manic period that is a tipping into depression – a feeling of listlessness, burnout, and loss of direction and hope. Further, lithium seems to have a direct effect on depressing the impact of nitric oxide (NO), a gas that acts as a transmitter between brain cells via receptors. This leads to an overall dampening effect across a field of neurons.

164    *Self-Literacy*

If we imagine the brain as a complex system, working at maximum complexity at the edge of chaos, then – crudely – overstimulation may lead to tipping into chaotic effects, where under-stimulation leads to a dulling that prevents maximum potential of the overall complex system of the brain (that is always in activity). The brain consumes about 20% of the body's energy supply – more than any other organ. One system overrides all others – the transmission of the chemical dopamine from the brain stem upwards and outwards across the brain to feed the prefrontal cortex that constitutes a third of the brain and is the primary location for planning ahead, coordinating, and reflecting. Locating an 'I' in the brain may be a fool's errand, but if we were forced to do so, the prefrontal cortex would be the best candidate for coordinator of activity that produces a sense of self.

Indeed, left-field thinkers such as Andy Clark locate selfhood in the near future, as the essence of prediction. The brain works by a feedback loop between predictive activity in the here-and-now informed by memory. Self is then an ever-changing field of predictive processing looking back on the fleshly being who struggles to stay in the here-and-now in light of being sandwiched between prediction and memory. Selfhood is the compromise between forward thinking and recollection that must be located a fraction of a fraction of a second in the future. For if selfhood is located too far in the future then we spin into unhinged, psychotic states of irreality; and if the self is too hinged to memory as anchor, then we become severely depressed, stuck in a mire.

The prefrontal cortex acts as inhibitor of 'lower' impulses, and so when dopamine is released in large quantities into this area, cognitive inhibitions are reduced, while emotional or affective states take control. Id replaces ego and superego. Here, a sense of sharp isolationist identity gives way to a sense of engagement or collectivity – not a separation from the world as an isolated viewer inhabiting perspective, but dissolving perspective for multiple perspectives or engagement. Persons who characteristically see themselves as embedded in the social show greater fMRI activation in the medial prefrontal cortex than those who are stubbornly individualistic. The distinction between the less and more inhibited states is often referred to using the metaphors of 'bread' (rational, more inhibited) and 'wine' (looser, less inhibited).

While analogies for the brain include the computer, these will all fall short, because machines, however complex, are not self-aware. The brain is like a weather system – complex, dynamic, adaptable, working at maximum complexity at the edge of chaos without falling into chaos, and able to spontaneously transform into higher levels of complexity – but with the added factor of producing self-awareness. The cortical brain is the main attractor in the system that includes the autonomic nervous system (fight-or-flight system controlled by adrenaline) and the enteric system, the nerve complex around the gut; while these systems are embedded in a muscular, skeletal, immune, vascular, and body organ system that is open to the outside world (the porous skin being the largest organ of the body and 'open' from mouth to anus). That world, specifically the *umwelt* or immediate environment, 'prepares' us at any one moment for activity, shaping us through the senses as a collective system. Thus, to 'locate' selfhood in the brain is to miss the point of existence, for location is multiple with a preferential drift to the abstract near future (Lacan's Real).

We might think of the brain not as the origin of the sense of self, but as part of the wider nexus in which selves are generated, debated, acted out, and understood. It is foolish to think about a neurological self without appreciation of an historical, ethical, aesthetic, political, and transcendental self that cannot be reduced to brain form and function. Brain is then a key attractor within a wider, nonlinear, complex, adaptive system. For example, a sense of embodiment is critical to self-awareness, but embodiment is self-location in space and time. For some, sense of self may appear to remain consistent across changing environments, times of day, and seasons. But this was not true for the poets Coleridge and Wordsworth for example, who felt that the authentic self could only be realised deeply immersed in – or at one with – nature. Selves experienced in other contexts were not inauthentic but dulled. Certainly, sense of self is quite different during sleep and dreaming in comparison with daylight awareness. Coleridge realised a separate self from the authentic person walking in nature many miles each day when writing his voluminous notebooks and when under the influence of laudanum. As Coleridge and Wordsworth searched for an authentic sense of self in identification with nature (as a holistic experience) they suffered a contradiction that the philosopher Arthur Koestler called a 'holon' – that everything in nature is at once both a whole (in itself) and a part of something else. Of course 'nature' itself is part of something more embracing and cannot be taken as the end-point container or self. Holons are ever-receding horizons in which our consciousness is embedded.

Again, we can map activity of brain areas during cognitive and emotive tasks through fMRI, where certain parts of the brain 'light up' or are seen to be activated for certain tasks. Such geographies are subject to technical languages that are literal and not metaphorical, and divisive as they are specialist languages excluding the vernacular (and then not democratic in intent). Here, information gains meaning only for an elite group.

For example, sensory information is integrated by the temporoparietal junction in the cortex while perception of embodiment is governed by the extrastriate body area in the lateral occipitotemporal cortex. The latter region is activated when people are shown images of body parts.

## 166   *Self-Literacy*

Specifically, the extrastriate body area is activated in response to body position, where the tempoparietal junction is activated when there is a sense of disembodied location. While there is information coding and processing for bodily position in one part of the brain, another part is processing memory that shapes a sense of an autobiographical self – what have I done in the past and how has this shaped a unique 'me'? Here, the left dorsolateral prefrontal cortex and the posterior cingulate cortex are involved in processing information. Again, of course the matter of identity cannot be reduced to matter and the philosophical question remains: how does electrical and chemical activity translate into experience? Meanwhile the brain, our Common Wealth, has been colonised by specialists and their obfuscatory languages.

# 45 The linguistic transactional self in surgical settings

In the late 1990s, I set up a research team to investigate communication patterns in surgical team settings as part of a new wave of 'patient safety' protocols. New evidence at the time showed that errors largely occurred in such teams not because of technical incompetence, but because of so-called 'non-technical' communication breakdown – both within the team and across teams (such as messages between the ward and theatre teams). More, we investigated conditions for potential errors ('near misses' or 'close calls') that did not result in harm to the patient because the potential error was nipped in the bud. These typically included the potential for wrong side/ wrong site surgery and unintentionally leaving instruments or swabs in the patient's body after surgery. Again, the source of such potential mishaps was not technical incompetence but communication incompetence. Further, the origin of such communication errors was almost wholly grounded in surgeons' talk and not in the talk of the nursing staff, and in the lack of protocols (such as briefing, debriefing, and instrument counts at the end of surgery and before the wound is closed) as front-line defence. The lack of uptake of safety protocols was also frustrated by surgeons' inbuilt historical arrogance as a culture, in which personal judgement was prized over what were perceived as time-consuming protocols such as checklists.

At this time, surgical teams were notoriously hierarchical, based on military structures with strict authority rules. Surgeons were mostly men and theatre nursing staff women. We noted that while the nursing staff used one predominant style of communication – dialogue and open-ended questions – the surgeons relied more on monologue and closed statements. It seemed obvious to us that authority-led closed statements did not present the best way of communicating in a clinical team setting and may generate surgical team climates where error leading to patient harm was more likely. But we had to demonstrate this with raw data. Which we did.

We videotaped (with the permission of patients, who in any case were not identifiable on screen, and theatre personnel) theatre staff during

DOI: 10.4324/9781003619901-46

# 168   *Self-Literacy*

operations, made transcripts of their communications, and analysed the video evidence with the teams. We also set up an ongoing educational programme to improve communication within and between teams introducing ideas such as pre-briefing of surgical lists and debriefing at the end of lists. We analysed the performance of a set of surgical teams over time, also comparing this with a control cohort of surgical teams who did not receive the educational intervention until later down the line.

In short, on several measures and through interview data, we found that, indeed, surgeons' styles of communication consistently veered to the authoritative, advertised by statements and demands rather than open-ended questions and discussions. Nurses' styles of communication typically veered towards collaborative, open-ended questioning. Over time, through educational sessions and adoption of briefing and debriefing protocols, in our study group surgeons' communication styles changed becoming less didactic, more open-ended, conversational, and democratic. The climate of such teams changed from autocracy to democracy and participation. Further, from 'close-call' reporting, the number of potential errors and incidents decreased. Surgeons reported changes in their communication styles and nurses reported better communication atmospheres in theatres. In short, a better patient safety climate had been established. In the control cohort with no intervention, authority-led, hierarchical habits persisted, and close-call reports noted no significant change in levels of 'near misses' in operating theatres.

Several years on, briefing and debriefing protocols such as the World Health Organisation's Surgical Safety Checklist have been introduced globally as standard practice. Many studies now show improvement in patient safety and care as better communication patterns are introduced within and between clinical teams. Here, selves are adapted and changed as new climates of patient safety are introduced and new cultures of clinical work are established. At the heart of this is talk: the linguistic, transactional self emerges from a previous authoritarian climate. Democracy is established.

This introduces Hegel and Marx to clinical contexts – in our work above, the operating theatre as a traditional hotbed of neoliberal fictions. In the neoliberal model, the more robust and talented entrepreneurs rise above the rest, maintaining their authority through a kind of imperialism. But the reality is that tradition and authoritarian bullying maintained a surgeon-led hierarchy, flying in the face of common sense and then experimental evidence that democratic structures work best for patients' safety, health outcomes, and staff work satisfaction. Nurses regularly report that working in more democratic teams brings better work satisfaction. Surgeons are now realising this, while patients benefit.

Let us rehearse this distinction in styles – the linguistic authoritative and the democratic with greater theoretical rigour. The psychologist Jerome

*The linguistic transactional self in surgical settings* 169

Bruner makes a key distinction concerning narrative – that there are two broad styles, and these suggest two broad personality dispositions, or senses of self as differing cognitive styles. First, there is the instrumental approach. This is reductive, logical, analytical, linear, and literal. It eschews metaphor and other literary tropes. It is reflected in language as the indicative mood ('this *is*'). This is the traditional speaking voice and (non)listening ear of the male surgeon. It is grounded in intolerance of ambiguity or uncertainty, also the mark of the authoritarian personality and the bully. Literalism is preferred over the metaphorical. The second style – adopted largely by nurses – is complex, nonlinear, expansive, expressive, and both ambiguous and contradictory (where both conditions serve as resources rather than hindrances) embracing metaphor. This style is reflected linguistically as the subjunctive mood ('this *could be*'), attracting modal auxiliaries for the verb: 'might', 'possibly', and 'maybe'.

Language does need both approaches, but where it comes to a dominant shaping of character through use of language, adoption of a predominantly instrumental indicative mood of 'telling' rather 'inquiring' and 'debating' shuts down communication and points to the dominance of an authoritarian voice. This also shuts down democratic habits. In contrast, language can be employed transactionally and translationally. For example, the Russian linguist and philosopher Mikhail Bakhtin proposes a model of the emergence of self through 'dialogism' – a multi-vocal or pluri-vocal polyphony of voices as we might find in an authentic democracy or a social encounter devoid of hierarchy. Here, selfhood is negotiated through social exchange or dialectic encounter. Self is a product of conversation. Where the dialogue is with a powerful institution, it may be one-way traffic in which self is a product of forced conversion rather than free conversation.

Such distinctions in styles of self-expression through linguistic registers and habits are important. For example, as noted, in surgical team contexts, typically surgeons use imperatives and authoritative rather than facilitative voices, based on dominance of the indicative mood. Such telling rather than asking or debating is seen as efficient, but it creates hierarchical teams that have been shown to be less efficient (in terms of patient safety, patient outcomes, and team worker satisfaction) than flattened hierarchies, or democratically inclined teams drawing on Bakhtinian dialogue. Importantly, linguistic styles of such surgeons can be modified to engage more with the subjunctive mood and facilitative manner to create more democratic working conditions. This requires adopting team habits such as briefing and debriefing in which open dialogue is encouraged.

At a granular level, what a shift from monologue to dialogue does is to embrace the creation of narrative understanding of events rather than a literal listing of facts. This opens the door to embrace of affect or emotion as a central register of language. This brings texture but also uncertainty

## 170   *Self-Literacy*

to the ongoing process of developing self. More, a self that is textured through appropriate catharsis (where release of emotions can be followed by insight) is robust, less likely to be prone to burnout. In the psycho-analytic tradition of confessing cathartically followed by analysis and then insight and regrouping of self, emotional lability is seen as an essential part of self-inquiry, rather than as destabilising. Freud, of course, saw such destabilising (developing symptom such as burnout, the 'yips' or loss of self-confidence) as a symptom of repression of uncomfortable and unre-solved affect – a loss of self and self-confidence.

Jerome Bruner insists that 'a well-formed logical argument differs radi-cally from that of a well-wrought story', constituting two modes of thought. The first is concerned with a search for truth based on information and knowledge, where the latter is about endowing experience with meaning based on knowledge morphing into wisdom. As far as self is concerned, the paradigmatic method and way of life based on objectivity requires dissolu-tion of self, or temporary suspension of self, where the narrative mode's primary role is to shape selves.

Bruner describes the self shaped by narrative as a 'transactional self' – conversational and intersubjective. Key to this is the ability for perspective-taking – where one intuitively understands another self. Self is not bounded, but porous, and mutable in the face of other selves. And this, precisely, is the character of self. It is already social. Self can be reduced to language or syntax, but it is more than this – self as transactional is a means for social encounters as hotbeds of language invention and reinven-tion: the coining of new words, the development of slang, specialist codes, and particular emphases such as the invention of metaphor in poetry. Self is shaped in the kingdom of the shared vernacular, the language of patients. Nurses know this, surgeons are only now realising it.

# 46 Subject to power/power runs through the subject

We are used to thinking about power as authority, or 'power over' someone. This includes legitimate authority – such as the captain of a team, an airline pilot, or a surgeon leading a team – as well as illegitimate authoritarian leaders backed by armies, or plain bullies. Here, power is essentially repressive or controlling of others, a 'sovereign power'. Sovereign power is primarily thought of as institutional – the all-consuming power of the Pharaoh in ancient Egypt; the Emperor in the Roman world or the ancient Chinese world; the king, the Church, and the State ruling over the population in medieval times; a string of political dictators up to the present day. Sovereign power also creates a self – as an authority – or fails to create a self where one is subject to a greater sovereign power. Here, selves are servants or subservient.

Challenging the hegemony of sovereign power, Michel Foucault suggested that in contemporary society, power also works in indirect, subtle and personal ways to subjugate and control but also to empower. An example is the widespread use of surveillance. The UK has up to 6 million CCTV cameras at work – 24 cameras every square kilometre. China is estimated to use 200 million CCTV camera systems. We are subject to extensive documentation and scrutiny. But such power is not exercised as 'power over' such as certain American states banning abortion. Rather, power runs through a system as 'capillary power' right to the finest elements of social interaction, such as how we greet a stranger, or how families engage in conversation through 'turn taking' or resort to plain argument. Capillary power also works as a means of resistance – how do women in American states who choose abortion gain access to the procedure in the face of authority? Capillary power can work as bland socialisation into conformity (table manners, everyday fashion in clothes), or as generative of innovative ways of being such as idiosyncratic expression of lovemaking. We can never make selves or identities from scratch, rather we are always working with historical smoking guns.

DOI: 10.4324/9781003619901-47

## 172 *Self-Literacy*

Importantly, where sovereign power is exercised over self-forming, this may result in conformism such as standard uniform dress codes during Mao's period of rule in China, but selves produced through capillary power can be idiosyncratic, stressing difference. Capillary power running through all social interactions, down to fine exchanges, can then be productive rather than repressive. This is advertised in the resistance shown by the LGBTQ+ movements globally.

Foucault questions three common assumptions about power: first, that it is oppressive and then must be countered through liberation politics (on the big stage as revolutions); second, that power is exercised formally through institutions, where in fact it is experienced informally through all social exchanges, right down to the smallest of details (as micro-practices) such as a handshake; and third, that power is to do with beliefs or ideology, where in fact it is about bodies communicating and as they do so, (re)producing the rules that govern such communication. Capillary power again is not about subjection and reproduction of traditions or laws, but about subjectivity and production of selves. Power at the capillary level innovates as the making of the subject. This is not just political, or power-related, but an ethical and aesthetic task through which life becomes a work of art.

Foucault asks: 'what are the conditions of possibility for the emergence of a particular discourse that allows production, experimentation, and innovation in the ethical and aesthetic realms of life?'. In other words, how are selves produced and maintained that deepen the qualities of experiences: their depths, breadths, and intensities? Here, interest in the self is about the rules that govern or shape legitimacy – what are the interpersonal forces that lead to one person considering another 'mad' or 'different', an 'outsider', or an 'outlaw'? How do constraints and opportunities arise beyond the sovereign power components of the exercise of ingrained custom, law, and authority?

These are questions of disciplinary practices, the key one of which again is surveillance. Surveillance seeps into our everyday lives now in ways that Foucault could never have imagined thanks to new technologies such as the Internet. Our selves are produced and reproduced according to capillary powers to which we collectively subscribe as we engage with social media such as Facebook, Instagram, or TikTok. Foucault would not moralise about this – it is neither 'good' nor 'bad' – but was more interested in the historical conditions of possibility for the emergence of such social practices.

An example of this is the intersection of two customs guided by capillary power. The first is the professional touching of patients by doctors, considered to facilitate a more intimate and trusting relationship. The second is the rise of strident feminism that refuses the touching of women by men unless invited. Male doctors now will not touch female patients on

*Subject to power/power runs through the subject*   173

principle, even where a light touch for reassurance, or a hug showing care, are invited. Indeed, historically, male doctors touching women patients has been a matter of changing codes through capillary power. The stethoscope was invented by the French physician René Laënnec in 1816 not just to hear otherwise hidden sounds in the body such as the heart's pulse, but to alleviate otherwise embarrassing intimacy with women patients.

Modern practices switch focus from sovereign power to capillary power to create new subjectivities. For example, historically, a king's directive acts to control subjects, but now we have a penetrating surveillance system such as a postal questionnaire or a census that gathers data. Micropractices such as psychotherapy, counselling, helplines, and visits to health professionals such as doctors and nurses produce confessing subjects with docile bodies: self as 'patient'. This echoes across social practices – particularly self as consumer where we believe we are exercising choice, but in fact are manipulated by advertising and fashion such that we conform. Modern power – as 'bio-power' – acts directly on bodies (fashions, exercise, health regimes). Under the direction of the colour supplements, self-help books, and Internet pornography, generations are growing up with 'expectations' – codes of how they should look and behave during sex, or how bodies can be turned into objects for the male gaze, following patriarchal scripts that exploit women. Capillary power operating at this level shapes bodies and activities rather than ideologies and values.

Self is then not a logical category or a concept (essence preceding existence), but a living self in action produced through social practices. This form of self is necessarily multiple. The self that votes is not the same self that makes love or fashions furniture. There is no superordinate, totalising, or transcendent self. Self is formed rather by reacting to events. One of those events, significant for contemporary scholars, is the work of Foucault. How do Foucault's words now shape selves? Or is that a question just for intellectuals?

# 47 Bodies that are no-bodies
## The biological self

Tucked away in a corner of an expanding universe (what is it expanding into is anybody's guess) humans are small specks, yet perhaps important because we have consciousness of, and knowledge about, the very universe we inhabit. It may be that such reflexive awareness is uncommon in the cosmos, even singular. But such self-reflexivity has also tricked us into believing that consciousness spells out singularity – an embodied and circumscribed self. The reality is that we are not closed-off and singular, but open beings physically reconstituted at regular intervals. As Tom Oliver says: 'most of the estimated 37 trillion cells' that make up a single body have a very short lifespan of weeks, if not days, so that 'there is a near continual turnover of material'. We are not static creatures yet live with the illusion of stasis. At any one moment we are both running down towards death (entropy), and regenerating, as new molecules flow through us.

These include atoms from the farthest reaches not just of our solar system, but the universe itself as it unfolds and expands since the Big Bang (a strange notion as there was no one there to hear the bang and the suddenly dense matter from which the expansion of the universe arose had collapsed down to an infinitely small and tight mass). Indeed, it is better to think of ourselves not as discrete bodies and identities, but as reconstituted flowing matter that has already been everywhere and our origins are in such atoms concentrated in two cells – a single sperm and an ovum. Skin cells renew every few weeks, at the rate of 500 million skin cells per day. Cells in skeletal muscles however renew every 15 years. Brain cells may be capable of regrowth. Whatever the time periods for renewal, our bodies are not strictly 'our' bodies at all as these renewal cycles set in (such cycles slow down as we get older).

Importantly, the greater mass of cells in the body is constituted by 'alien' bacteria. These are not inert but have proven effects on our physiology and then our moods. To briefly amplify the notion that we cannot logically claim singularity – and then ego identity, or a bounded self – we are at root social beings grounded in the zoological history of evolving humankind

DOI: 10.4324/9781003619901-48

*Bodies that are no-bodies: the biological self* 175

and connected at once to a mass of persons, artefacts, and other lifeforms. How can we talk of singularity when every day we connect with animal and plant forms through foods, breathe from the atmosphere, and depend upon a human web to transport us, make a dwelling, and create art and science? We are not primarily selfish, but social beings.

The puzzle, of course, is that knowing these facts about immersion in a nonlinear, complex, dynamic world seems to make no dent on the experience we have of being largely static (I don't feel my millions of skin cells shedding each day, although I can occasionally see a skin 'snowfall' or a dandruff display), singular and separate, or contained. But this illusion is both historically and socially conditioned. Languages and social traditions create readymade points of identification into which we are quickly socialised, and this becomes the norm. Anthropology in particular shows us how different the sense of identity is between an urban person in Boston, an Inuit herding reindeer while treading tundra in the Arctic Circle, and a forest dweller in the Amazon living in a small tribal context prior to contamination from intruders.

Importantly, we are (again) nonlinear, open, dynamic, complex systems living at the edge of chaos with a possibility of spontaneously reformulating at higher levels of complexity. This, rather than closed, linear systems. We breathe air and eat from the world, not cut off from the world. We urinate and excrete back into the world. Our skin is a protective layer and not an exclusive barrier. Even within our body, between organ systems, the microbiome permeates most of our tissues, and we have a 'virome' that travels throughout the body, composed of viral particles. This forms an inner ecosystem that is in constant regeneration.

Our languages are systems that precede us and into which we are born. And when and as we die, molecules are released that join the dance of molecules across the universe so that chemically we have eternal life. Before we get too cosmic, the miracle of the human body – again, derived from a single-cell ovum fertilised by a single-cell sperm – is that cells are arranged into differing levels of complexity as 'strange attractors', or relatively stable bodies with many characteristics of more mechanical, linear closed systems, such as our organs. Organs, and the brain is the most complex of these, are still systems subject to entropy (or running down) as we get older or injured, but they are substantial and consciously 'felt' as substantial mass (e.g., the rising and falling of the chest as the lungs expand and deflate). The great puzzle, of course, is the gap between our anatomical and physiological knowledge of systems such as the nervous system and brain and our experience of living. While a fMRI scan can show a portion of brain activity related to a task of which the person is aware, there is a disconnect between the instrumental activity of neurons firing in patterns and the experience that this produces.

## 176    *Self-Literacy*

We also have no direct knowledge or experience of the constant regeneration of bodily matter except for skin wounds healing and as noted some shedding of dandruff. Cells in the gut lining live only five days before they are renewed, and red blood cells live four months. Yet our experience of being does not necessarily correlate with this everyday death and renewal. If 'we' are constantly in a state of shedding and recycling, why is the self in many cultures experienced as bounded and consistent? Perhaps we have been looking for our lost keys under the streetlight rather than where we dropped them. It may be, as philosophers and geographers rather than neuroscientists tell us, that we should be focusing on concepts of space, place, and time ahead of, or instead of, 'selfhood'.

Being placed in space (grounded, posture, localised, in a dwelling, in a locality, at school, shopping, walking, commuting, travelling) or being displaced (homeless, travelling, temporary homes, refugees) is perhaps a fruitful way to frame identity and self. This goes some way to explaining why a stable self may have coalesced as people on the move (hunter-gatherers following herds or shoals) start to dwell – to put down roots and build homes (agriculturalists with domesticated crops and animals). Settlements bring containment and boundary, and this perhaps has a knock-on effect for body and mind as a separate sense of stable (rather than nomadic) self emerges.

While knowledge of our symbiotic relationship with micro-organisms such as gut bacteria is a recent product of scientific inquiry, so we are now familiar with the hacking of our bodies through external infections, viral or bacterial. Perhaps this knowledge of alien invasion promising illness and disease has led to a stronger sense of an isolated self as a fortification. As popular science becomes entertainment, more people will gain knowledge of the biology that is the body and possibly the sense of a stable, unique, interior self will be displaced, even blown out of the water. There is an old joke: if we didn't have time, would everything happen at once? Maybe it does, in a sense, for the non-conscious elements of what is shed from the body and what lives in us, supposedly non-human.

Another source for a strong sense of self paradoxically may come from the increasing knowledge of connectivity between humans across the globe. Self may be a psychological defence against drowning in interconnectivity – the 64 million kilometres of roads that pattern the planet, or the nearly 2 million people per day being transported by 6,000 commercial flights between 41,000 airports, and the half a million commercial ships creating wakes on our oceans and waterways daily. Increasingly seen in the sky at night, 13,000 satellites circumnavigate Earth helping us to communicate at distance (Elon Musk has launched over half of such satellites – around 7,000). Self can surely only be described as a web or a net where augmented by technologies, yet it would be arrogant to

*Bodies that are no-bodies: the biological self* 177

see any one of us as a spider inhabiting that web. For some, the historical human self is explained in evolutionary terms – our biological adaptation has allowed exponential growth of our species and is thus an evolutionary success. In 10,000 BCE the world population stood at around a million. By 5000 BCE (just a blink away in evolutionary time) the world population stood at around 5 million. By 1800 AD this figure had swollen to 1 billion. The current population is 7 billion, predicted to rise to 10 billion during this century. We will meet an extremely small proportion of these people, but we are connected by our common destiny of death and, of course, Elon Musk's cohort of satellites.

Evolution by natural selection has now given way to a cultural gaffe – thanks to a combination of global warming and overpopulation in relation to resources – that promises extinction of humanity (along with many other species) such that, yes, the self of humanity may be fully dissipated across the universe. This is the evolution of the bio-illogical. The sovereign ego has become a mad king plotting his own demise. And this ruler, obsessed of course by currency and economics, has invented cryptocurrency to add to the eco-misery. The cryptocurrency industry needs vast computer resources that will soon be consuming as much as 1% of annual global electricity. This puts a big strain on local electricity grids. A single crypto transaction consumes more energy than that required to power up to ten average UK households in a day, and this figure will almost double annually. We go under haunted by our own follies.

# 48  The universal SELF

Cosmologists tell us, that for mathematical reasons, there are 18 possibilities for the shape of the universe – the BIGSELF that encompasses all selves. SpaceTime has different possible personalities, although of course it contains all selves. Our shelf life, the span of the self, is relatively short, but we are all implicated in the shelf life of the universe from which we came and to which we return as spinning matter. The life of the universe is infinity. The paradox of the self that is the universe, our Mother Self, is that it has finite volume but no edges. Travel to what you think is beyond the edge of the universe and you will, paradoxically end up where you started! That you might stick in certain places at certain times is due to gravity. Einstein showed that space is curved because of large objects creating gravitational fields. So, we have some sense of the universe's personality. It is a sticky and recursive being.

One possible shape for the universe is a torus or doughnut – fall into its centre and you come back on yourself. Endlessly. There are no holes, and so no leakage; surfaces are infinite. SpaceTime is self-contained. The universal SELF is recursive, so that each time self meets self, a more complex self emerges. Such complexity has no limits in space or time. This production of complexity might be thought of as the expanding universe since the Big Bang, where matter collapsed on itself with such concentration that it was forced to blow out. This expanding SELF cannot be compared to deity (in whose image we are supposed to exist) because the Big Bang long preceded the human image. I cannot think of a greater conceit than claiming that humanity is created in God's image because humanity is a mere speck cosmologically. One certainty is that our residue after death will have no capability to sense, in fact it will be wholly non-sensical and inhabiting the bio-illogical.

Some cosmologists think that the universe is flat, like an expanding sheet of paper with no limits, but metaphorically that is a bore. I prefer the doughnut – more personality. The problem with investigating the shape of the universe is that you would have to be able to travel at the speed of

DOI: 10.4324/9781003619901-49

*The universal SELF*   179

light and would, no doubt, see images of yourself all around like a hall of mirrors because you would be everywhere at once, as would all other matter. Does it matter? Only when we die. The common assumption is that the body dies while the mind, in some form, may go on to infinity. The reality (whose reality?) is that the body will go on, distributed across the cosmos, without unity. Looking at some doughnut images of the cosmos, you cannot help thinking that our cosmic home looks like an arsehole. This short ride called LIFE might be an immense joke.

# 49  Subject to the abject

The controversial 16th-century German priest Martin Luther, the scourge of the Catholic Church, infamously described humanity as the excrement from God's anus: castoff, degraded, marginalised, surplus to needs, and neither subject nor object but abject. The abject is extremely bad, the pits of suffering, but it also describes the person who has been marginalised or ostracised. These are the wretched of the earth, unable to reach a place of pride or gain any self-esteem. The abject self is a non-self, neither subject nor object, a self *in extremis*.

For the French feminist and poststructuralist writer, psychoanalyst, and philosopher Julia Kristeva, the abject is the experience of horror as a breakdown in meaning caused by a breakdown in the distinction between self and other. The self is engulfed by the other or is overshadowed and loses all sense of moral purpose. The singular example is the Holocaust as a vortex into which many ordinary people were sucked and which they chose to block out even as they knew of the horror of Hitler's mission; while many other examples of genocide exist. The abject is experienced too in disgust – for example, at the sight of a corpse, or in the presence of putrid or foul matter.

Where psychoanalysts usually focus on the place where meaning emerges – such as a recognition of self as distinct from another, or in the moments of moral reflections on the plight of others who are in difficulties, or sick – the abject refers to the place where meaning collapses. For Freud, the abject – especially terror – is a primary condition of the unconscious. Where the ego of the conscious mind becomes an object of knowledge open to its own conceptualisations, the subject of the unconscious is beyond comprehension. Indeed, this subject is likely to be repulsive to the ego. Dreams are the royal road to the unconscious, and nightmares are familiar to us all as pollutants, viruses, or infectious agents that kidnap and torture conscious agency.

The abject, as horror, is experienced in our very early recognition of separation from the world of animals. Here, we are ejected from the

DOI: 10.4324/9781003619901-50

*Subject to the abject*  181

Garden of Eden or the place of absolute innocence, to discover that we have responsibility and a conscience. However, while the animal self is stripped away in a period of horror at the loss, we are still connected with the mother as a nourisher. Second, we are separated from the mother and a new level of abjection emerges. We are abject because we recognise the horror that such separation heralds. We must find our individuality out of the safety of the mother-net. Third, we enter a world in which horror precedes us – many things are encountered that disturb identity as system and order. We recognise that the world is unpredictable, unpalatable, dangerous, disturbing, and sometimes very dark.

In facing such harsh realities, our emotional response is unpleasant. Our idyll is broken. Culturally, we will be drawn to the abject – or excremental selfhood – time and time again in ways that are cathartic through fairy story, myth, literature, theatre, cinema, and television news. These provide media for catharsis that protect us from the reality of abjection. But soon, we face a death or serious accident in the family. As we grow, so the abject accompanies our relationships – the terror of loneliness and rejection, the sickness we experience in rejection, or falling in love and being jilted, or being loved and not being able to return the feeling. In relationships, sex pitches us deeply into a mixture of elation and abjection – the orgasm as 'little death' can be a deep pleasure or become a compulsion and we are torn between desire for another, satisfying our own needs, and unselfishly addressing the needs of the other.

# 50 The final straw
## The self's last sip of life's juice

'I'm not afraid of death, I just don't want to be there when it happens' said actor and film director Woody Allen. In the UK, there is a move to 'put death on the curriculum' for younger schoolchildren, where most children will experience a bereavement in the family (usually a grandparent) without knowing how to deal with this, or how to identify with the grief of their elders. They will see previously robust selves hollowed out of their elders as grief plays out. They will see despair in their mother's or father's eyes as a loved one is lost, a partner, relative, or child cruelly ripped out of life through a fatal accident or illness. Freud posited *eros*, life force, as the main instinctual driver early in his writings. But later, he gave as much presence to *thanatos* – the death wish. This is based not just on the fact that some people seek harmful and aggressive behaviours, but that we generally seek risk rather than regulation. We like to shake hands, or flirt, with death even as we don't want to be there when it happens. For many, poverty is the royal road to an earlier death than they might like, while for many others, a bad diet paves that royal road to an early exit.

For some, the death wish (Thanatos) is always stronger than life force (Eros). The most talented fiction writer of his generation David Foster Wallace grew up as a strapping 6'2" athlete, a star tennis player, but abandoned sports when the writing bug infected him. After *Infinite Jest* – one of the most important novels of ideas of the late 20th century – Wallace was courted by eager publishers, awarded a MacArthur genius grant, got married, and then hung himself at age 46. He was a lifelong depressive. Sometimes, entropy marks us at an early age.

Following the course of entropy, the body inevitably runs down. The heart has a sell-by date. Death is our only certainty in life, and our biggest uncertainty – most of us don't know how it will happen and we have no idea what will happen thereafter, although we might have faith in an afterlife. Biology tells us that our tissues will decay and join the matter of the universe, so that materially, in a sense, there is no death, just a recycling of matter at the atomic level. This may be compromised somewhat if we

DOI: 10.4324/9781003619901-51

The final straw: the self's last sip of life's juice    183

opt for cremation. Cindering seems a brutal way to end our existence, to offer a full stop to our death sentence. In 1900 in the UK cremation rates were 1%. They are now at 80%, reflecting a need for efficiency or quick turnover even in death. The corpse is a commodity.

Cremation is cheaper than burial but it is also more polluting – in the UK at the time of writing, around £1,500 per body as opposed to £5,000 for a burial (£6,000 in London). You can get a 'bargain funeral' on the thefuneralmarket.com (good to know). In the USA, average prices for funeral ceremony and cremation are between $7,000 and $12,000. Undertakers will remind you that these are basic costs and do not include a cemetery, monument, marker, or flowers. Better start saving now.

In life, our immediate sense of self is bodily presence, sensation. At death we become nobodies. Self is cancelled. Some believe the mind, spirit, or soul continues. The journey is uncertain. Tickets cannot be bought beforehand, and it is unlikely that those used to first-class travel will gain first-class entry to an afterlife as the infamous Protestant Elect believed (where piety gains you entry – although Calvinists believe that the list has already been drawn up and it is basically a lottery, you may or may not be on that list whatever your deeds in life). Life on earth is laced with this terror of the uncertainty of death, yet we mostly shelve dwelling on this as discomfiting. The body is destined to become nobody. Further, who will remember us in two generations' time unless we are celebrities?

The rich are jostling for ways in which they can maintain longevity, to even live forever. The posthuman movement promises eternal life through technology. But how strange life would be if we all hung around forever. Very cluttered, very hard to imagine the younger generations tolerating a pile of redundant oldies. Communication would be impossible across multiple generations. People who want to live forever are surely narcissists.

Let's leave bodies to their natural courses. If a dead body were left to decay naturally it first bloats as bacteria aerate the flesh. Carrion flies and blow flies will lay their eggs in the rotting flesh, prompting active and advanced decay as the bones' surfaces powder. The larvae of maggots or flies multiply to eat the soft tissue only to be eaten themselves by ants and wasps. As months pass, the body is licked back to cartilage, the bones gnawed clean by voles and mice, offering a feast for springtails and earthworms, millipedes, woodlice, maggots, beetles, slime moulds, and fungi. Their feet numbering in the thousands, tread-safe millipedes will walk and waste here too, crusting over.

Shakespeare surely had it right in *King Lear*. As Lear dies, Edgar steps up to revive him, but Kent intervenes: 'Vex not his ghost, O, let him pass! / He hates him / That would upon the rack of this / tough world / Stretch him out longer'. Being some body, any body, means that we have selfhood in flesh, whatever the state of our bodies. Some invest deeply in bodies

184    *Self-Literacy*

through bodybuilding, sports, body-based performance, and so forth, but some will take the path of bodily abuse.

Body as self comes in and out of focus here – cultivation through exercise or performance brings the body to the fore as the key element of self-presentation. Abuse sets the body as background to some other factor of self, such as personality, or identification with a social group. How bodies are celebrated changes with history: the ideal of the male body in Greek sculpture related to sports, the ideal of the body in contemporary North European culture related to youth. Bodies are not given as finished objects but cry out to be improved or adapted. How bodies function changes across cultures and through history: sex and toilet functions now private, where once they were more public through necessity (large families sharing rooms, the water closet not invented until 1596 and not widely available until the mid-19th century).

Intimacy with the dead body is a way of life for some (undertakers, morgue assistants, pathologists) and once a rite of passage for medical students. Today, anatomy is increasingly taught through simulation and as surface and living anatomy (live bodies, such as artists' models). Cadaver dissection is getting more difficult as donated corpses are scarce. Some believe that the corpse must be buried whole, untouched. The Ancient Egyptians made a sensual feast of embalming and wrapping the body of royalty to send it on a journey to the other world, the sarcophagus as first-class cabin for the journey within the elite tomb as a private jet. Around the sarcophagus were multiple items for the journey – from plush furniture to food.

The boxed and bandaged royal person is configured as a travelling self in another world adjacent to this: embalmed and salted, wrapped in resin and cloth, and sent on the otherworld journey. The boxed body is accompanied by gold, clay, quartz, jasper-red and lapis-blue glass, turquoise glass, feldspar, animal skin, bronze, resin, ebony, ivory, shell, dried fruit, palm nuts, reed, papyrus, linen, alabaster, silver, granite, calcite, obsidian, gypsum, olive leaves, cornflowers, lotus petals, pomegranate, iron, silt, corn seed, amethyst, carnelian, serpentine, lapis-lazuli, steatite, turquoise, leather, sesame oil, sandstone, lead, tin, copper, chalk, galena, malachite, red and yellow ochres, frankincense, arsenic, wine, bread, garlic, meat, chickpeas, lentils, wheat, barley, juniper berries, peas, coriander, fenugreek, sesame, honey, dates, black cumin, grape juice, watermelon seeds, almonds, and an array of humming, winged perfumes.

When the Pharaoh dies, the brain is extracted through the nose and the skull's interior is washed with solvent followed by hot resin. The major organs of the body are removed and placed in canopic jars to accompany the corpse. The chambers of the body are sweetened with palm wine and spices, while the chest and belly are packed with linen pouches bursting

*The final straw: the self's last sip of life's juice* 185

with myrrh, garlic, and onions, thought to preserve the flesh. The remaining cavities are filled with sawdust and sealed with beeswax and then gold plate. Cedar oil, cumin, wax, and various unguent and pungent oils are rubbed into the skin, along with gums, milk, and wine. The skin shines in a mini rebirth and is further coated with spices to give it a pleasant odour for the journey ahead. The body is then set in resin, and the embalmer's job is nearly done. The priest then joins the embalmer in wrapping the body in linen, with the toes and fingers wrapped separately. The priest then shouts, 'You live again! You are young again! And forever!'

# Appendix
## The disposable self as 'worm'

There are bits of the bodily self that have been considered as redundant and can readily be discarded: a disposable self. The oldest definition of 'appendix' appears in English in the 1540s, and is derived from the Latin *appendere*, 'to cause to hang from something'. It referred to anything from a necklace pendant to a hanged man on the gallows, but primarily was used to describe supplementary material at the end of a book.

In the human body, the appendix is a thin tube that hangs from the large intestine. It rests in the lower right part of your belly or abdomen. Long thought to be vestigial, the appendix was regularly removed if it became inflamed. It was labelled as a useless object, an evolutionary hangover. Darwin believed that the appendix was an evolutionary anomaly, a leftover from when early human ancestors switched diets from leaf-based to fruit-based. Worse, in 1928 the American doctor Miles Breuer went on record as saying that people with infected appendices should be left to die, thus removing their inferior genes from the gene pool. Breuer called such people 'candidates for extinction'.

Nearly five hundred years passed between the first anatomical description of the appendix and knowledge of its function – still incomplete. An Italian surgeon based in Bologna, Berengario de Carpi, provided the first complete anatomical description of the appendix. Two hundred years later, in 1735, a French surgeon Claudius Amyand performed the first removal of the appendix, an appendectomy. But it was only at the turn of the millennium that the appendix's role was set out. The appendix provides a storehouse for a 'back up' batch of beneficial bacteria that can be released into the gastrointestinal (GI) tract should that stretch of gut become deficient in necessary gut flora. This function was outlined by a research group at Duke University, North Carolina in 2007.

Appendicitis, an inflamed appendix, can be life-threatening if the appendix bursts, and common practice has been to whip it out. Over 300,000 appendices are removed every year in the USA. But we know that as a young child the appendix is a functional part of the immune system,

Appendix 187

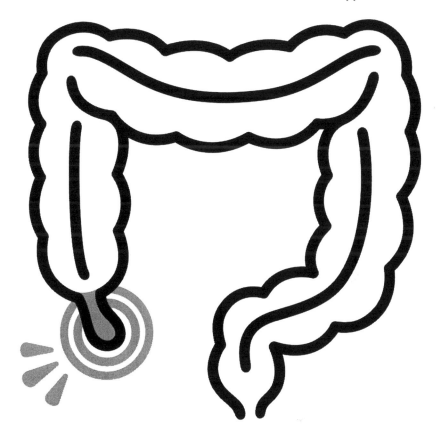

*Figure A.1* Appendix.

helping the body to fight disease. New thinking suggests that antibiotic treatment could be an alternative therapy to appendectomy.

New thinking also suggests that removing the appendix can raise risk for GI diseases such as colorectal cancer and irritable bowel syndrome. The appendix, also colloquially known as 'the worm', is a habitat for gut bacteria essential to the immune system response. These bacteria provide protection from a variety of conditions including ulcerative colitis and may play a part in preventing the development of colorectal cancer, and even Type 2 diabetes and the autoimmune disease lupus. One study of 258 species of mammals showed that those with an appendix live longer than those without. The possible explanation for this is that the appendix has a common role of preventing diarrhoea. This factor was particularly marked in primates, suggesting that it would apply to humans.

## 188  *Appendix*

The appendix might be an important organ in preventing human bowel problems. Young adult persons who had undergone an appendectomy have been compared with a matched population with an intact appendix and found to have double the risk of developing a serious infection with non-typhoidal *Salmonella* serious enough to require hospitalisation. The appendix may then act as a 'safe house' for gut bacteria that are beneficial. If the colon (a tube or pipe) becomes contaminated with a pathogen such as *Salmonella*, diarrhoea follows. The colon gets flushed repeatedly, wiping everything clean, including the resident gut microbiome. However, just off-set from the colon is the appendix, a haven for these positive microbiome organisms with a thick layer of 'good' bacteria. The flow through the colon does not manage to get into the appendix as the opening is restrictive. This microbiome collective can then repopulate the colon once the attack of diarrhoea is complete. Initial, albeit small scale, studies show that people who have had an appendectomy end up with a less diverse microbiome. While suggestive, such studies need to be carried out on larger populations to confirm or challenge these early findings.

Further, the appendix may serve as a preparatory stimulus for the rest of the immune system, where it is rich in 'M cells' that act as 'scouts' in first detecting and then immobilising invasive viruses and bacteria. These are then handed over to the more powerful T lymphocytes that do the heavy lifting of immunological defence. Initial studies suggest that removing the appendix may also reduce the population of CD3+ and CD8+ T cells, central to immune 'surveillance', where the immune system spots and acts to address potential harmful intrusions such as bacterial infections.

This 'worm' that is disposable, a throwaway self, may just be essential to health, and again antibiotics may be a good alternative treatment to surgery. The paradox is that extensive antibiotic use compromises the immune system generally. It may be that we should take probiotics along with antibiotics in case of treatment. In any case, Darwin was certainly wrong – the 'worm' is not useless. It is an essential part of bodily selfhood.

# Further reading

## Composite List

### A

Abrams D, Hogg MA. (Eds.) 1999. *Social Identity and Social Cognition*. Oxford: Blackwell.

Agamben G. 1999. *The Man without Content*. Stanford, CA: Stanford University Press.

Agamben G. 2004. *The Open: Man and Animal*. Stanford, CA: Stanford University Press.

Agamben G. 2005. *State of Exception*. Chicago, IL: University of Chicago Press.

Alcoff LM, Mendieta E. (Eds.) 2003. *Identities: Race, Class, Gender, and Nationality*. Oxford: Blackwell.

Ameriks K, Sturma D. (Eds.) 1995. *The Modern Subject: Conceptions of the Self in Classical German Philosophy*. New York: State University of New York (SUNY) Press.

Arikha N. 2022. *The Ceiling Outside: The Science and Experience of the Disrupted Mind*. London: Basic Books.

Arnold K, Peto J. Undated. *Identity & Identification*. London: Black Dog Publishing.

Ashley C. 1997. *Being on Line: Net Subjectivity*. New York: Lusitania Press.

### B

Badiou A. 2009. *Theory of the Subject*. London: Continuum.

Balsamo A. 1997. *Technologies of the Gendered Body: Reading Cyborg Women*. Durham, NC: Duke University Press.

Barfield O. 1926/1953. *History in English Words*. London: Faber & Faber.

Barker-Benfield GJ. 1992. *The Culture of Sensibility: Sex and Society in Eighteenth-Century Britain*. Chicago, IL: University of Chicago Press.

Barthes R. 1977. *Image, Music, Text*. London: Fontana Press.

Barthes R. 2013. *How to Live Together*. New York: Columbia University Press.

Bauman Z. 2004. *Identity*. Cambridge: Polity.

Bayer B, Shotter J. (Eds.) 1998. *Reconstructing the Psychological Subject: Bodies, Practices and Technologies*. London: Sage.

## 190  Further reading

Bell JA. 1998. *The Problem of Difference: Phenomenology and Poststructuralism.* Toronto: University of Toronto Press.

Bellah RN, Madsen R, Sullivan W, et al. 2008. *Habits of the Heart: Individualism and Commitment in American Life.* Berkeley: University of California Press.

Benhabib S. 1992. *Situating the Self: Gender, Community and Postmodernism in Contemporary Ethics.* Cambridge: Polity Press.

Bermúdez JL. 1998. *The Paradox of Self-Consciousness.* Cambridge: MIT Press.

Berryman, J. 1973. *Recovery.* London: Faber & Faber.

Binkley S, Capetillo-Ponce J. 2010. *A Foucault for the 21st Century: Governmentality, Biopolitics and Discipline in the New Millennium.* Newcastle Upon Tyne: Cambridge Scholars Press.

Blackburn S. 2014. *Mirror, Mirror: The Uses and Abuses of Self-Love.* Princeton, NJ: Princeton University Press.

Bless H, Fiedler K, Starck F. 2004. *Social Cognition: How Individuals Construct Social Reality.* Hove: Psychology Press.

Bogard W. 1996. *The Simulation of Surveillance: Hypercontrol in Telematic Societies.* Cambridge: CUP.

Bollas C. 2018. *The Shadow of the Object: Psychoanalysis of the Unknown Thought.* Abingdon: Routledge.

Bourdieu P. 2001. *Masculine Domination.* Stanford, CA: Stanford University Press.

Bracher M, et al. 1994. *Lacanian Theory of Discourse: Subject, Structure and Society.* New York: New York University Press.

Broadhead RS. 1983. *The Private Lives and Professional Identity of Medical Students.* New Brunswick, NJ: Transaction.

Brooks P. 2011. *Enigmas of Identity.* Princeton, NJ: Princeton UP.

Brothers L. 2001. *Mistaken Identity: The Mind-Brain Problem Reconsidered.* Albany: State University of New York (SUNY) Press.

Brown NO. 1966. *Love's Body.* New York: Random House.

Bruner J. 1986. *Actual Minds, Possible Worlds.* Cambridge, MA: Harvard University Press.

Burke C, Schor N, Whitford M. (Eds.) 1994. *Engaging with Irigaray.* New York: Columbia University Press.

Butler J. 1990. *Gender Trouble: Feminism and the Subversion of Identity.* London: Routledge.

Butler J. 1997. *The Psychic Life of Power.* Stanford, CA: Stanford University Press.

Butler J. 2005. *Giving an Account of Oneself.* New York: Fordham University Press.


## C

Cadava E, Connor P, Nancy J-L. (Eds.) 1991. *Who Comes after the Subject?* London: Routledge.

Calarco M, DeCaroli S. (Eds.) 2007. *Giorgio Agamben: Sovereignty & Life.* Stanford, CA: Stanford University Press.

Campbell J. 1989. *Renewal Myths and Rites of the Primitive Hunters and Planters.* Eranos Lectures 9. Dallas, TX: Spring Publications.

Capoza D, Brown R. (Eds.) 2000. *Social Identity Processes: Trends in Theory and Research.* London: Sage.

*Further reading* 191

Cascardi AJ. 1992. *The Subject of Modernity*. Cambridge: CUP.

Cixous H. 1991. *Coming to Writing and Other Essays*. Cambridge, MA: Harvard University Press.

Cixous H. 1991. *Promethea*. University of Nebraska Press.

Cixous H. 1992. *Readings*. Hemel Hempstead: Harvester Wheatsheaf.

Cixous H. 1993. *Three Steps on the Ladder of Writing*. New York: Columbia University Press.

Cixous H. 1998. *Stigmata: Escaping Texts*. London: Routledge.

Cixous H, Clément C. 1986. *The Newly Born Woman*. Minneapolis: University of Minnesota Press.

Cixous H, Calle-Gruber M. 1997. *Rootprints: Memory and Life Writing*. London: Routledge.

Clark A. 1997. *Being There: Putting Brain, Body, and the World Together Again*. Cambridge: MIT Press.

Clark A. 2008. *Supersizing the Mind: Embodiment, Action, and Cognitive Extension*. Oxford: OUP.

Clark A. 2016. *Surfing Uncertainty: Prediction, Action and the Embodied Mind*. Oxford: OUP.

Clark A. 2023. *The Experience Machine: How Our Minds Predict and Shape Reality*. London: Allen Lane.

Clément C. 1994. *Syncope: The Philosophy of Rapture*. Minneapolis: University of Minneapolis Press.

Cohen RA, Marsh JL. (Eds.) 2002. *Ricouer as Another: the Ethics of Subjectivity*. Albany: State University of New York (SUNY) Press.

Conrad P. 1998. *Modern Times, Modern Places: Life & Art in the Twentieth Century*. London: Thames & Hudson.

Copjec J. (Ed.) 1994. *Supposing the Subject*. London: Verso.

Costandi M. 2022. *Body Am I: The New Science of Self-Consciousness*. Cambridge: MIT Press.

Critchley S, Dews P. (Eds.) 1996. *Deconstructive Subjectivities*. Albany: State University of New York (SUNY) Press.

Crossley ML. 2000. *Introducing Narrative Psychology: Self, Trauma and the Construction of Meaning*. Buckingham: Open University Press.

Curry M. 2004. *Difference*. London: Routledge.


*D*

Davis C. 1996. *Levinas: An Introduction*. Cambridge: Polity Press.

DeLillo D. 2016. *Zero K*. London: Picador.

Derrida J. 2007. *Psyche: Inventions of the Other*. Vol. 1. Stanford, CA: Stanford University Press.


*E*

Eakin JP. 1999. *How Our Lives Become Stories: Making Selves*. Ithaca, NY: Cornell University Press.

Elias N. 2000. *The Civilizing Process* (2nd ed.). Oxford: Blackwell.

## 192 *Further reading*

Elkin L. 2016. *Flâneuse*. London: Penguin Books.

Ellemers N, Spears R, Doosje B. (Eds.) 1999. *Social Identity*. Oxford: Blackwell.

Elliott A. 1996. *Subject to Ourselves: Social Theory, Psychoanalysis and Postmodernity*. Oxford: Polity Press.

Engeström Y. 2008. *From Teams to Knots: Activity-Theoretical Studies of Collaboration and Learning at Work*. Cambridge: Cambridge University Press.

### F

Faubion JD. (Ed.) 1995. *Rethinking the Subject: An Anthology of Contemporary European Social Thought*. Boulder, CO: Westview Press.

Featherstone M. (Ed.) 2000. *Body Modification*. London: Sage.

Fink B. 1995. *The Lacanian Subject: Between Language and Jouissance*. Princeton, NJ: Princeton University Press.

Foucault M. 1985. *The Use of Pleasure: The History of Sexuality*. Vol. 2. London: Penguin.

Foucault M. 1986. *The History of Sexuality. Vol Three: The Care of the Self*. London: Penguin.

Foucault M. 1990. *The History of Sexuality*. Vol. 1: *An Introduction*. London: Penguin.

Foucault M. 1997. *Ethics*. London: Allen Lane, The Penguin Press.

Foucault M. 2001. *Fearless Speech*. Los Angeles, CA: SemiotextI.

Foucault M. 2005. *The Hermeneutics of the Subject: Lectures at the Collège de France 1981–1982*. New York, NY: Palgrave Macmillan.

Foucault M. 2010. *The Birth of Biopolitics: Lectures at the Collège de France 1978–1979*. London: Palgrave Macmillan.

Foucault M. 2011. *The Courage of Truth: The Government of Self and Others. Lectures at the Collège de France* 1983-1984. London: Palgrave Macmillan.

Freeman M. 1993. *Rewriting the Self: History, Memory, Narrative*. London: Routledge.

Freeman J. 2015. *Remaking Memory: Autoethnography, Memoir and the Ethics of Self*. Faringdon: Libri.

Freud S. 1962. *The Ego and the Id*. London: Hogarth Press.

Frueh J. 1996. *Erotic Faculties*. Berkley: University of California Press.

Fryer DR. 2004. *The Intervention of the Other: Ethical Subjectivity in Levinas and Lacan*. New York: Other Press.

### G

Gasché R. 1986. *The Tain of the Mirror: Derrida and the Philosophy of Reflection*. Cambridge, MA: Harvard University Press.

Gay P. 2007. *Modernism: The Lure of Heresy*. London: William Heinemann.

Geary J. 2011. *I Is an Other: The Secret Life of Metaphor and How It Shapes the Way We See the World*. New York: Harper Perennial.

Gent L, Llewellyn N. (Eds.) 1990. *Renaissance Bodies: The Human Figure in English Culture c.1540-1660*. London: Reaktion Books.

Gergen KJ. 2001. *Social Construction in Context*. London: Sage Publications.

Further reading   193

Ginzburg C. 1980. *The Cheese and the Worms: The Cosmos of a Sixteenth-Century Miller*. New York: Dorset Press.

Glover J. 1988. *I: The Philosophy and Psychology of Personal Identity*. London: Penguin.

Glück L. 2017. *American Originality: Essays on Poetry*. New York: Farrar, Strauss & Giroux.

Goffman E. 1956. *The Presentation of Self in Everyday Life*. London: Pelican.

Granta 39. 1992. *The Body*. London: Granta Books.

Greenblatt S. 1980. *Renaissance Self-Fashioning: From More to Shakespeare*. Chicago, IL: University of Chicago Press.

Greenfield S. 2011. *You and Me: The Neuroscience of Identity*. London: Notting Hill Editions.

## H

Haig D. 2020. *From Darwin to Derrida: Selfish Genes, Social Selves, and the Meanings of Lives*. Cambridge: MIT Press.

Hamachek DE. 1987. *Encounters with the Self*. New York: Holt, Rinehart and Winston.

Hans JS. 1995. *The Site of Our Lives: The Self and the Subject from Emerson to Foucault*. Albany: State University of New York (SUNY) Press.

Haraway D. Situated Knowledges: The Science Question in Feminism and the Privilege of Partial Perspective. *Feminist Studies*. 1988;14:575–99.

Haraway DJ. 1991. *Simians, Cyborgs and Women: The Reinvention of Nature*. London: Routledge.

Haraway DJ. 1997. *Modest_Witness@Second_Millenium. Female_Man©_Meets_Oncomouse™: Feminism and Technoscience*. London: Routledge.

Harré R. 1984. *Personal Being: A Theory for Individual Psychology*. Cambridge, MA: Harvard University Press.

Harré R. 1998. *The Singular Self: An Introduction to the Psychology of Personhood*. London: Sage.

Hayles NK. 1999. *How We Became Posthuman: Virtual Bodies in Cybernetics, Literature, and Informatics*. Chicago, IL: University of Chicago Press.

Hecht JM. 2003. *The End of the Soul: Scientific Modernity, Atheism, and Anthropology in France*. New York: Columbia University Press.

Henriques J, et al. (Eds.) 1984. *Changing the Subject: Psychology, Social Regulation and Subjectivity*. London: Routledge.

Hillman J. 1980. *Egalitarian Typologies versus the Perception of the Unique: Eranos Lectures 4*. Dallas, TX: Spring Publications.

Holland R. 1977. *Self & Social Context*. London: Macmillan.

Holland NN. 1992. *The Critical I*. New York: Columbia University Press.

## I

Illouz E. 2007. Cold *Intimacies: The Making of Emotional Capitalism*. Cambridge: Polity Press.

Irigaray L. 1985. *The Sex Which Is Not One*. Ithaca, NY: Cornell University Press.

## 194  Further reading

Irigaray L. 1991. *Marine Lover of Friedrich Nietzsche*. New York: Columbia University Press.
Irigaray L. 1992. *Elemental Passions*. London: The Athlone Press.
Irigaray L. 1993. *je, tu, nous: Toward a Culture of Difference*. New York: Routledge.
Irigaray L. 1999. *The Forgetting of Air*. London: The Athlone Press.
Ives K. 2007. *Cixous, Irigaray, Kristeva: The Jouissance of French Feminism* (2nd ed.). Maidstone: Crescent Moon Publishing.


### K

Kant I. 1934. *Critique of Pure Reason*. London: JM Dent.
Kapuscinski R. 2008. *The Other*. London: Verso.
Kiesler CA, Kiesler SB. 1970. *Conformity*. Reading, MA: Addison-Wesley.
Kirsch A. 2023. *The Revolt against Humanity: Imagining a Future without Us*. New York: Columbia Global Reports.
Klemm DE, Zöller G. (Eds.) 1997. *Figuring the Self: Subject, Absolute, and Others in Classical German Philosophy*. Albany: State University of New York (SUNY) Press.
Krakauer EL. 1998. *The Disposition of the Subject: Reading Adorno's Dialectic of Technology*. Evanston, IL: Northwestern University Press.
Kristeva J. 1982. *Powers of Horror: An Essay on Abjection*. New York: Columbia University Press.
Kristeva J. 1991. *Strangers to Ourselves*. New York: Columbia University Press.
Kristeva J. 2017. *The Enchanted Clock*. New York: Columbia University Press.
Kristeva J. 2018. *Passions of Our Time*. New York: Columbia University Press.


### L

Lacquer T. 1992. *Making Sex: Body and Gender From the Greeks to Freud*. Cambridge, MA: Harvard University Press.
Lieberman MD. 2013. *Social: Why Our Brains Are Wired to Connect*. Oxford: OUP.
Lingis A. 2005. *Body Transformations: Evolutions and Atavisms in Culture*. New York: Routledge.
Lacan J. 1977. *Écrits: A Selection*. London: Tavistock Publications.
Lacan J. 1977. *The Four Fundamental Concepts of Psychoanalysis*. London: Penguin Books.
Lacoue-Labarthe P. 1993. *The Subject of Philosophy*. Minneapolis: University of Minnesota Press.
Lasch C. 1979. *The Culture of Narcissism: American Life in an Age of Diminishing Expectations*. New York: WW Norton.
Lee P, Goldberg C, Kohane I. 2023. *The AI Revolution in Medicine: GPT-4 and Beyond*. London: Pearson.
Levin DM. 1985. *Phenomenological Psychology and the Deconstruction of Nihilism*. London: Routledge & Kegan Paul.
Levin DM. 1988. *The Opening of Vision: Nihilism and the Postmodern Situation*. London: Routledge.

Levinas E. 1998. *Otherwise Than Being: Or Beyond Essence*. Pittsburgh, PA: Duquesne University Press.

Levinas E. 2006. *Humanism of the Other*. Urbana & Chicago: University of Illinois Press.

Lilly J. 1972. *The Centre of the Cyclone*. London: Paladin.

Lipsky D. 2010. *Although of Course You End Up Becoming Yourself: A Road Trip with David Foster Wallace*. New York: Broadway Books.

Lowes JL. 1951. *The Road to Xanadu: A Study in the Ways of the Imagination*. London: Constable.

## M

MacMurray J. 1961. *Persons in Relation*. London: Faber.

Marar Z. 2012. *Intimacy*. Durham: Acumen.

Marcus L. 1994. *Auto/biographical Discourses: Theory, Criticism, Practice*. Manchester: Manchester University Press.

Matthews PR, McWhirter D. (Eds.) 2003. *Aesthetic Subjects*. Minneapolis: University of Minnesota Press.

Meyers DT. 1994. *Subjection and Subjectivity: Psychoanalytic Feminism and Moral Philosophy*. London: Routledge.

Mithen S. 2024. *The Language Puzzle: How We Talked Our Way Out of the Stone Age*. London: Profile Books.

Mlodinow L. 2012. *Subliminal: The Revolution of the New Unconscious and What It Teaches Us about Ourselves*. London: Allen Lane.

Moore HL. 1994. *A Passion for Difference*. Oxford: Polity Press.

Moore HL. (Ed.) 1999. *Anthropological Theory Today*. Cambridge: Polity Press.

Morris B. 1994. *Anthropology of the Self: The Individual in Cultural Perspective*. London: Pluto Press.

Mukherjee S. 2022. *The Song of the Cell: An Exploration of Medicine and the New Human*. London: Random House.

## N

Nicolson A. 2019. *The Making of Poetry: Coleridge, the Wordsworths and Their Year of Marvels*. London: William Collins.

Nietzsche F. 1984. *Human, All Too Human: A Book for Free Spirits*. Lincoln: University of Nebraska Press.

Nietzsche F. 1956. *The Birth of Tragedy & The Genealogy of Morals*. New York: Anchor Books/Doubleday.

Nietzsche, F. 1968. *The Will to Power*. New York: Vintage/Random House.

Norris M. 1985. *Beasts of the Modern Imagination: Darwin, Nietzsche, Kafka, Ernst, & Lawrence*. Baltimore, MD: The Johns Hopkins University Press.

Nussbaum FA. 1989. *The Autobiographical Subject: Gender and Ideology in Eighteenth-Century England*. Baltimore, MA: The Johns Hopkins University Press.

# 196  *Further reading*

## O

Oatley K. 1984. *Selves in Relation: An Introduction to Psychotherapy and Groups.* London: Methuen.

Oliver T. 2020. *The Self Delusion: The Surprising Science of How We Are Connected and Why That Matters.* London: Weidenfeld & Nicolson.

## P

Paechter C, et al. (Eds.) 2001. *Learning, Space and Identity.* London: Sage.

Pagel M. 2012. *Wired for Culture: The Natural History of Human Cooperation.* London: Penguin.

Parfit D. 1984. *Reasons and Persons.* Oxford: Clarendon Press.

Park K. 2006. *Secrets of Women: Gender, Generation, and the Origins of Human Dissection.* New York: Zone Books.

Pesic P. 2002. *Seeing Double: Shared Identities in Physics, Philosophy, and Literature.* Cambridge: MIT Press.

Polanyi M. 1983. *The Tacit Dimension.* Gloucester: MA, Peter Smith.

Porter R. (Ed.) 1997. *Rewriting the Self: Histories from the Renaissance to the Present.* London: Routledge.

Portmann A. 1948. *Animal Forms and Patterns: A Study of the Appearance of Animals.* London: Faber and Faber.

Portmann A. 1959. *Animal Camouflage.* Ann Arbor: University of Michigan Press.

Poster M. 2001. *The Information Subject.* Amsterdam: G+B Arts International.

Pyle F. 1995. *The Ideology of Imagination: Subject and Society in the Discourse of Romanticism.* Stanford, CA: Stanford University Press.

## R

Reber AS. 1993. *Implicit Learning and Tacit Knowledge: An Essay on the Cognitive Unconscious.* Oxford: Oxford University Press.

Reber AS, Allen R. (Eds.) 2022. *The Cognitive Unconscious: The First Half Century.* New York: Oxford University Press.

Redgrove P. 1979. *The Sleep of the Great Hypnotist.* London: Routledge & Kegan Paul.

Regosin RL. 1977. *The Matter of My Book: Montaigne's Essais as the Book of the Self.* Berkeley: University of California Press.

Renaut A. 1997. *The Era of the Individual: A Contribution to the History of Subjectivity.* Princeton, NJ: Princeton University Press.

Richards RJ. 2002. *The Romantic Conception of Life: Science and Philosophy in the Age of Goethe.* Chicago, IL: The University of Chicago Press.

Ricoeur P. 2005. *The Course of Recognition.* Cambridge, MA: Harvard University Press.

Roberts N. 2012. *A Lucid Dreamer: The Life of Peter Redgrove.* London: Jonathan Cape.

*Further reading* 197

Roma V et al. 2009. *The Unavowable Community*. Institut Ramon Lull.
Romanyshyn RD. 1989. *Technology as Symptom and Dream*. London: Routledge.
Romero M. 2018. *Introducing Intersectionality*. Cambridge: Polity Press.
Rose N. 1996. *Inventing Our Selves: Psychology, Power and Personhood*. Cambridge: CUP.
Ryan J. 1991. *The Vanishing Subject: Early Psychology and Literary Modernism*. Chicago, IL: The University of Chicago Press.

### S

Sadoff DF. 1998. *Sciences of the Flesh: Representing Body and Subject in Psychoanalysis*. Stanford, CA: Stanford University Press.
Sartre J-P. 1957. The *Transcendence of the Ego: An Existential Theory of Consciousness*. New York: Noonday Press.
Sartre J-P. 1969. *Being and Nothingness*. London: Methuen.
Sartwell C. 2004. *Six Names of Beauty*. London: Routledge.
Sass L. 1992. *Madness and Modernism: Insanity in the Light of Modern Art, Literature, and Thought*. Cambridge, MA: Harvard University Press.
Schmidt J. (Ed.) 1996. *What is Enlightenment? Eighteenth-Century Answers and Twentieth-Century Questions*. Berkeley: University of California Press.
Schrag CO. 1997. *The Self after Postmodernity*. New Haven, CT: Yale University Press.
Sellers S. (Ed.) 1994. *The Helene Cixous Reader*. London: Routledge.
Sennett R. 2011. *The Foreigner: Two Essays on Exile*. London: Notting Hill Editions.
Sennett R. 2012. *Together: The Rituals, Pleasures and Politics of Cooperation*. London: Allen Lane.
Siedentop L. 2015. *Inventing the Original: The Origins of Western Liberalism*. London: Penguin Books.
Smith R. 1995. *Derrida and Autobiography*. Cambridge: CUP.
Sparrow T. 2014. *The End of Phenomenology: Metaphysics and the New Realism*. Edinburgh: Edinburgh University Press.
Steele M. 1997. *Theorizing Textual Subjects: Agency & Oppression*. Cambridge: CUP.
Storr W. 2017. *Selfie: How We Became So Self-obsessed and What It's Doing to Us*. London: Picador
Surowiecki J. 2005. *The Wisdom of Crowds: Why the Many Are Smarter Than the Few*. London: Abacus.

### T

Tauber A. 2022. *The Triumph of Uncertainty: Science and Self in the Postmodern Age*. Budapest: Central European University Press.
Taylor D, Vintges K. (Eds.) 2004. *Feminism and the Final Foucault*. Chicago: University of Illinois Press.
Tester K. (Ed.) 1994. *The Flâneur*. London: Routledge.
Trueit D. (Ed.) 2012. *Pragmatism, Post-Modernism, and Complexity Theory: The "Fascinating Imaginative Realm" of William E. Doll, Jr*. London: Routledge.

## 198  *Further reading*

### V

Varela FJ, Thompson E, Rosch E. 2016. *The Embodied Mind: Cognitive Science and Human Experience* (2nd ed.). Cambridge: MIT Press.
Vila-Cabanes I. 2018. *The Flaneur in Nineteenth-Century British Literary Culture: "The Worlds of London Unknown"*. Newcastle-Upon-Tyne: Cambridge Scholars Publishing.

### W

Wetherell M. (Ed.) 1996. *Identities, Groups and Social Issues*. London: Sage.
White M, White L. 1964. *The Intellectual versus the City*. New York: Mentor.
Whitford M. 1991. *Luce Irigaray: Philosophy in the Feminine*. London: Routledge.
Williams J. 2017. *The Visiting Privilege*. London: Serpent's Tail.

## By Topics

### Archaeology

Mithen S. 2024. *The Language Puzzle: How We Talked Our Way Out of the Stone Age*. London: Profile Books.

### Anthropology

Campbell J. 1989. *Renewal Myths and Rites of the Primitive Hunters and Planters*. Eranos Lectures 9. Dallas, TX: Spring Publications.
Kapuscinski R. 2008. *The Other*. London: Verso.
Moore HL. 1994. *A Passion for Difference*. Oxford: Polity Press.
Moore HL. (Ed.) 1999. *Anthropological Theory Today*. Cambridge: Polity Press.
Morris B. 1994. *Anthropology of the Self: The Individual in Cultural Perspective*. London: Pluto Press.
Vila-Cabanes I. 2018. *The Flaneur in Nineteenth-Century British Literary Culture: "The Worlds of London Unknown"*. Newcastle-Upon-Tyne: Cambridge Scholars Publishing.

### Biology

Arikha N. 2022. *The Ceiling Outside: The Science and Experience of the Disrupted Mind*. London: Basic Books.
Brothers L. 2001. *Mistaken Identity: The Mind-Brain Problem Reconsidered*. Albany: State University of New York (SUNY) Press.
Costandi M. 2022. *Body Am I: The New Science of Self-Consciousness*. Cambridge: MIT Press.
Greenfield S. 2011. *You and Me: The Neuroscience of Identity*. London: Notting Hill Editions.
Haig D. 2020. *From Darwin to Derrida: Selfish Genes, Social Selves, and the Meanings of Lives*. Cambridge: MIT Press.
Lieberman MD. 2013. *Social: Why Our Brains are Wired to Connect*. Oxford: OUP.

*Further reading* 199

Mukherjee S. 2022. *The Song of the Cell: An Exploration of Medicine and the New Human*. London: Random House.

Portmann A. 1948. *Animal Forms and Patterns: A Study of the Appearance of Animals*. London: Faber and Faber.

Portmann A. 1959. *Animal Camouflage*. Ann Arbor: University of Michigan Press.

Tauber A. 2022. *The Triumph of Uncertainty: Science and Self in the Postmodern Age*. Budapest: Central European University Press.

### Contemporary Cognitive Psychology

Clark A. 1997. *Being There: Putting Brain, Body, and the World Together Again*. Cambridge: MIT Press.

Clark A. 2008. *Supersizing the Mind: Embodiment, Action, and Cognitive Extension*. Oxford: OUP.

Clark A. 2016. *Surfing Uncertainty: Prediction, Action and the Embodied Mind*. Oxford: OUP.

Clark A. 2023. *The Experience Machine: How Our Minds Predict and Shape Reality*. London: Allen Lane.

Mlodinow L. 2012. *Subliminal: The Revolution of the New Unconscious and What It Teaches Us about Ourselves*. London: Allen Lane.

Polanyi M. 1983. *The Tacit Dimension*. Gloucester: MA, Peter Smith.

Reber AS. 1993. *Implicit Learning and Tacit Knowledge: An Essay on the Cognitive Unconscious*. Oxford: Oxford University Press.

Reber AS, Allen R. (Eds.) 2022. *The Cognitive Unconscious: The First Half Century*. New York: Oxford University Press.

Varela FJ, Thompson E, Rosch E. 2016. *The Embodied Mind: Cognitive Science and Human Experience* (2nd ed.). Cambridge: MIT Press.

### Cultural Studies

Alcoff LM, Mendieta E. (Eds.) 2003. *Identities: Race, Class, Gender, and Nationality*. Oxford: Blackwell.

Barthes R. 1977. *Image, Music, Text*. London: Fontana Press.

Barthes R. 2013. *How to Live Together*. New York: Columbia University Press.

Bauman Z. 2004. *Identity*. Cambridge: Polity.

Binkley S, Capetillo-Ponce J. 2010. *A Foucault for the 21st Century: Governmentality, Biopolitics and Discipline in the New Millennium*. Newcastle Upon Tyne: Cambridge Scholars Press.

Broadhead RS. 1983. *The Private Lives and Professional Identity of Medical Students*. New Brunswick, NJ: Transaction.

Brooks P. 2011. *Enigmas of Identity*. Princeton, NJ: Princeton UP.

Copjec J. (Ed.) 1994. *Supposing the Subject*. London: Verso.

Faubion JD. (Ed.) 1995. *Rethinking the Subject: An Anthology of Contemporary European Social Thought*. Boulder, CO: Westview Press.

Featherstone M. (Ed.) 2000. *Body Modification*. London: Sage.

Foucault M. 1985. *The Use of Pleasure: The History of Sexuality*. Vol. 2. London: Penguin.

## 200    Further reading

Foucault M. 1986. *The History of Sexuality. Vol Three: The Care of the Self*. London: Penguin.

Foucault M. 1990. *The History of Sexuality*. Vol. 1: *An Introduction*. London: Penguin.

Foucault M. 1997. *Ethics*. London: Allen Lane, The Penguin Press.

Foucault M. 2001. *Fearless Speech*. Los Angeles, CA: Semiotext(e).

Foucault M. 2005. *The Hermeneutics of the Subject: Lectures at the Collège de France 1981–1982*. New York, NY: Palgrave Macmillan.

Foucault M. 2010. *The Birth of Biopolitics: Lectures at the Collège de France 1978–1979*. London: Palgrave Macmillan.

Foucault M. 2011. *The Courage of Truth: The Government of Self and Others. Lectures at the Collège de France 1983–1984*. London: Palgrave Macmillan.

Haraway D. Situated Knowledges: The Science Question in Feminism and the Privilege of Partial Perspective. *Feminist Studies*. 1988;14:575–99.

Kirsch A. 2023. *The Revolt against Humanity: Imagining a Future without Us*. New York: Columbia Global Reports.

Lingis A. 2005. *Body Transformations: Evolutions and Atavisms in Culture*. New York: Routledge.

Matthews PR, McWhirter D. (Eds.) 2003. *Aesthetic Subjects*. Minneapolis: University of Minnesota Press.

Norris M. 1985. *Beasts of the Modern Imagination: Darwin, Nietzsche, Kafka, Ernst, & Lawrence*. Baltimore, MD: The Johns Hopkins University Press.

Oliver T. 2020. *The Self Delusion: The Surprising Science of How We Are Connected and Why That Matters*. London: Weidenfeld & Nicolson.

Pagel M. 2012. *Wired for Culture: The Natural History of Human Cooperation*. London: Penguin.

Pesic P. 2002. *Seeing Double: Shared Identities in Physics, Philosophy, and Literature*. Cambridge: MIT Press.

Romero M. 2018. *Introducing Intersectionality*. Cambridge: Polity Press.

Sartwell C. 2004. *Six Names of Beauty*. London: Routledge.

Sass L. 1992. *Madness and Modernism: Insanity in the Light of Modern Art, Literature, and Thought*. Cambridge, MA: Harvard University Press.

Sennett R. 2012. *Together: The Rituals, Pleasures and Politics of Cooperation*. London: Allen Lane.

Steele M. 1997. *Theorizing Textual Subjects: Agency & Oppression*. Cambridge: CUP.

White M, White L. 1964. *The Intellectual versus the City*. New York: Mentor.


### *Feminisms*

Balsamo A. 1997. *Technologies of the Gendered Body: Reading Cyborg Women*. Durham, NC: Duke University Press.

Benhabib S. 1992. *Situating the Self: Gender, Community and Postmodernism in Contemporary Ethics*. Cambridge: Polity Press.

Bourdieu P. 2001. *Masculine Domination*. Stanford, CA: Stanford University Press.

Burke C, Schor N, Whitford M. (Eds.) 1994. *Engaging with Irigaray*. New York: Columbia University Press.

## Further reading    201

Butler J. 1990. *Gender Trouble: Feminism and the Subversion of Identity*. London: Routledge.

Butler J. 1997. *The Psychic Life of Power*. Stanford, CA: Stanford University Press.

Butler J. 2005. *Giving an Account of Oneself*. New York: Fordham University Press.

Cixous H. 1991. *Coming to Writing and Other Essays*. Cambridge, MA: Harvard University Press.

Cixous H. 1991. *Promethea*. University of Nebraska Press.

Cixous H. 1992. *Readings*. Hemel Hempstead: Harvester Wheatsheaf.

Cixous H. 1993. *Three Steps on the Ladder of Writing*. New York: Columbia University Press.

Cixous H. 1998. *Stigmata: Escaping Texts*. London: Routledge.

Cixous H, Clément C. 1986. *The Newly Born Woman*. Minneapolis: University of Minnesota Press.

Cixous H, Calle-Gruber M. 1997. *Rootprints: Memory and Life Writing*. London: Routledge.

Clément C. 1994. *Syncope: The Philosophy of Rapture*. Minneapolis: University of Minneapolis Press.

Elkin L. 2016. *Flâneuse*. London: Penguin Books.

Frueh J. 1996. *Erotic Faculties*. Berkley: University of California Press.

Haraway DJ. 1991. *Simians, Cyborgs and Women: The Reinvention of Nature*. London: Routledge.

Irigaray L. 1985. *The Sex Which Is Not One*. Ithaca, NY: Cornell University Press.

Irigaray L. 1991. *Marine Lover of Friedrich Nietzsche*. New York: Columbia University Press.

Irigaray L. 1992. *Elemental Passions*. London: The Athlone Press.

Irigaray L. 1993. *je, tu, nous: Toward a Culture of Difference*. New York: Routledge.

Irigaray L. 1999. *The Forgetting of Air*. London: The Athlone Press.

Ives K. 2007. *Cixous, Irigaray, Kristeva: The Jouissance of French Feminism* (2nd ed.). Maidstone: Crescent Moon Publishing.

Kristeva J. 1982. *Powers of Horror: An Essay on Abjection*. New York: Columbia University Press.

Kristeva J. 1991. *Strangers to Ourselves*. New York: Columbia University Press.

Kristeva J. 2018. *Passions of Our Time*. New York: Columbia University Press.

Meyers DT. 1994. *Subjection and Subjectivity: Psychoanalytic Feminism and Moral Philosophy*. London: Routledge.

Nussbaum FA. 1989. *The Autobiographical Subject: Gender and Ideology in Eighteenth-Century England*. Baltimore, MA: The Johns Hopkins University Press.

Park K. 2006. *Secrets of Women: Gender, Generation, and the Origins of Human Dissection*. New York: Zone Books.

Sellers S. (Ed.) 1994. *The Helene Cixous Reader*. London: Routledge.

Taylor D, Vintges K. (Eds.) 2004. *Feminism and the Final Foucault*. Chicago: University of Illinois Press.

Whitford M. 1991. *Luce Irigaray: Philosophy in the Feminine*. London: Routledge.

202   *Further reading*

## History

Barker-Benfield GJ. 1992. *The Culture of Sensibility: Sex and Society in Eighteenth-Century Britain*. Chicago, IL: University of Chicago Press.

Conrad P. 1998. *Modern Times, Modern Places: Life & Art in the Twentieth Century*. London: Thames & Hudson.

Elias N. 2000. *The Civilizing Process* (2nd ed.). Oxford: Blackwell.

Gay P. 2007. *Modernism: The Lure of Heresy*. London: William Heinemann.

Gent L, Llewellyn N. (Eds.) 1990. *Renaissance Bodies: The Human Figure in English Culture c.1540–1660*. London: Reaktion Books.

Ginzburg C. 1980. *The Cheese and the Worms: The Cosmos of a Sixteenth-Century Miller*. New York: Dorset Press.

Greenblatt S. 1980. *Renaissance Self-Fashioning: From More to Shakespeare*. Chicago, IL: University of Chicago Press.

Hecht JM. 2003. *The End of the Soul: Scientific Modernity, Atheism, and Anthropology in France*. New York: Columbia University Press.

Lacquer T. 1992. *Making Sex: Body and Gender from the Greeks to Freud*. Cambridge, MA: Harvard University Press.

Porter R. (Ed.) 1997. *Rewriting the Self: Histories from the Renaissance to the Present*. London: Routledge.

Pyle F. 1995. *The Ideology of Imagination: Subject and Society in the Discourse of Romanticism*. Stanford, CA: Stanford University Press.

Regosin RL. 1977. *The Matter of My Book: Montaigne's Essais as the Book of the Self*. Berkeley: University of California Press.

Richards RJ. 2002. *The Romantic Conception of Life: Science and Philosophy in the Age of Goethe*. Chicago, IL: The University of Chicago Press.

Sennett R. 2011. *The Foreigner: Two Essays on Exile*. London: Notting Hill Editions.

Siedentop L. 2015. *Inventing the Original: The Origins of Western Liberalism*. London: Penguin Books.

## Literature/Literary Criticism

Barfield O. 1926/1953. *History in English Words*. London: Faber & Faber.

Berryman, J. 1973. *Recovery*. London: Faber & Faber.

Cascardi AJ. 1992. *The Subject of Modernity*. Cambridge: CUP.

Crossley ML. 2000. *Introducing Narrative Psychology: Self, Trauma and the Construction of Meaning*. Buckingham: Open University Press.

DeLillo D. 2016. *Zero K*. London: Picador.

Eakin JP. 1999. *How Our Lives Become Stories: Making Selves*. Ithaca, NY: Cornell University Press.

Freeman J. 2015. *Remaking Memory: Autoethnography, Memoir and the Ethics of Self*. Faringdon: Libri.

Geary J. 2011. *I Is an Other: The Secret Life of Metaphor and How It Shapes the Way We See the World*. New York: Harper Perennial.

Further reading 203

Glück L. 2017. *American Originality: Essays on Poetry*. New York: Farrar, Strauss & Giroux.

Granta 39. 1992. *The Body*. London: Granta Books.

Kristeva J. 2017. *The Enchanted Clock*. New York: Columbia University Press.

Lipsky D. 2010. *Although of Course You End Up Becoming Yourself: A Road Trip with David Foster Wallace*. New York: Broadway Books.

Lowes JL. 1951. *The Road to Xanadu: A Study in the Ways of the Imagination*. London: Constable.

Marcus L. 1994. *Auto/biographical Discourses: Theory, Criticism, Practice*. Manchester: Manchester University Press.

Nicolson A. 2019. *The Making of Poetry: Coleridge, the Wordsworths and Their Year of Marvels*. London: William Collins.

Redgrove P. 1979. *The Sleep of the Great Hypnotist*. London: Routledge & Kegan Paul.

Roberts N. 2012. *A Lucid Dreamer: The Life of Peter Redgrove*. London: Jonathan Cape.

Ryan J. 1991. *The Vanishing Subject: Early Psychology and Literary Modernism*. Chicago, IL: The University of Chicago Press.

Williams J. *The Visiting Privilege*. 2017. London: Serpent's Tail.

### New Technologies

Ashley C. Undated. *Being On Line: Net Subjectivities*. New York: Lusitania Press.

Bogard W. 1996. *The Simulation of Surveillance: Hypercontrol in Telematic Societies*. Cambridge: CUP.

Haraway DJ. 1997. *Modest_Witness@Second_Millenium. Female_Man©_Meets_ Oncomouse™: Feminism and Technoscience*. London: Routledge.

Hayles NK. 1999. *How We Became Posthuman: Virtual Bodies in Cybernetics, Literature, and Informatics*. Chicago, IL: University of Chicago Press.

Krakauer EL. 1998. *The Disposition of the Subject: Reading Adorno's Dialectic of Technology*. Evanston, IL: Northwestern University Press.

Lilly J. 1972. *The Centre of the Cyclone*. London: Paladin.

Poster M. 2001. *The Information Subject*. Amsterdam: G+B Arts International.

Trueit D. (Ed.) 2012. *Pragmatism, Post-Modernism, and Complexity Theory: The "Fascinating Imaginative Realm" of William E. Doll, Jr*. London: Routledge.

### Philosophy

Agamben G. 1999. *The Man without Content*. Stanford, CA: Stanford University Press.

Agamben G. 2004. *The Open: Man and Animal*. Stanford, CA: Stanford University Press.

Agamben G. 2005. *State of Exception*. Chicago, IL: University of Chicago Press.

Ameriks K, Sturma D. (Eds.) 1995. *The Modern Subject: Conceptions of the Self in Classical German Philosophy*. New York: State University of New York (SUNY) Press.

## 204  *Further reading*

Badiou A. 2009. *Theory of the Subject*. London: Continuum.

Bell JA. 1998. *The Problem of Difference: Phenomenology and Poststructuralism*. Toronto: University of Toronto Press.

Cadava E, Connor P, Nancy J-L. (Eds.) 1991. *Who Comes after the Subject?* London: Routledge.

Calarco M, DeCaroli S. (Eds.) 2007. *Giorgio Agamben: Sovereignty & Life*. Stanford, CA: Stanford University Press.

Cohen RA, Marsh JL. (Eds.) 2002. *Ricouer as Another: The Ethics of Subjectivity*. Albany: State University of New York (SUNY) Press.

Critchley S, Dews P. (Eds.) 1996. *Deconstructive Subjectivities*. Albany: State University of New York (SUNY) Press.

Curry M. 2004. *Difference*. London: Routledge.

Davis C. 1996. *Levinas: An Introduction*. Cambridge: Polity Press.

Derrida J. 2007. *Psyche: Inventions of the Other*. Vol. 1. Stanford, CA: Stanford University Press.

Fryer DR. 2004. *The Intervention of the Other: Ethical Subjectivity in Levinas and Lacan*. New York: Other Press.

Gasché R. 1986. *The Tain of the Mirror: Derrida and the Philosophy of Reflection*. Cambridge, MA: Harvard University Press.

Hans JS. 1995. *The Site of Our Lives: The Self and the Subject from Emerson to Foucault*. Albany: State University of New York (SUNY) Press.

Holland NN. 1992. *The Critical I*. New York: Columbia University Press.

Illouz E. 2007.Cold *Intimacies: The Making of Emotional Capitalism*. Cambridge: Polity Press.

Kant I. 1934. *Critique of Pure Reason*. London: JM Dent.

Klemm DE, Zöller G. (Eds.) 1997. *Figuring the Self: Subject, Absolute, and Others in Classical German Philosophy*. Albany: State University of New York (SUNY) Press.

Lacoue-Labarthe P. 1993. *The Subject of Philosophy*. Minneapolis: University of Minnesota Press.

Levin DM. 1985. *Phenomenological Psychology and the Deconstruction of Nihilism*. London: Routledge & Kegan Paul.

Levin DM. 1988. *The Opening of Vision: Nihilism and the Postmodern Situation*. London: Routledge.

Levinas E. 1998. *Otherwise than Being: Or Beyond Essence*. Pittsburgh, PA: Duquesne University Press.

Levinas E. 2006. *Humanism of the Other*. Urbana & Chicago: University of Illinois Press.

Nietzsche F. 1956. *The Birth of Tragedy & The Genealogy of Morals*. New York: Anchor Books/Doubleday.

Nietzsche, F. 1968. *The Will to Power*. New York: Vintage/Random House.

Nietzsche F. 1984. *Human, All Too Human: A Book for Free Spirits*. Lincoln: University of Nebraska Press.

Parfit D. 1984. *Reasons and Persons*. Oxford: Clarendon Press.

Renaut A. 1997. *The Era of the Individual: A Contribution to the History of Subjectivity*. Princeton, NJ: Princeton University Press.

Ricoeur P. 2005. *The Course of Recognition*. Cambridge, MA: Harvard University Press.

Further reading   205

Roma V. 2009. *The Unavowable Community*. Institut Ramon Lull.

Sartre J-P. 1957. The *Transcendence of the Ego: An Existential Theory of Consciousness*. New York: Noonday Press.

Sartre J-P. 1969. *Being and Nothingness*. London: Methuen.

Schmidt J. (Ed.) 1996. *What Is Enlightenment? Eighteenth-Century Answers and Twentieth-Century Questions*. Berkeley: University of California Press.

Schrag CO. 1997. *The Self after Postmodernity*. New Haven, CT: Yale University Press.

Smith R. 1995. *Derrida and Autobiography*. Cambridge: CUP.

Sparrow T. 2014. *The End of Phenomenology: Metaphysics and the New Realism*. Edinburgh: Edinburgh University Press.

### Psychoanalysis

Bollas C. 2018. *The Shadow of the Object: Psychoanalysis of the Unknown Thought*. Abingdon: Routledge.

Bracher M, et al. 1994. *Lacanian Theory of Discourse: Subject, Structure and Society*. New York: New York University Press.

Brown NO. 1966. *Love's Body*. New York: Random House.

Elliott A. 1996. *Subject to Ourselves: Social Theory, Psychoanalysis and Postmodernity*. Oxford: Polity Press.

Fink B. 1995. *The Lacanian Subject: Between Language and Jouissance*. Princeton, NJ: Princeton University Press.

Freud S. 1962. *The Ego and the Id*. London: Hogarth Press.

Hillman J. 1980. *Egalitarian Typologies versus the Perception of the Unique: Eranos Lectures 4*. Dallas, TX: Spring Publications.

Lacan J. 1977. *Écrits: A Selection*. London: Tavistock Publications.

Lacan J. 1977. *The Four Fundamental Concepts of Psychoanalysis*. London: Penguin Books.

Sadoff DF. 1998. *Sciences of the Flesh: Representing Body and Subject in Psychoanalysis*. Stanford, CA: Stanford University Press.

### Psychology and Sociology

Abrams D, Hogg MA. (Eds.) 1999. *Social Identity and Social Cognition*. Oxford: Blackwell.

Arnold K, Peto J. Undated. *Identity & Identification*. London: Black Dog Publishing.

Bayer B, Shotter J. (Eds.) 1998. *Reconstructing the Psychological Subject: Bodies, Practices and Technologies*. London: Sage.

Bellah RN, Madsen R, Sullivan W, et al. 2008. *Habits of the Heart: Individualism and Commitment in American Life*. Berkeley: University of California Press.

Bermúdez JL. 1998. *The Paradox of Self-Consciousness*. Cambridge: MIT Press.

Blackburn S. 2014. *Mirror, Mirror: The Uses and Abuses of Self-Love*. Princeton, NJ: Princeton University Press.

Bless H, Fiedler K, Starck F. 2004. *Social Cognition: How Individuals Construct Social Reality*. Hove: Psychology Press.

Bruner J. 1986. *Actual Minds, Possible Worlds*. Cambridge, MA: Harvard University Press.

## 206 *Further reading*

Capoza D, Brown R. (Eds.) 2000. *Social Identity Processes: Trends in Theory and Research*. London: Sage.

Ellemers N, Spears R, Doosje B. (Eds.) 1999. *Social Identity*. Oxford: Blackwell.

Engestrom Y. 2008. *From Teams to Knots: Activity-Theoretical Studies of Collaboration and Learning at Work*. Cambridge: Cambridge University Press.

Freeman M. 1993. *Rewriting the Self: History, Memory, Narrative*. London: Routledge.

Gergen KJ. 2001. *Social Construction in Context*. London: Sage Publications.

Glover J. 1988. *I: The Philosophy and Psychology of Personal Identity*. London: Penguin.

Goffman E. 1956. *The Presentation of Self in Everyday Life*. London: Pelican.

Hamachek DE. 1987. *Encounters with the Self*. New York: Holt, Rinehart and Winston.

Harré R. 1984. *Personal Being: A Theory for Individual Psychology*. Cambridge, MA: Harvard University Press.

Harré R. 1998. *The Singular Self: An Introduction to the Psychology of Personhood*. London: Sage.

Henriques J, et al. (Eds.) 1984. *Changing the Subject: Psychology, Social Regulation and Subjectivity*. London: Routledge.

Holland R. 1977. *Self & Social Context*. London: Macmillan.

Kiesler CA, Kiesler SB. 1970. *Conformity*. Reading, MA: Addison-Wesley.

Lasch C. 1979. *The Culture of Narcissism: American Life in an Age of Diminishing Expectations*. New York: WW Norton.

MacMurray J. 1961. *Persons in Relation*. London: Faber.

Marar Z. 2012. *Intimacy*. Durham: Acumen.

Oatley K. 1984. *Selves in Relation: An Introduction to Psychotherapy and Groups*. London: Methuen.

Paechter C, et al. (Eds.) 2001. *Learning, Space and Identity*. London: Sage.

Romanyshyn RD. 1989. *Technology as Symptom and Dream*. London: Routledge.

Rose N. 1996. *Inventing Our Selves: Psychology, Power and Personhood*. Cambridge: CUP.

Storr W. 2017. *Selfie: How We Became So Self-obsessed and What It's Doing to Us*. London: Picador.

Surowiecki J. 2005. *The Wisdom of Crowds: Why the Many Are Smarter Than the Few*. London: Abacus.

Tester K. (Ed.) 1994. *The Flâneur*. London: Routledge.

Wetherell M. (Ed.) 1996. *Identities, Groups and Social Issues*. London: Sage.

# Index

Note: *Italic* page numbers refer to figures.

abjection 180–181
absent self 147–148
accountability sink 148
actions, legitimacy of 100
active questioning 14
adaptive systems 77, 108, 148, 165
addicted self 3
advertising 2, 6–7, 11, 54, 100, 149, 173
aesthetic: discrimination 17; nature 6; sensibility 104; surgery 14–15; surplus 6
Agamben, Giorgio 65
Alberti, Leon Battista: *De Pictura* 27
Albrecht Durer's grid *28*
alchemical self 29–33
alchemists 29, 31–33, 37
alchemy 32–33; Jung 29–30; material aspects of 30; speculative 37
alcoholism 128
*Alice in Wonderland* (Lewis) 4
Allen, Woody 182
Altamont Festival 142–143
alterity 155
alternative truth 12, 46, 73
Alzheimer's 91, 147 148
ambiguity 2, 76–77, 83, 108, 169
*Americana* (DeLillo) 95–96
American behaviourism 132
Amis, Martin: *The Information* 98
anatomical geography 53
anatomy 52–53, 184
animal: concealment 5; forms 23; magnetism *48*, 49; self 9, 34–36; shows 6; spirit 35

Anthropocene 152
anthropology/anthropologists 34, 175
antihumanist: Anthropocene 152; pessimism 152–153
anti-metaphorical qualities 100–101
anti-psychiatry 99
anxiety 54, 137, 160
appearance, semiotics of 9
aristocracy 38–40, 45
Aristotle 109–110
art exhibition 134
artificial intelligence (AI) 8–9, 152; developments in 153; piecemeal regulation of 153; thinking 152
asceticism 14, 26
Ashbery, John 71
Assange, Julian 12, 66
*As You Like It* (Shakespeare) 25
athletics 14, 17
Attention Deficit Hyperactivity Disorder (ADHD) 119
Attlee, Clement 144
Augustine of Hippo 26, 86; *Confessions* 43, 85–87
authentic/authenticity 10, 12, 82, 132; alchemists 31; existence 10; identity 129–130, with muscle 20–22, self 8, 11, 72, 159, 165; selves 10–12
authoritarian/authoritarianism 41, 54, 64, 169
autobiographical self 3, 109, 166
autobiography 26, 43, 85–86, 89, 92, 98
autonomic nervous system 80–81, 164–165

## 208 Index

autonomy 25–26, 85, 119, 132
ayahuasca ceremony 116

Bablet, Mathieu 153–154; *Carbon and Silicon* 153–154
bad faith 10
Bakhtin, Mikhail 169
Balzac, Honoré de: *Le Colonel Chabert* 61
Barfield, Owen: *History in English Words* 51
Barker-Benfield, G. J.: *The Culture of Sensibility*: *Sex and Society in Eighteenth-Century Britain* 13
Barthes, Roland 92–93
Bates, Henry Walter 7
Bateson, Gregory 101
Baudelaire, Charles 18–19
Baudrillard, Jean 94
Bauman, Z. 3
Beat generation 139, 141
Beckett, Samuel 78
Begum, Shamima 65–66
behaviour 5, 8, 10, 78, 133, 162; aggressive 182; American 132; obsessive-compulsive 101
*Being and Nothingness* (Sartre) 10
Bernays, Martha 52, 129
Berners-Lee, Tim 113
Bevan, Aneurin 144
'Beyond the Pleasure Principle' 52–53
bias 2, 42, 90, 94, 129–130
Biden, Joe 137
Big Bang 79, 174, 178
biohybrid 114
biological/biology 6, 9, 52, 176, 182; self 174–177; typologies 61
bio-power 173
black box 133
*The Black Goddess and the Sixth Sense* (Redgrove) 104
block patterns 142
Bloom, Molly 160
bodies 3, 174–177, 179, 184; boxed 184; embalming and wrapping 184; limits 111–112; and mind dualism 44; modification 112; preserving 184–185; reclamation of 112, 126; regeneration of 176; self-forming 111; systems 80
Boswell, James 86

bounded self 131, 174–175
bourgeois capitalism 87
brain 164; development 62; networks in 162
Brando, Marlon 142–143
bricoleur 4
Brunelleschi, Filippo 27
Bruner, Jerome 61, 82, 168–170
Brutalism 149
bullying 10, 53, 131, 149, 151, 168
Bunyan, John 86
burial 183
Burroughs, William 76, 160
Butler, Judith 127–130

Cade, John 163
Callery, Ben 149–150
Calvinists 183
camouflaged self 5–8
Campbell, Joseph: *The Hero with a Thousand Faces* 21–22
cancelling the self 95–98
capabilities 62, 97, 108, 110
capillary power 126, 171–173
*Carbon and Silicon* (Bablet) 153–154
care of self 14–16, 56
Carnegie, Andrew 58–59
Carroll, Lewis: *Alice in Wonderland* 4
Carson, Kit 57
Cartesian: *cogito* 117; mantra 97
casual friendships 123
Catholic tradition of nuns suffering 112
central nervous system 80
ceremony 31, 35, 115–116, 183
Channing, Cornelia 147
chaos 68–69, 77–79, 108, 116, 148, 164–165, 175
chaotic system 78
character 2–3, 9, 26, 78, 83, 129, 131; development of 25, 95–96; eccentric 8; fashioning 25; minor 20; physiognomy and typologies of 45; primary 151; self-deprecation 13; shaping of 34, 169; studies of 44
Charcot, Jean-Martin 49–50
choking 136–137
Christian/Christianity 14, 25–26, 29, 39, 44–45
Cicero 17
circumscribed self 174

## Index 209

citizenship 64–67, 86
*The Civilizing Process* (Elias) 13
Civil Rights movement 134
Cixous, Hélène 126, 129
Clark, Andy 164
'close-call' reporting 168
cognitive/cognition 108; behavioural therapy 121; psychologists 137; strategies 62; styles 169; unconscious 108
Coleridge, Samuel Taylor 38, 51, 165
collateral damage 64
*Le Colonel Chabert* (Balzac) 61
colour: of animals 5; persons of 64
common sense 109, 168
communal meeting 121
communication 168, 172; errors 167; incompetence 167; information and 114; nurses' styles of 168; patterns 167; predominant style of 167
community interests 132
complex systems 77–81, 108, 110, 162, 164, 175
compliance, indirect 128
Comte, August 61
Conan Doyle, Sir Arthur: *The Sign of the Four* 44
'concealing colouration' 5
confessional/confessionalism 89; narratives 87; self 85–88
*Confessions* (Augustine of Hippo) 43, 85–87
*Confessions* (Rousseau) 43, 85
confidentiality 89
consciousness 30, 42, 94, 106–111, 163, 174; signal recognition of 91; surplus of 108
consumerism 92
contemporary: feminisms 130, narcissistic culture 73; self 3
Cooper, David 99–100
core self 56, 109–110, 132
cosmologists 178–179
cremation 182–183
critical: 'erotics' 129; pedagogy 129; psychiatry 99
Cromwell, Oliver 39
cross-dressing 112
cryptocurrency industry 177
Cubism 27–28

cultural/culture 53; habits 14; language of 73; of nerves 52; signs 127; style 59; symbols of 73, 127
*The Culture of Sensibility: Sex and Society in Eighteenth-Century Britain* (Barker-Benfield) 13
cyberspace 114–115

Damasio, Antonio 109
Darwin, Charles 5, 59, 62
Darwin, Erasmus 5
Davis, Miles 139
dead body, intimacy with 183–184
death 182; and disintegration 78; exercise 15–16; uncertainty of 183; wish 182
decision-making 137, 148
deconstructive: literary criticism 150; postmodernism 150; style 80
deep insulin treatment 103
defence mechanisms 53–54, 75
deferral/deference 71, 155; forms of 156; of judgement 157
Deleuze, Gilles 94
DeLillo, Don 76, 92; *Americana* 95–96; *Players* 97
delusions 75, 99, 103, 148
dementia 147–148
democracy 59, 113, 153–154, 156, 168
democratic dictatorship 65
*De Pictura* (Alberti) 27
depression 11, 54, 163
Derrida, Jacques 85–86, 111, 149, 155–157
Descartes, René 30–31, 42, 44, 75–76; *Discourse on Method* 42
desire: sexual 52; unconscious 53–54
despair 11, 182
developing self 169–170
Dewey, John 59
*Diagnostic and Statistical Manual of Mental Disorders* (DSM) 100–101
dialogism 169
Dickens, Charles: *Hard Times* 4
Dickinson, Emily 71
dignity 41
disciplinary practices 172
*Discourse on Inequality* (Rousseau) 43
*Discourse on Method* (Descartes) 42
discrimination 17, 119
disembodied location 166

## Index

disposable self 187–189
dissociation 49, 102–103
doctors 107, 145–146
'do it yourself' 4
Donne, John 61
double binds 41, 101, 123
'doughnut' economy 79
dramaturgical self 28
Duchamp, Marcel 18, 28
Durkheim, Émile 61
duty of candour 11

earprints 44
ego 53, 75, 78; a-hysterical 54;
    defence mechanisms of 54; fragile
    75; identity 174–175; inflation 46;
    super-defended 75; territory of 52;
    women's 48–49
Egypt 126, 171, 184; myth 36;
    patriarchal politicians 126
electric shock 133–134
Elemental House, Melbourne *150*
Elias, Norbert: *The Civilizing Process*
    13
Elkin, Lauren 18
embodied/embodiment 163;
    metaphorical 30, 107–108; nature
    159; perception of 165–166; self 174
emotion/emotional 78; hostility 135;
    labour 79; sensitivity 153
employment 65, 79, 105, 120, 128
enlightenment self 37–43
enteric (gut) system 80
entropy 78, 80, 175, 182
environmentalism 152–153
equality 29, 73, 79, 113
equity 73, 79
erotic role play (ERP) function 121
erotic transference 49, 50
*An Essay Concerning Human
    Understanding* (Locke) 42
essentialism 94
Esterson, Aaron 100
ethnic cleansing 59, 64
ethnographers 34–35
Euripides 11–12
European Renaissance 25, 39
'European' self 2–3
evolution, theory of 83
excremental selfhood 181
exhibitionism 100–101, 111

existential/existentialism 10–11, 98
expectations 8, 96, 173
experimental psychology 132
experimenters 133–134
expositional biography 11
externalism 109

faith 76, 133–134, 182
familiars 8, 12, 23, 24, 96, 100–101,
    109–110, 116, 123, 176, 180
family 120, 140, 182; dysfunctional
    conversations 101; fashioning of
    123–125; setting 123
fashion/fashioning 7, 25–26, 73, 139;
    families 124–125; of human identity
    25–26; industry 8
fatigues 6
fear of shame 161
feelings 14, 21, 30, 34, 49, 51, 61,
    93, 96, 108, 112, 120, 127, 136,
    163, 181
feminine/feminist/feminism 128–131,
    172–173; genealogy 94; literature
    87; movements 112; selves 126–130
fictions 82, 90, 93, 95, 154, 159, 168,
    174, 182
fingerprint identification 44
*flâneur* 17–19
*The Flaneur in Nineteenth-Century
    British Literary Culture*: "*The
    Worlds of London Unknown*"
    (Vila-Cabanes) 17–18
folk: art 17; lore 26; music 140, 142
forest-dwelling communities 35
foster families 124
Foucault, Michel 14, 25–26, 56, 58,
    126, 171–173
Franklin, Benjamin 49
Frazer, James George: *The Golden
    Bough* 31
Freud, Sigmund 50–53, 75, 96–97,
    129; bias to male sexuality 129;
    The Ego and the Id 53; personal
    unconscious 36
friendship 119–120, 123–124
frontiersman 57–60, 73, 85, 119
Frueh, Joanna 129
functional magnetic resonance imaging
    (fMRI) scanning 162, 164–165
functional writing 82
future self 114

## Index 211

Gallop, Jane 129
Galton, Francis 44
Galvani, Luigi 162
gender: identification 3, 126; trouble 130
gendered self 112
Generative Pre-trained Transformer-4 (GPT-4) 152
genres of story 90
Gibbon, Edward 86
Ginzburg, Carlo 25
global warming 32, 177
Glück, Louise 71
Goffman, Erving 8, 28, 73
good faith 10, 90
Grand Narrative of Modernism 91
grand narratives 92, 156
*The Grapes of Wrath* (Steinbeck) 79
Great Depression in America (1929–39) 79
Greek: autobiography 86; pan 68–70; Pan 69; sculptures 14
Greenblatt, Stephen 25–26
Greenfield, Susan 163
group, interest 123–124
guardedness 75
Guattari, Félix 94
gymnasium 14–15, 17

habits/habitual 8, 13–15, 45, 85, 111, 114, 168–169, 191; identities 112; shaping 34; unconscious 137
*Habits of the Heart: Individualism and Commitment in American Life* (Bellah) 2
Haig, David 63
hallucinations 91, 102, 148
Haraway, Donna 1
*Hard Times* (Dickens) 4
Hegel, Georg Wilhelm Friedrich 113–114, 128, 168
Heidegger, Martin 85–86, 94, 146, 149, 160
hero/heroic: confessional writing 130; individualism 58; masculinism 53; myths 21
*The Hero with a Thousand Faces* (Campbell) 21–22
heteronomy 93–94, 98
Hillman, James 31
*History in English Words* (Barfield) 51

Hobbes, Thomas: *Leviathan* 38, 39
Holocaust 157, 180
Holzinger, Florentina 111
Homer 12, 20–21, 32; *Iliad* 20, 22, 32, 129; *Odyssey* 129
homeric: characterisations 21; heroes 21
horror 180–181
*The Hour of the Star* (Lispector) 97
House, Gregory 9
Huichol Indians 31
human/humanism 26–27; animal 5–6; culture 20; evolution 7; self-display 8; sexuality 52
humanistic personalism 89
humanist political maturity 63
humanoids 114
Hume, David 76, 95–96
hunting cultures 31, 36
hysterics 49–50

idealism, Hegel's model of 115
idealistic cleansing 93
identity 72, 90, 131–132, 156; construction 25; cultural forming of 151; fashioning of 25–26; formation 15; imitation as basis for 7–8; overlapping 124; personal ownership of 93; politics 18; postmodern and poststructuralist 156; professional 145
*Iliad* (Homer) 20, 22, 32, 129
illegal immigrants 65
illeism 46–47
imagination 16, 30–31, 35, 51, 93, 101–102, 108–109
immortality, dreaming of 20
immune system 80–81, 99
impartiality 1, 79
imperialism 93, 168
impersonal 120, 149
imposition 10, 40–41, 76
impression management 8, 10
inauthentic: existence 10; selves 10–12
incest 123
inclusivity 1, 79, 92
individual/individualism 2, 25, 57, 59; capacity 15; cultural value of 2; spirit 59
inequalities 41, 43, 80
inequities 43, 59, 80, 100
*The Information* (Amis) 98

## 212    *Index*

insanity 100
intersectionality 2
intersubjective identity 61, 170
*In the Country of the Skin* (Redgrove)
    103
intimacy 34, 96, 118, 120, 173, 184
intuition 90, 106, 108–109
'invasive' organisms 80–81
Irigaray, Luce 94

Jackson, Andrew 59
Jakobson, Roman 127
James, Alice 97–98
James, Henry 97
James, William 97
Japanese self 2–3
jazz 139–141, 143
Jencks, Charles 149–151
Joux, Armede 44
Joyce, James 78, 95, 159–160; *Ulysses*
    159–160
Julius Caesar 46–47, 131
Jung, Carl Gustav 29, 33, 36

Kant, Immanuel 4, 40–42, 76, 97, 109,
    113–115
Keats, John 117
Khamseh, Moghadam *119*
Kierkegaard, Søren 10–11
*King Lear* (Shakespeare) 27–28,
    183–184
'kiss-and-tell' journalism 87–88
knowledge 106, 170, 174–176; of
    literary forms 83; of self 127
know thyself/yourself 14, 117
Koestler, Arthur 165
Kristeva, Julia 130, 155, 180

labour markets 79
Lacan, Jacques 72, 158–161
Laënnec, René 173
Laing, R. D. 99–101
language 3, 46, 62, 93, 109, 127–128,
    155–156, 158, 169–170; combative
    73; games 77–78; inherent
    indeterminacy 91; invention and
    reinvention 170; of patients 170;
    performative 93; register 107–108;
    technical or instrumental 83–84
Lasch, Christopher 73
Lavater, Johann Kaspar 44

Lawrence, D. H. 117
Layard, John 104
learning process 81
Lee, Peter 152
*Leviathan* (Hobbes) 39
Levinas, Emmanuel 62, 94, 157
LGBTQ+ 131, 172
liberation 41, 90–91, 172
life on earth 152, 183
linear/nonlinear 27, 77, 78, 103, 110,
    148, 163, 165, 169, 175
linguistic: registers 107, 169;
    transactional self 167–170
Lispector, Clarice: *The Hour of the
    Star* 97
listening 14, 67, 91, 98, 101, 169
literalism 93, 105, 169
literary psychology 33
Locke, John 43, 76; *An
    Essay Concerning Human
    Understanding* 42
Logue, Christopher 20–21
Lombroso, Cesare 44
loneliness 118–122
Losey, Joseph 128
Lowell, Robert 71
Luther, Martin 180

madness 99–100
*Madness and Modernism* (Sass) 105
magnetism 48, 49, 104, 162; animal
    48, *48*, 49
Manning, Chelsea 12
Marden, Orison Swett 57–59; New
    Thought 58; *Pushing to the Front*
    57–58
market economy socialism 144
Marx, Karl 94, 168
Marxism 156
Maslow, Abraham 58
Massachusetts Institute of Technology
    (MIT) 114
mathematical theory 77
Mayer, Johann Christoph Andreas 44
McCarthyism 53
medical: gaze 54; students 145
medieval: art 27; self 2–3
*Memoirs of a Woman Doctor*
    (Saadawi) 126–127
*Memorial* (Oswald) 21
memory 15, 81, 147–148

*Index* 213

mercury 30–31, 99
Mesmer, Franz Anton *48*, 48–49
meta-affect 108–109
meta-cognition 108–109, 153
metaphors 30, 53, 62, 75, 78–81,
    83–84, 105, 148
metonymic chain 54, 160
micro-organisms 176
migrants 34, 119, 131–132
Milgram, Stanley 133–134
Milton, John 149
mindfulness 60, 121
minimalism 149–150
Miskin, Lionel 104
modernist/modern/modernist 42, 92,
    150–151, 156; academic psychology
    131; ego 51–55; humanism 87; jazz
    140; practices 173; psychotherapy
    105; relational self 62; self of
    13, 54–55, 92–94; sensibility 12;
    structuralism 54; subject 77
mods 139–143, *140*; culture 139;
    identity 142–143
Möhsen, Johann Karl Wilhelm 40
monologic 93; bias 94
moral reasoning 153
morbid environmentalism 152–153
mortality 16, 20–21
multiplicity 2, 18, 96, 130
Murthy, Vivek 119
muscle memory 136
music 23, 49, 139–140, 142
Musil, Robert 96
Musk, Elon 115–116
myths 20–21, 35–36, 59–60, 68, 149,
    181; *see also* religion

narcissism/narcissistic 10, 31, 46–47,
    71–73, 75, 91; gratification 98;
    personality traits of 64; root cause
    of 73; self 15, 18, 73
narrative: knowing 83; self 84, 86–87
Nasseri, Mehran Karimi 66–67
national security 12
*Nausea* (Sartre) 10
neoliberal/neoliberalism 58; capitalism
    56, 59, 92; capitalist economies
    79; economics 144; growth 80–81;
    political movement of 73
nerves 51–52
neurological self 162–166

neurology 162–163
neurons 54, 163
*The New York Times* 147
NHS *see* UK National Health Service
    (NHS)
Nietzsche, Friedrich 17, 96
nightmares 70, 180
nomadic settler 115
normality 99, 131–132
Northern Soul 139–141

obedience 134
objectivity: geographies of 1;
    scientific 1
Object-Oriented Ontology 154
obsessive-compulsive behaviour 101
*Odyssey* (Homer) 12, 20, 22, 129
Oe, Kenzaburo 96
Oliver, Tom 174
online self 3
opportunistic capitalism 58
oppression 127
organised crime 124
orgasmic self 129
Oswald, Alice: *Memorial* 21
otherness 155
overpopulation 177
over-thinking 138

Palaeolithic cave artists 27
panic 68–70
paranoia 75–76, 120, 148; definition
    of 76; escaping 76; issue of 76;
    self-imposed 76
parrhesia 11, 21, 90
patient safety 167
patriarchal/patriarchy 112, 118,
    127–130; dominant power of 53;
    pornography 128; views 87
Penfield, Wilder 162
Pepper, Art 139
performance art 111
performative language 93
performed self 3, 93
persistence 21, 58
personal/personalism 31; branding 46;
    confessional styles 71; consciousness
    114–115; growth cultures 56;
    identity 42, 61–62
personality 8, 86, 178
personhood 2–3, 26

## 214 Index

perversion 101–102
Petrarch 87–88
phallogocentrism 149
phrenology 44, 162
*phronesis* 109–110
physical ability 137
physiognomy 44–45
plant/planting: self 34–36; societies 35–36
*Players* (DeLillo) 97
Pleasure Principle 53, 96–97
Plutarch 14
poetry 30–31, 102–104, 110, 159, 170
*poiesis* 109
political/politicians 148; enlightenment 146; identity 145–146
politicised junior doctors 144–146
pop-therapeutic culture 90
Portmann, Adolf 7
possessed and absent selves 48–50
posthumanism/posthumanist 153; literature 151; moment 83; movement 183; radical perspective of 154; relational self 63; selves 77–78; sensibility 12; style 80; subject 77; thinkers 113; voices 92
post-industrial cultures 116
postmodernity/postmodern/ postmodernism 78, 149, 151, 156; climate 83; differing strands of 150; fictions 93; 'reconstructive' 149
power 23, 91, 96–97, 145, 171; as aesthetic display 6–7; assumptions about 172; over 171
practical wisdom 110–111
practice managers 144–145
pre-conscious process 109–110
prefrontal cortex 162–164, 166
prejudice 40, 65, 126
*Prelude* (Wordsworth) 86
prisoners 134–135
privacy 8, 85
private: healthcare 144; self 2
privilege, abuse of 11
Protestant Elect 183
psyche, tripartite structure of 53
psychiatry 99–100
*Psychiatry and Anti-Psychiatry* (Cooper) 99
psychoanalysis 54, 102, 129–130
psychobiography 98

psychology 131, 135
psychosis 91, 160
psychosomatic 51
public: manners 13; self 2
'puffers' 31–32
punishment 64, 133–134
puritanism 129

quickening, in alchemy 32–33

racism 77, 119; *see also* discrimination
rationality/rationalisation 53, 75, 92
Reagan, Ronald 73
realities 3, 42, 73, 117, 168, 174, 179, 181
Reality Principle 53, 96–97
'real' self 4
recession 79
recognition 3, 20, 71, 91, 98, 107–108, 110, 114, 159, 180
Redgrove, Peter 101–104; *The Black Goddess and the Sixth Sense* 104; *In the Country of the Skin* 103
reflection 72, 97–98
reinforcement 133
relational self 3, 61–63
relationship 71, 81, 86, 122, 172–173, 181; on demand 121; virtual 122
relearning 137
religion 25, 29, 61, 89–91, 156; *see also* secular
Renaissance 27; European self during 25; humanism 153; painters 27–28, 28; self 2–3, 25–28
resilience 58
robots 112–114, 116–117, 122, 152; silicon-based lifeforms 115, 116
Romanyshyn, Robert 27
Roquentin, Antoine 10–11
Rorty, Richard 83
Rousseau, Jean-Jacques 86, 90, 92; *Confessions* 43; *Discourse on Inequality* 43
Ryan, Judith 95; *The Vanishing Subject* 95

El Saadawi, Nawal 127; *Memoirs of a Woman Doctor* 126–127
sacrifice 20–21, 31, 35–36, 65, 94, 113
salt 30–31, 129, 184
Sarkel, Manfred 103

Index 215

Sartre, Jean-Paul: *Being and Nothingness* 10; *Nausea* 10
Sass, Louis 105; *Madness and Modernism* 105
saunterer *see flâneur*
sceptics 19, 37, 59
schizophrenia 102–103
Schmitt, Carl 64–65
scientific objectivity 1
screen addiction 118
scripts 8, 12, 15, 26, 129–130
secular: humanistic confession 89; personal confessional style 86–87
self 2, 6, 68, 155; absorption 71–73, 98, 105; awareness 164–165; body location of 4; change over time 2–3; confidence 2; definitions of 66, 163; description of 68; development of 56; displays 6; engulfed by panic 68–70; esteem 118, 121; experience of 96; expression 132, 169; *in extremis* 180; forming 13–17, 26, 39, 84; fragmentation of 130; improvement 14, 17, 26–27, 97, 157; insight and regrouping of 170; interest 72, 87, 109; knowing 15, 26, 97; as laboratory rat 131–135; narrative construction of 82–84; of personalistic humanism 94; in pieces 136–138; pleasure 128, 158; presentation 184; qualifications of 3; recognition of 72–73, 180; reference 46–47, 71–72; reflection 162–163; reliance 2; respect 2; revelation 98; righteous narcissist 71–74; sense of 2, 18, 35, 39, 84, 111, 139, 146, 155, 162–163, 165, 176, 183; shared expressions of 72; stripped of rights 64–67; surveillance 89; techniques of 73, 'writing out' of 17
self-harming practices 70, 111
self-help 56, 60; culture of 60; journal 57–58; modern traditions of 57; movement 42, 59, 73; origins of 56–60
*Self-Help* (Smiles) 59
selfhood 2–3, 40, 131, 164
selfishness 15
selflessness 62
self made 38

self-making 15
selves *see* self
sensitivity: of men towards women 13
sexual/sex: desire 52; orientations 127; workers 120
Shakespeare, William 29; 'All the world's a stage' 28; *King Lear* 27–28, 183–184; spectator self 27–28; *The Tempest* 31; *As You Like It* 25
shamans 23, 35
Sherman, Cindy 8–9
*The Sign of the Four* (Conan Doyle) 44
*The Simpsons* 121
simulacrum 121, 163
Singer, Judy 99–100
singularity 85, 174–175
skin, electrification of 103
Skinner, B.F. 132
slave/slavery 64, 124–125, 130
sly civility 128
Smiles, Samuel 57; *Self-Help* 59
Smith, Adam 62–63, 87; *The Theory of Moral Sentiments* 62–63
social/sociological: artefacts 127; habits 128; injustice 11; media 56, 87, 121; practices 127, 173; relations 160; selves 62; structure 39
sociology 61
Socrates 14, 65
solipsism 95, 109, 127
sovereign power 171–173
space/place 34
SpaceTime 178
Spall, Peter 101–102
spirit/spiritual 37; confessional cleansing 86; teachings 29
Stanford University 134
Steinbeck, John: *The Grapes of Wrath* 79
Stevens, Wallace 3
stories/storying/storytelling 26, 82, 89
strange attractors 78, 175
'stream of consciousness' approach 151
street philosophers 14
streetwalkers 18
strolling *see flâneur*
structuralism 92
subjects/subjectivity 90–91, 97–98, 113–117, 132, 171–173, 180–181; 'hermeneutic' 15; multiple forms of 116; ownership of 91

## 216 *Index*

subservience 39, 112, 128
succession 123–124
suffering 13, 31, 70, 98, 102, 111–112, 147, 180
suffocation 70, 158
surgeons 107–108, 117–119, 136, 145, 162, 167–171, 187
surveillance 45, 171–173, 189
Swift, Jonathan 78

tacit: knowing 108–109; reasoning 106
taste 13, 17, 100, 104–105
taxation 144
technical competence 108
technology 114, 176–177; development of 37; of self 14, 58
*The Tempest* (Shakespeare) 31
tenderness 13
Thatcher, Margaret 73
*The Theory of Moral Sentiments* (Smith) 62–63
therapeutic self-discovery 18–19
Thiel, Peter 154
Thoreau, Henry David 85–86, 92, 130
toroidal attractors 78
tradition 17, 21, 23, 25, 27, 34–35, 37, 39, 42, 61, 66, 80–81, 102, 112, 115–116, 119, 124, 128, 141, 145, 168–170, 172, 175
transactional self 61, 168–170
transcendental idealism 109
transcendent self 4, 76
transhumanism 153–154
translational self 76–81
transpersonal self 3
tribe leaders 115
Triquetra knot 159, *161*
Trump, Donald 12, 46, 72, 154
truth-telling 11–12, 21, 41
Tundra dwellers 35

UK National Health Service (NHS) 144–146
*Ulysses* (Joyce) 159–160
uncertainty 76, 169
unconscious 94; desires 53–54, 96–97; life 52–53; process 109–110
unique identifiers 44–45
universal self 178–179

values 63, 76, 116
*The Vanishing Subject* (Ryan) 95
Vila-Cabanes, Isabel: *The Flaneur in Nineteenth-Century British Literary Culture: "The Worlds of London Unknown"* 17–18
*A Vindication of the Rights of Woman: with Strictures on Political and Moral Subjects* (Wollstonecraft) 13
violence 123, 135
virtual: girlfriend 122; identities 115; relationships 122

Wallace, David Foster 77, 182
Western culture 14, 20, 85
whistleblowers/whistleblowing 11–12; high-profile 11–12; in politics 11
white supremacy 130
Whitman, Walt 71
WikiLeaks 11–12, 66
Williams, Joy 17, 95; 'The Girls' 17
Wollstonecraft, Mary: *A Vindication of the Rights of Woman: with Strictures on Political and Moral Subjects* 13
womb 3, 34, 123
women 112; human trafficking of 130; hyper-sexualisation and domestication of 54; identity 127–128; rights of 57
Woodstock Festival (1969) 142
Woolf, Virginia 18, 78, 95, 120
Wordsworth, William 38, 165; *Prelude* 86
work ethic 58–59
World Health Organisation (WHO) 118, 168
World Wide Web (WWW) 113
worthlessness, sense of 119
writing 94; personal confessional 93; therapy of 93; *see also* poetry

Yanomami 35
yourself 149–151

Zen Buddhism 100
Zöllner, Johann Friedrich 40

Printed in the United States
by Baker & Taylor Publisher Services